Multinational Strategic Alliances

Wiley Series in Practical Strategy

Published titles

Business Unit Strategy
Segev

Virtual Organizations and Beyond: Discover Imaginary
Systems
Hedberg et al

Strategic Market Planning: A Blueprint for Success
McNamee

Forthcoming titles

Competitive Intelligence Turning Analysis into Success
Hussey and Jenster

Multinational Strategic Alliances

Robert J. Mockler

JOHN WILEY & SONS, LTD
Chichester • New York • Weinheim • Brisbane • Singapore • Toronto

Copyright © Robert J. Mockler
Published in 1999 by John Wiley & Sons Ltd,
Baffins Lane, Chichester,
West Sussex PO19 1UD, England

National   01243 779777
International (+44) 1243 779777
e-mail (for orders and customer service enquiries): cs-books@wiley.co.uk
Visit our Home Page on http://www.wiley.co.uk
             or http://www.wiley.com

Other Wiley Editorial Offices

John Wiley & Sons, Inc., 605 Third Avenue,
New York, NY 10158–0012, USA

WILEY-VCH Verlag GmbH, Pappellallee 3,
D-69469 Weinheim, Germany

Jacaranda Wiley Ltd, 33 Park Road, Milton,
Queensland 4064, Australia

John Wiley & Sons (Asia) Pte Ltd, 2 Clementi Loop #02–01,
Jin Xing Distripark, Singapore 129809

John Wiley & Sons (Canada) Ltd, 22 Worcester Road,
Rexdale, Ontario M9W 1L1, Canada

Library of Congress Cataloging-in-Publication Data

Mockler, Robert J.
    Multinational strategic alliances / Robert J. Mockler.
        p.   cm. — (Wiley series in practical strategy)
    Includes bibliographical references (p.   ) and index.
    ISBN 0-471-98775-1 (cloth: alk. paper)
    1. Strategic alliances (Business)   2. International business
enterprises — Management. I. Title. II. Series.
    HD69.S8M66   1999
    658'.044 — dc21   98–37306
                                              CIP

British Library Cataloguing in Publication Data

A catalogue record for this book is available from the British Library

ISBN 0-471-98775-1

Typeset in 11/13 pt Times by Vision Typesetting, Manchester
Printed and bound in Great Britain by Biddles Ltd, Guildford and King's Lynn.
This book is printed on acid-free paper responsibly manufactured from systainable forestry, in which at least two trees are planted for each one used in paper production.

Dedicated to the late Colman M. Mockler, former Chief Executive Officer of the Gillette Company, brother and mentor of the author, one of business's truly great leaders, and an extraordinary human being.

Contents

Series Foreword

The aim of this series is to provide managers with books on strategy, strategic management and strategic change, which are helpful, practical, and provide guidance for the application of sound concepts in real situations.

In the mid-1960s when the subject of planning began to emerge, the whole literature could have been listed on one or two sheets of paper. It was easy to decide which books to read, because so few were available. This state of affairs changed rapidly, and the scope of the subject has moved from a focus on formal planning to a broader view which merges with the literature of leadership, change management, strategic analysis and organization. Modern writing sees the organization and its strategies in an integrated way, and there are many, often conflicting, theories about the 'right way' to formulate strategies and practice strategic management.

Management does not take an academic interest in theories, but is concerned about what works best in the situation in which it operates. Hence this series. Each book is conceptually sound, and gives proper acknowledgement to the originators of concepts and ideas, but the emphasis is on using the concepts or methods, rather than academic argument.

Business school faculty and students are also concerned with the application of theories and will find much in these books to supplement the more academic texts.

In this series the aim is to give readers clear guidance on how to make the subject of the book work in their own situation, while at the same time taking care to ensure that the books do not oversimplify situations. Checklists and questionnaires are included when they aid the aims of the book, and examples are given. The experience of the author in actually applying the concepts, rather than just knowing about them, is intended to show through the writing.

The series will make complex matters understandable. We hope that it will become a catalyst that helps managers make a difference to the strategic performance of their organizations.

David Hussey
David Hussey & Associates
Editor of *Journal of Strategic Change*

Preface

This book provides working guidelines for understanding and using strategic alliances in multinational businesses. It is written for international managers and students of international management to help them do their jobs more effectively, no matter what the size of their enterprise. The diversity, complexity and rapidly changing context of multinational management, as well as the growing and widespread use of strategic alliances in international management, dictates a need for a book such as this one.

The book is based on the experiences of the author and of multinational companies working with overseas joint venture operations. The disciplined systematic processes and contingency frameworks given throughout this book, and the best practices guidelines and situation analysis checklists given in the concluding sections of Chapters 2–6 and in Appendix A, are based on these experiences. In addition, a substantial body of contingency theory, research and practice provides a theory basis for this work (Chandler, 1962; Donaldson, 1995, 1996; Egeloff, 1982; Lawrence and Lorsch, 1967; Rumelt, 1974; Stopford and Wells, 1972; Vancil, 1980; Mockler, 1989, 1992a,b).

The multinational area has become important to success in business today, because the markets in many developed countries are maturing and growth is being sought in new markets by companies of all sizes. Strategic alliances are a major enabling tool of multinational firms, as they are for domestic ones. These alliances have a number of unique characteristics which make them difficult to use effectively.

One book, of course, cannot adequately cover all aspects of multinational strategic alliances in detail. This book is, therefore, intended only to provide an introduction to the subject, as well as systematic processes, guidelines and checklists to guide and stimulate the reader's work in the field. As much as space has permitted, the book provides a wide range of examples of both successful and unsuccessful experiences to provide an experience base for improving day-to-day management skills.

While it is useful to develop best practices guidelines, these experiences show that each situation is in some ways unique. Because of the contingent nature of strategic alliance formulation and implementation, guidelines, like rules, are made to be broken. The ultimate guideline is to use the approach which best meets the individual situation's specific requirements. Such a contingency perspective is the unifying theme of this book.

REFERENCES

Chandler, A.D. Jr (1962). *Strategy and Structure.* Cambridge, MA, MIT Press.

Donaldson, L. (1995). *American Anti-Management Theories of Organization.* New York, Cambridge University Press.

Donaldson, L. (1996). *For A Positivist Organization Theory.* Thousand Oaks, CA, Sage Publications.

Egeloff, W.G. (1982). Strategy and structure in multinational corporations: An information processing approach. *Administrative Science Quarterly*, **27**, pp. 435–458.

Lawrence, P.R. and Lorsch, J.W. (1967). *Organization and Environment: Managing Differentiation and Integration.* Boston, MA, Division of Research, Harvard Business School.

Mockler, R.J. (1989). *Knowledge-Based (Expert) Systems for Management Decisions.* Englewood Cliffs, NJ, Prentice-Hall.

Mockler, R.J. (1992a). *Developing Knowledge-Based Systems Using an Expert Systems Shell.* Englewood Cliffs, NJ, Prentice-Hall/Macmillan.

Mockler, R.J. and Dologite, D.G. (1992b). *Expert Systems: An Introduction to Knowledge-Based Systems.* Englewood Cliffs, NJ, Prentice-Hall/Macmillan.

Rumelt, R.P. (1974). *Strategy, Structure, and Economic Performance.* Boston, MA, Division of Research, Harvard Business School.

Stopford, J.M. and Wells, L.T. (1972). *Managing the Multinational Enterprise.* New York: Basic Books.

Vancil, R. (1980). *Decentralization: Managerial Ambiguity by Design.* New York, Financial Executives Research Foundation.

Acknowledgements

Many people have contributed to this book. I wish to thank (in alphabetical order) the many acquaintances, associates and friends in business who helped me: Krister Ahlstrom (President and CEO, A. Ahlstrom Corporation), Tony C.K. Au Young (General Manager and Director, Gillette (Shanghai) Ltd), Warren Buffett (Chairman, Berkshire Hathaway, Inc.), John Patrick Casey (Partner, Peat Marwick), Manuel Jorge Cutillas (Chairman and CEO, Bacardi Ltd), Michael Eisner (Chairman and CEO, The Walt Disney Company), Jack Eyman (China Rhome and Haas), Loo Kim Fa (Marketing and Sales Director, Gillette (Shanghai) Ltd), Werner Fischer (Vice President, Brother International Corporation), Patrick Gilmore (former President, Brother International Corporation), Roberto Goizueta (late Chairman and CEO, The Coca-Cola Company), David Hussey (David Hussey and Associates), Raymond J. Lane (President and COO, Oracle Corporation), Robert Lutz (President and COO, Chrysler Corporation) and Ernest S. Micek (Chairman, President and CEO, Cargill, Inc.).

Others who helped include: Rupert Murdoch (Chairman, News Corporation), Patrick Purcell (Publisher, *Boston Herald*), David Puttruck (President and CEO, Charles Schwab & Co., Inc.), Joseph Saggese (Chairman, President and CEO, Borden Chemicals), Donald J. Schneider (President, Schneider International, Inc.), Peter Senge (Director, MIT's Center for Organizational Learning), Roberto Servitje (Chairman and CEO, Groupo Industrial BIMBO), Don Tapscott (President, Alliance of Converging Technologies), Daniel Tully (Chairman and CEO, Merrill-Lynch and Co., Inc.),

Charles R. Walsh (Executive Vice President, Chemical Bank), Jack Welch, Jr (Chairman and Chief Executive Officer, General Electric Company), Alfred Zeien (Chairman and CEO, The Gillette Company) and Lorenzo Zambrano (President and General Director Grupo Cementos Mexicanos–CEMEX.)

My thanks are also extended to my many professional friends and associates and to my graduate students who contributed to the development of this book – at St John's University (New York and Rome), University of Sao Paulo (Brazil), Bocconi University (Milan, Italy), the State Universities in St Petersburg and Moscow, and Renmin and Tsinjhua Universities (Beijing, China). I also want to thank my many workshop participants around the world, who used drafts of this text (and its accompanying support material) and so helped make it a more useful teaching and learning tool. I am especially grateful to Natasha Carnevali for her help with British Airways/American Airlines case study.

1
Introduction: Strategic Alliances and Multinational Management

Webster's dictionary defines strategic as 'important' and alliance as 'association of interests'. *Strategic alliances*, then, are associations important to alliance partners and formed to further their common interests. They can involve franchising and licensing agreements, partnership contracts, equity investments in new or existing joint ventures and consortia.

Strategic alliances are well-known tools available to, and used by, multinational business managers. For example, of the more than 167 000 foreign-funded investments in China in the mid-1990s, 64% were joint ventures and 15% were cooperative partnerships (Wong et al, 1996). In the auto industry, more than 1000 alliances have been created worldwide; in the airline industry, the number exceeds 300. Strategic alliances have proven to be important to both domestic and multinational businesses, as well as to the economies of the countries involved.

The question appears to be not *whether* multiple partnerships and joint ventures should be used, but *how* to develop and manage them effectively (CE Roundtable, 1997; CEO Brief 1997a,b). Jim Kelly, CEO of United Parcel Services (USA), for example, believes that developing a core competency in alliance management is critical to success in multinational business. In his view, UPS' development of such a core competency in strategic alliance capabilities through its many multinational alliances has given his company a major competitive edge (Kelly, 1997).

A 1997 Booz-Allen and Hamilton survey reports that

- Alliances account for 15% of the revenue generated by America's top 1000 firms
- The number of such deals between US firms and partners in Europe, Asia and Latin America is growing 25% annually
- 60% of US CEOs viewed alliances as successful as opposed to 20% in 1990
- Return-on-investment is higher in companies active in alliances (Harbison, 1997a,b)
- A company's success with alliances improves with experience and that 90% of the most successful alliance companies studied are making efforts to institutionalize best alliance practices, efforts this book is designed to support (Harbison, 1997a,b)

NATURE OF STRATEGIC ALLIANCES: CONTINUING PARTNERSHIPS

The term 'strategic alliance' is used to describe a wide range of cooperative partnerships and joint ventures. Strategic alliances have three distinguishing characteristics:

- Two or more entities unite to pursue a set of important, agreed-upon goals while in some way remaining independent subsequent to the formation of an alliance
- The partners share both the benefits of the alliance and control over the performance of assigned tasks during the life of the alliance. This is the most distinctive characteristic of alliances and the one that makes them so difficult to manage.
- The partners contribute on a continuing basis in one or more key strategic (that is, important to them) areas, for example, technology or products

Many kinds of alliances exist and there are many ways to manage them. In addition, when these alliances cross national borders, cross-cultural complexities impact on their effectiveness. An alliance's success, therefore, is highly dependent on contingent thinking and entrepreneurial skills.

STRATEGIC ALLIANCES COME IN MANY SHAPES, SIZES AND KINDS

Alliances can involve substantial investments in *joint ventures*. For example, in 1997 British Petroleum (BP) joined with Mobil Oil in a refining, distribution and marketing joint venture, a $5 billion organization with 12% of the service station business and 18% of the lubricants market in Europe. The two companies, which were not in themselves market leaders, expected to gain scale benefits and scale economics.

In an effort to exploit the new markets in the former USSR, PepsiCo Inc. initially formed joint ventures with state-owned firms, which controlled production and distribution. In spite of the resulting poor quality products and poor service, PepsiCo achieved a four-to-one lead over rival Coca-Cola. Since the breakup of the Soviet Union in 1991, Coca-Cola has invested $240 million in Russia, working through and with aggressive local joint venture private companies. As a result, Coca-Cola was close to equalling Pepsi's market share in Russia in 1997.

In 1996, PepsiCo announced plans to invest $550 million in Russia to regain its dominant position, by working with and through independent private bottlers and distributors. Pepsi, in conjunction with two joint venture partners, planned to add 11 plants, 30 production lines and 5000 employees over a 5–year period. In spite of such moves, PepsiCo was having problems overseas in late 1997. In 1996 Coca-Cola announced a joint venture with PepsiCo's present distributor in Venezuela. This alliance gave Coca-Cola instant access to 80% of the Venezuelan market and reduced PepsiCo's market share to less than 25%.

Strategic alliances also include *cooperative partnerships*. International airline alliances, such as the one proposed between British Airways (BA) and American Airlines (AA) in 1998 involving operational and sales activities, are a familiar type of alliance partnership which does not involve equity investment. British Airways also is involved in several continuing *franchise partnerships*, some of which involve equity investments.

Governments worldwide encourage and stimulate strategic alliances. In cooperation with multinational firms, governments use strategic alliances in many ways:

- To privatize state-owned companies while continuing to profit from and to some degree control the businesses
- To attract capital while nurturing local businesses
- To bring technology to their country
- To improve overall economic performance quickly, especially in developing countries, without entirely relinquishing control of local businesses to foreign operators

Government interest in joint ventures is one of the major drivers that encourage domestic and multinational businesses to enter strategic alliances. For example, in 1997, the Bolivian government privatized Samapa, its capital's water supply company, through a joint venture led by France's Lyonnaise des Eaux and a subsidiary of Argentina's Comercial del Plata. The new owners invested $360 million in upgrading facilities. Also, Brazil continues to revitalize its telecommunications and energy industries by privatizing them through joint ventures.

When Matav, Hungary's state-owned telephone company, was privatized, the Hungarian government retained an interest in the new joint venture company formed with Ameritech Corp. (US) and Deutsche Telekom AG (Germany). This multibeneficial arrangement enabled Hungary to continue to participate in profits from the business, to acquire capital for the percentage of Matav that it sold, and to introduce advanced telecommunications technology into the country.

In late 1997, almost 50% of the assets of Hungary's state-owned banking system were controlled by non-Hungarians and buying was still being pursued aggressively. Belgian, German, Austrian, Irish, American, Japanese and French financial institutions all had established some form of joint venture or other kind of equity investment with Hungarian state-owned banks.

> All this foreign money has been a boon for Hungarian consumers and companies, as investors inject fresh capital and know-how into the system, roll out new products, and push lending rates to record lows. Compared to the debt-ridden state of most Hungarian banks just five years ago, the transformation is stunning (Reed, 1997).

Airbus Industrie, founded in 1969 by a *consortium* of the governments of Britain, France, Germany and Spain, was originally a marketing alliance venture that sold the planes manufactured jointly by its four partners: Aerospatiale (France, 37.9%, state-owned, manufactured the cockpit and parts of the fuselage and assembled finished plane), Daimler-Benz Aerospace (Germany, 37.9%, privately-owned, manufactured portions of the fuselage and assembled some planes), British Aerospace (20%, privately-owned, manufactured most of the wings and some small fuselage parts), and Construcciones Aeronauticas (Spain, 4.2%, state-owned, manufactured horizontal tail stabilizers).

In late 1997, China signed a $600 million agreement for its first foreign-controlled power station under a build/operate/transfer joint venture agreement. Electricite de France (EdF) will own 60% of the plant and GEC Alsthom 40%. EdF will operate the plant in partnership with the Guangzi provincial government and French firms will supply most of the $330 million in equipment. The venture will own and operate the facility for 15 years, after which China will be given control. A complex contract guaranteeing purchase of electricity and specifying other agreement obligations was developed to ensure that the venture will earn a return that justifies the investment.

Understanding strategic alliances also requires understanding what they are not. Because they do not involve two or more independent firms sharing benefits and control over a continuing time period, mergers and acquisitions are not considered strategic alliances, nor are wholly-owned subsidiaries of multinational corporations. Joint ventures also may or may not be true strategic alliances, depending on the circumstances. For example, the Fuji Photo Film Company brought little to the Fuji–Xerox joint venture in Japan beyond its initial capital contribution. The venture functioned as a relatively independent subsidiary of Xerox because Fuji did not have access to the technology and contributed no technology of its own (Gomes-Cassares and McQuade, 1991; Jacobson and Hillkirk, 1986). As a result, this joint venture only nominally can be considered a strategic alliance. An agreement through which a firm grants a license for using technology in exchange for a royalty also is not considered a strategic alliance *except* when there is continuing contribution and control among two or more independent firms. For example, REFRAC Technology Development Corporation in 1952 began *licensing* worldwide patented and trademarked technologies for specialized products and manufacturing processes under such names as Heli-Coil, Econo-O-Lift and Bellofram. In addition to the existing products, processes and trademarks that were patented and registered, the agreements included ongoing updating of product technology, as well as assistance with updating manufacturing technology and knowledge, all of which are characteristic of a continuing *franchising alliance arrangement* (REFRAC, 1996).

Strategic alliances in business then range from those having minimal interaction – as in licensing agreements that require only some updating of technologies – to large, highly interactive, and continuing joint ventures, such as the one between British Petroleum and Mobil Oil in the mid-1990s. In addition, alliances can range from having a very important (strategic) effect for each partner to only marginally affecting a firm's future.

The essential concept of sharing control and management on a continuing basis is what makes managing strategic alliances such a critical, difficult and demanding task. This concept is relatively new for many companies. Until the 1980s, Borden, for example, resisted entering into strategic alliances, preferring to retain 100% control over overseas ventures. Other companies, such as General Motors, insisted on majority control wherever feasible to protect technology, facilitate integration and simplify management and control.

Such attitudes have changed dramatically. In the 1980s and 1990s, General Motors formed many different kinds of strategic alliances and hundreds of others have been formed among major automakers. Some firms, however, including Fujitsu (Japan), Drummond Company (USA) and Siemens (Germany), still prefer to operate wholly-owned overseas subsidiaries in countries such as Great Britain and Colombia which allow them.

WHY MULTINATIONAL STRATEGIC ALLIANCES?

Strategic alliances appeal to multinational firms for reasons other than because many countries require foreign investors to use them. If planned and managed effectively, they can:

- Enable overseas expansion and provide access to new markets
- Add value to a firm's product line
- Expand distribution and provide access to materials
- Develop and improve operations, facilities and processes, and provide access to new capabilities, new knowledge and new technologies
- Provide additional financial resources

- Decrease risks and enable relatively rapid adaptation to changing competitive market forces,
- Create new opportunities when faced with increasingly intense global competition
- Reduce competition

Strategic alliances often are useful in establishing a comprehensive integrated package of enablers, including marketing and production, organization, financial and accounting, and telecommunications/information systems operations. These enablers can help companies rapidly penetrate new markets or expand in existing ones. Through an alliance with Mobil, British Petroleum was able to establish a strong market position in Europe in 2–3 years. Doing this on their own had been estimated to take 8 years. Daewoo's Auto Group moved quickly into Eastern Europe between 1994 and 1997 by investing over $2 billion in equity-sharing joint ventures. Worldwide, Daewoo had varying interest in more than 100 alliances (from single digit to over 90%) in over 40 countries in many different industries (Brzezinski, 1997a,b; Kraar, 1996; 'Overseas Projects', 1997). America Online Inc. (AOL) used alliances in 1998 to establish a major position in Europe when competing against strongly entrenched telecommunications companies.

Another key trend driving strategic alliance growth is the globalization of business and of knowledge used in business. The importance of knowledge – in addition to the traditional economic forces of labor, land and capital – to wealth accumulation has received considerable attention recently. The rapidity with which knowledge can be communicated and translated globally into new products and services has contributed to the growing use of strategic alliances in today's highly competitive, global environment (Badaracco, 1991; Davenport and Prusak, 1998; Roos et al, 1997).

Strategic alliances also enable adaptation of common global frameworks to diverse local requirements. For example, the Gillette Company markets well-known global brands and products. Gillette has used alliances, especially in the distribution area, to expand rapidly worldwide. Gillette views strategic alliances as an effective way to move quickly into different countries in an adaptive, flexible way, while still retaining global brand identities. Hundreds of other multinational companies have used strategic alliances to balance and synergistically use local diversity.

Although strategic alliances are an effective management tool, they are not appropriate for all companies or all industry situations. As of 1997, Japan's largest telecommunications operation, Nippon Telegraph and Telephone, had developed international markets independently and had shown little interest in joining global telecommunications alliances (Nakamota, 1997). While Hungary benefited greatly from foreign-investor joint ventures in their banking sector, state-owned banks in Estonia, a Baltic state with little foreign-bank competition, were prospering because of a thriving economy (over 11% annual growth), which provided a well-regulated, open trading environment (Thornhill 1997). In the mid-1990s, Russian banks used wholly-owned subsidiaries and branches on the island of Cyprus rather than strategic alliances to do their offshore business and avoid the chaotic conditions in Russia after the break-up of the USSR (Gregoriou 1996). About the same time in 1997 that the US tobacco firm Philip Morris was increasing (to 50%) its equity investment in Cigatem, a large Mexican tobacco firm, BAT Industries, the UK tobacco group, chose a wholly-owned investment approach and repurchased Cigarrera La Moderna, a large Mexican tobacco company, for almost $2 billion.

One critic of multinational strategic alliances is Michael Porter, who believes that they are transition devices, tend to insure mediocrity and are destined to fail. In his view, they involve significant costs in terms of coordinating, reconciling goals and giving up profits (Porter, 1990). While many disagree with these views, Porter correctly points out that strategic alliances are in many cases transitional and can terminate as strategic requirements change and/or insurmountable operational problems arise.

British Telecommunications (BT) provides another multinational perspective on strategic alliances, since the company has used a *mixed strategy*. In 1984, BT, a large, inefficient, government-owned utility, was privatized (sold to the public). BT subsequently entered into alliances with rivals of existing and former state-owned monopolies in Spain, Italy, the Netherlands, Sweden, France and Germany. BT's strategy was to capitalize on Great Britain's head start (core competency) in deregulating telecommunications and to leapfrog the monopolies when barriers to competition came down across Europe in 1998. Through acquisitions, mergers and joint ventures, BT was transformed from a bloated government monolith to an agile competitor. This was stimulated in part by an increasingly

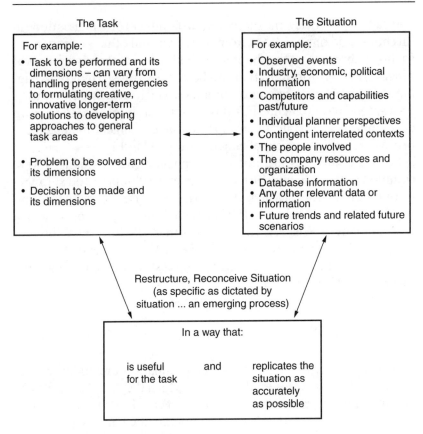

The Task

For example:

- Task to be performed and its dimensions – can vary from handling present emergencies to formulating creative, innovative longer-term solutions to developing approaches to general task areas

- Problem to be solved and its dimensions

- Decision to be made and its dimensions

The Situation

For example:

- Observed events
- Industry, economic, political information
- Competitors and capabilities past/future
- Individual planner perspectives
- Contingent interrelated contexts
- The people involved
- The company resources and organization
- Database information
- Any other relevant data or information
- Future trends and related future scenarios

Restructure, Reconceive Situation (as specific as dictated by situation ... an emerging process)

In a way that:

is useful and replicates the for the task situation as accurately as possible

Figure 1.1 A Basic Emergent Entrepreneurial Contingency Process

competitive free market, a condition which often stimulates rapid growth in the overall market and in individual firm performance.

General Motors Corp. also uses a mixed strategy, wholly owning many of its overseas plants and entering into joint ventures where required (as in China), as it expands worldwide operations with the goal of eventually having some 50% of its production capacity overseas.

Because they can serve as a major balancing and integrative enabler, strategic alliances can be difficult to manage successfully. Skills in conflict resolution, diversity integration, and crisis management are essential to the management of strategic alliances. The entrepreneurial decision making and action, such as the process shown in Figure 1.1, is required to meet these skill needs.

It can help to review the successes and failures of others, as is done in this book, and one can learn from one's own and other's experiences, as shown throughout the chapters of this book. But the experiences of others are rarely formulas that can be directly transferred to managing new situations at different companies, which most often have their own special requirements. For this reason, this book also focuses on developing reader skills in entrepreneurial contingent management processes, one key aspect of which is outlined in Figure 1.1.

Strategic alliances are not a new phenomenon. Alliances were common in the 18th and 19th centuries in the shipping and shipping insurance industries (Lynch, 1993). NEC, a major Japanese technology firm, was established in 1899 as Japan's first joint venture with a US company – Western Electric. Another US firm, ITT, bought Western Electric's interest in 1925. The ITT alliance ended in 1965, even though ITT remained NEC's largest stockholder until the early 1970s (Kobayashi, 1991).

PLANNING AND MANAGING STRATEGIC ALLIANCES

In addition to explaining what strategic alliances are and how they work, this book focuses on the ways in which they can be developed and managed more effectively. Four aspects of this task are introduced in this section and discussed in detail in Chapters 2–6.

Determining Strategic Fit: Enterprise-Wide Strategic Alignment

Strategic alliances can be a useful method or enabler for multinational growth for many enterprise-wide strategic reasons. For example, airlines use strategic alliances frequently to meet changing worldwide market needs. In September 1995, Delta Air Lines received approval and antitrust immunity to further its partnership with Austrian Airlines, Sabena and Swissair. This partnership was strengthened and expanded in 1997. Similar immunity was also granted to an alliance of United Airlines, Lufthansa, Air Canada, Scandinavian Airlines and Thai Airways. In addition to permitting the integration of passengers on selected flights, such immunity allows airlines to integrate flight schedules, marketing plans and sales promotions.

Such alliances allow airline partners to function as one major worldwide carrier without investing in one another. The partners remain separate firms and preserve capital. Competing airlines sometimes form alliances, as in early 1997, when Alitalia (Italy) and Air France formed a marketing alliance. Such alliances are not always easy to manage, however. Disputes arose in the mid-1990s between KLM and Northwest during their alliance, and many complaints and obstacles have arisen concerning the proposed 1998 British Airways/American Airlines partnership.

Automakers have used all kinds of strategic alliances – with suppliers, competitors, non-competitors and potential competitors. For example, Mitsubishi used such ventures to move into Asia ahead of stronger competitors, since it was unable to compete with these entrenched competitors in the US and Japan. In early 1997, Volkswagen (Germany) and General Motors (USA) announced joint venture plans with Finnish, Swedish and Central European partners to make cars in Russia.

In 1996, the Raisio Group, a 57-year old, farmer-owned company in a small Baltic Sea village in Finland, was deciding whether and how it might use strategic alliances to exploit a new margarine it had developed. The margarine, Benecol, contains a pine tree extract determined by medical testing to control and lower cholesterol levels. Demand for the product was so great that the company built a new factory to increase production and begin overseas sales.

Raisio faced many decisions. First, Raisio had to explore a possible link with a large European or US partner with worldwide marketing capabilities. Second, it had to find new sources of sterol and sitostanol, key ingredients in Benecol, since 5 tons of waste pulp must be processed at paper mills to distill one pound of the oil that is turned into sitostanol. Third, the product would have to be tested by regulatory agencies in the US and Europe. Fourth, a number of competitive products had been shown to be equally effective (Burt and William, 1998).

Within this situational context, the Raisio Group explored the place of strategic alliances within its existing conservative strategy and debated how to structure, negotiate and manage multinational alliances if it chose to expand overseas with its limited resources in a rapidly growing market (Echikson, 1997; Ibrahim, 1996; Ipsen, 1997). In 1997, the company announced an alliance with McNeil Consumer Products, a division of Johnson & Johnson (USA), for the use of Benecol in McNeil products (Molvor, 1997). A month later, Raisio announced an agreement with Westvaco Corporation (a US paper company) to build a joint venture plant in South Carolina to make sterol, a key ingredient of Benecol (Bloomberg, 1997).

Motorola provides an integrated example of different ways a multinational company has used strategic alliances: resource leveraging; speed of entry; access to customer markets; legal compliance; and access to technology. Motorola has used many kinds of strategic alliances, both joint ventures and different types of partnerships, as well as using exporting and wholly-owned subsidiaries as its strategic needs have changed.

Strategic alliances do not fit all company strategies. Citibank, for example, has successfully expanded in Asia on its own, both because of the nature of the banking business and because of its supporting computer and telecommunications technologies which enable creating and servicing banking outlets quickly without local partner support. Citibank also has the capital resources to support these moves. Industry, market and company strategic-fit and operational-fit requirements not only dictate the type of strategic alliances used, they also dictate whether or not strategic alliances are needed.

Negotiating Strategic Alliances and Selecting Compatible Partners (People and Company or Government Body)

The negotiation process for strategic alliances often is complex and lengthy. For example, the process General Motors went through in trying to put together a billion-dollar joint venture in China in the mid-1950s was without a predetermined script and lasted several years (Naughton et al, 1995; Stern, 1995), as did Tambrands' negotiations for a joint venture in Russia.

In 1996, a major chemical company with one joint venture in China in 1996, was planning four more. Based on its experience, the company thought each deal would take at least 2 years to complete. The complexities arose because the deals involved negotiating supply contracts with local companies, upgrading existing facilities, renegotiating labor contracts, complying with international environmental codes and waste disposal regulations and reducing the workforce.

Selecting partners involves matching a company's needs, values and capabilities with those of the partner firm(s) or government body. In addition, an alliance's success may depend on the type of people involved – their personal characteristics, values and capabilities – as well as on the personal chemistry among partners. Arne de Keijzer, a consultant specializing in prescreening individuals to identify the entrepreneurial, forthright, honest, innovative and adaptable characteristics which are likely predictors of effective alliance partners (de Keijzer, 1995). Observing and gaining insight into the traits of the individuals and firms involved is critical to the partner negotiation and selection process. Personal relations and trust must be cultivated and nurtured to make the alliance a success over the years.

Determining Specific Type and Structure of a Strategic Alliance That Enables an Effective Operational Fit

Many of the factors discussed in the preceding sections – strategic fit, negotiating processes and partner selection factors – can affect the type and structure of a strategic alliance. Other factors which help determine and develop an effective operational fit through the alliance structure include:

- The type of business – The structural needs of the banking, auto and airline industries differ greatly. Airline alliances are largely co-marketing and co-service partnerships, auto alliances most often involve manufacturing joint ventures, and banking alliances normally involve financial services systems.
- The enterprises involved – The Airbus consortium formed to build jet airliners involved four companies in four different countries with each doing a different part of the manufacturing process, and so required a different structure from that of the government agency and foreign firms involved in the first foreign-controlled power project in China.
- The potential for misuse of proprietary knowledge – Gillette imported its advanced technology razor, the Sensor, and manufactured only carbon and steel blades and older razor models in China in order to protect proprietary knowledge.

- The people involved – Special skills requirements and trust-worthiness of available local help can affect the management, operational and financial controls built into the structure.
- The importance of the alliance to each party – A foreign municipality may be interested only in the income from a venture, and not in ways it can provide growth for other related businesses the municipality is involved in. This was the case with Gillette where its joint venture partner retained only a 30% financial interest and did not require interlocking supply contracts. In contrast, a US chemical firm's venture in China used the Chinese partner's manufacturing facilities and had raw material supply contracts with the Chinese firm's other plants.
- Potential rivalry – The benefits of the learning potential in the General Motors alliance with Toyota in Fremont, California, apparently outweighed the fact that the automobiles produced were to be sold competitively under both the General Motors and Toyota brands. The deal was structured to terminate in the 1990s in order to tailor the structure to the logical time limits of the learning benefits.

Developing detailed alliance structures involves defining: percentage of ownership; mix of financing; kinds of material, technology, and machinery to be contributed by each partner; division and sharing of activities; staffing; location; autonomy; controls (not just for operations but also for measuring and controlling each partner's contributions over time); and guidelines for management after alliance inception.

The best structure is the organizational arrangement which most effectively meets strategic fit, operational fit and personal chemistry situation requirements *and* which is accepted through negotiation by all parties concerned. Negotiators should be convinced that the structure will enable both parties to improve their chances of obtaining the desired benefits from the relationship. The alliance must fulfill four basic criteria for each partner: it must add value, enable learning, protect and enhance core competencies and competitive advantages, and enable the operational flexibility needed for the venture to be successful.

Making Multinational Strategic Alliances Work: Leading and
Managing

Managing and leading strategic alliances involves doing whatever is
necessary to get the job done, within well-defined strategic frameworks. This task often involves reconciling and balancing diverse,
conflicting and often paradoxical forces on a continuing basis in a
complex and rapidly changing environment.

The tasks include staffing decisions, for example, the balance
between expatriate and local management. Solutions depend on
such situational factors as the nature of the product and business,
competitive market pressures, available personnel, alliance partner
relationships and their respective strategic goals, country cultures
involved, local laws and regulations, and existing pay scales. Other
tasks include managing cultural differences, developing organization structures, personnel administration, monitoring on a continuing basis and coordinating strategic alliance and home country
operations.

AN ITERATIVE EMERGING PROCESS

The four key strategic alliance activities listed above are not always
in practice discrete and sequential. For example, British Airways
selected American Airlines as a partner during the planning phase
(#1). After negotiating with them (#2), an alliance proposal with a
tentative structure suitable to airline operations was announced
(#3). More negotiations were, however, needed with the various
governments involved and with the European Economic Union
(#2). If the strategic alliance is approved, which it had not yet been in
early 1999, the alliance might have to be restructured to meet
regulatory requirements (#3). The details of managing the alliance
would then have to be worked out (#4), requiring further negotiations (#2) and refinements of the structure (#3).

The discrete and sequential process task list in the preceding
section and chapters following is for discussion and learning purposes only, so readers should keep its dynamic, iterative nature in
mind. This process is not unlike the overall strategic leadership and
management process cycle shown in Figure 1.2. Readers should note
also that strategic alliances are only one aspect of management. As

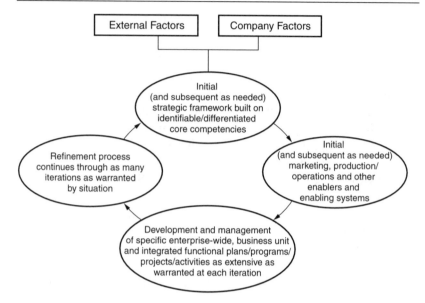

Figure 1.2   Strategic Management Process Cycle

such, they must be understood within the context of the overall strategic leadership and management process outlined in Figure 1.3.

TYPES OF ALLIANCE: AN OVERVIEW SUMMARY OF THE MAJOR KINDS

Types of interenterprise relationships are outlined in Figure 1.4. The bracket at the bottom of the figure indicates the types that are considered strategic alliances.

As seen in Figure 1.4, strategic alliances can vary along a broad continuum. *Licensing agreements* may or may not be strategic alliances, as explained in the discussion of REFRAC on page 93. International airlines have developed a wide range of *nontraditional nonequity contractual arrangements*, mainly in the marketing area. These continuing contracts are considered by many to be strategic alliances (Bryant, 1996). In 1996, long-time competitors General Electric and Rolls-Royce plc formed a *co-development partnership alliance* to develop a jet engine. The companies' goal was to compete in a program created to develop and build a new military strike aircraft for both the USA and Great Britain. The engine contracts

The Focus: An Emergent Entrepreneurial Leadership Process
The Process
1. *Strategic vision/mission:*
   'I knew exactly what kind of company I envisioned; I Just didn't know precisely what it would look like.' Precise definitions, in other words, often emerge over time, through the experiences involved in doing it.
2. *Strategic guidelines:*
   This is the map, the path, the planned steps. The secret here is KISS – 'Keep It Short and Simple.' That means one page written, five minutes oral, maximum length.
3. *Implementation:*
   'Doing whatever was necessary to get the job done, within well-defined general moral, legal, ethical and policy guidelines.' This often involves reconciling and balancing diverse, conflicting and often paradoxical forces, on a continuing basis, in a complex and rapidly changing competitive market environment.

The Activities
• Creating an overall vision (values, mission, strategic focus on core competencies, opportunities in future) and strategic framework (the guidelines or map). Specific strategies and strategic plans (enterprise-wide and in business units and functional areas) often emerge over time, through the enabling systems and processes.
• Activating, energizing, putting into place and monitoring enabling systems and processes, such as: functional area operations; telecommunications/information systems; accounting and finance systems; organization and business structures, processes and cultures; and strategic alliances.
• Nurturing enabling human resources and processes through: organization development; understanding cultural diversity, staffing, training, and communicating; and effective flexible leadership and integrative management at all levels.
• Ensuring that a core management staff (with appropriate interpersonal, communication, entrepreneurial and management skills and potential) is in place and functioning.
• Communicating and implementing the strategic framework, as well as the cultural benchmarks that are needed to enable the core management staff to translate the desired vision into action. The actual process involves superior visionary and pragmatic leadership appropriate for both the managers and people/groups involved in the situation.
• Leaving managers relatively free to manage, and pushing decision making as close to the customer as possible, but intervening where appropriate to make certain integrative activities are operating efficiently and effectively to achieve the company's strategic short- and long-term objectives.

Figure 1.3   Strategic Management: Multinational and Domestic

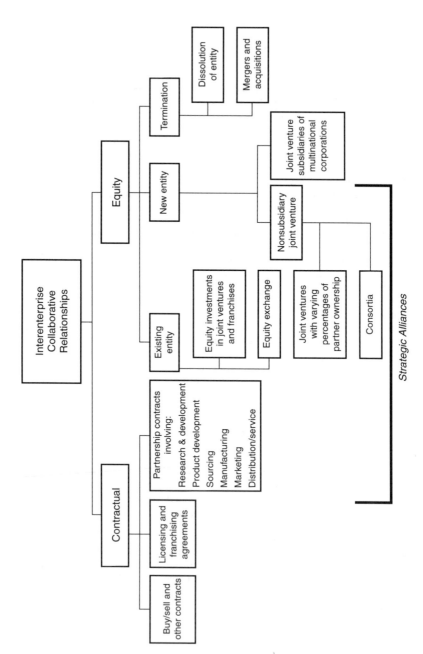

Figure 1.4 Types of Interprise Collaborative Relationships

for the new jets totaled $90 billion. Such alliance partnerships – among competitors, customers, suppliers and manufacturers – are becoming more common (Brandenburger and Nalebuff, 1996).

To enter Asian markets, Mitsubishi Motors used various alliance structures. In addition to building a dozen parts and assembly plants throughout Asia, Mitsubishi had 10 *joint ventures* in Asia, and others in Australia and New Zealand. These ranged from limited *equity investments* (from a 6.7% stake in Korea's Hyundai Motor Co. to a 32% stake in Indonesia's Mitsubishi Kram Yudka) to major *joint ventures* (Vina Star Motors – a three-way venture with the Vietnamese government, Mitsubishi and Malaysia's state-owned Perisajaam Otomobil Nasional (Proton) – which started selling vans in Vietnam in May 1995) (Updike 1995).

Daewoo's Auto Group used a different strategy in its effort to become a leading global automaker (in 1994 it ranked 24th in the world). Between 1994 and 1997, Daewoo obtained a controlling interest (50.2% to 70%) in all its automobile *joint ventures* in Poland, the Czech Republic, the former Soviet Republics and Romania. The wide range and large number of auto industry alliances are shown in Figure 1.5.

Appliance manufacturer, Whirlpool Corp., has spent $265 million since 1994 to buy *controlling interest* in four *existing competitors* in China and two in India in an effort to rapidly secure its competitive position in Asia. Airbus Industrie, founded in 1969, sells the airplanes manufactured jointly by *a consortium of four partners*: Aerospatiale (France); Daimler-Benz (Germany); British Aerospace (Great Britain); and Construcciones Aeronauticas (Spain).

In 1996, Chrysler entered into a *shared distribution* agreement in Japan (Pollack, 1995). Gillette has entered into different kinds of cooperative distribution/marketing agreements in many countries. For example, in an effort to reduce national distributors' control over price in China, Gillette entered into joint venture alliances with regional and local distributors.

Other alliances involve *research and development consortia*, a type popular and effective during the 1980s among Japanese and American companies (Bransletter and Sakakibara, 1997). More recently, multimillion-dollar consortia alliances have been formed for fuel cell research (US and Russian government agencies), advanced network technology (nine different consortia, 27 companies), gene research (three companies and an academic center) and

Company	Equity arrangement	Joint venture	Supplies or buys major components	Marketing/distribution arrangement	Technology arrangement	Manufacturing/assembly arrangement
General Motors (USA) (Includes Opel, Vauxhall Holden's, Saturn)	Isuzu Suzuki	Chrysler Daewoo Ford Isuzu Mercedes Saab Suzuki Toyota Volvo	AutoVaz BMW Fiat Honda Isuzu Mitsubishi Nissan Renault Saab Suzuki Toyota Volvo	CAC Isuzu Nissan Renault Saab	AutoVaz Chrysler Ford Isuzu Renault Toyota	Bertone CAC Isuzu Renault Suzuki Toyota
Ford (USA) (Includes Aston-Martin, Jaguar)	Kia Mazda	Fiat GM Kia Mazda Volkswagen Volvo	Fiat Mazda Nissan Volkswagen	Kia Suzuki	Chrysler GM Mazda Nissan	BMW Kia Mazda Nissan Suzuki
Toyota (Japan)	Daihatsu	Daihatsu GM Renault	Daihatsu GM Isuzu Nissan	Volkswagen	Daihatsu GM Honda Isuzu Mazda Mercedes Mitsubishi Volkswagen	Daihatsu GM Volkswagen

Volkswagen (Germany)	BAZ Skoda	First Auto Works Ford Shanghai Auto	BMW First Auto Works Ford Mercedes-Benz Nissan Shanghai Auto Skoda Volvo	Skoda Toyota	First Auto Works Mercedes-Benz Shanghai Auto Skoda Toyota	First Auto Works Toyota
Fiat (Italy) (Includes Alfa Romeo, Autobianchi, Ferrari, Iveco Lancia)	FSM	Ford Peugeot	Chrysler FSM Ford Fuji Heavy GM Pininfarina Renault Steyr	Mazda	FSM Nissan Peugeot	Bertone FSM Mazda Pininfarina
Nissan (Japan)	Fuji Heavy Yulon		Daewoo Dongfeng Ford Fuji Heavy GM Isuzu Peugeot Samsung Toyota Volkswagen Yulon	Daewoo Fuji Heavy GM	Daewoo Dongfeng Fiat Ford Honda Isuzu Mazda Mitsubishi Samsung Toyota	Ford Fuji Heavy Isuzu Mazda Yulon

Figure 1.5 Interrelationships among the World's Major Automaker (as of April 1997). Reproduced by permission, © 1997 Ward's *Automotive International*

Company	Equity arrangement	Joint venture	Supplies or buys major components	Marketing/ distribution arrangement	Technology arrangement	Manufacturing-/assembly arrangement
Peugeot (France) (Includes Citroën)		BMW Daihatsu Dongfeng Fiat Renault Suzuki	Honda Mitsubishi Nissan Renault Steyr	CAC Mazda	Daihatsu Dongfeng Fiat Mitsubishi Proton	CAC Chrysler Honda Isuzu Pininfarina
Renault (France)		Hyundai Mercedes Peugeot Toyota	Fiat GM Mitsubishi Peugeot Volvo	GM	Hyundai Peugeot	GM Isuzu
Honda (Japan)		Mitsubishi	BMW Daewoo GM Isuzu Mitsubishi Peugeot	Chrysler	BMW Daewoo Mazda Mitsubishi Nissan Toyota	China Motors Isuzu Mercedes-Benz Mitsubishi Peugeot
Chrysler (USA)		BMW Beijing Auto GM Mitsubishi Steyr-Daimler-Puch	BMW Beijing Auto Fiat Mitsubishi Steyr-Daimler-Puch	AutoVaz Honda	Beijing Auto Ford GM Mitsubishi	Mitsubishi Peugeot Steyr-Daimler-Puch

Mazda (Japan)	Ford
	Kia
		Ford
		Isuzu
			Ford
			Isuzu
			Kia
			Mitsubishi
			Suzuki
				Cycle & Carriage
				  Bintang
				Fiat
				Kia
				Peugeot
					Ford
					Kia
					Mercedes-Benz
					Nissan
					Toyota
						Cycle & Carriage
						  Bintang
						Fiat
						Ford
						Nissan
						Suzuki

Mitsubishi (Japan)	China Motors Hyundai Lotus Proton	Chrysler Honda Isuzu Mercedes-Benz Suzuki Volvo	Chrysler GM Honda Hyundai Mazda Mercedes-Benz Peugeot Proton Renault Volvo	Volvo	China Motors Chrysler Honda Hyundai Mazda Mercedes-Benz Nissan Peugeot Proton Toyota Volvo	China Motors Chrysler Honda Isuzu Pininfarina
Hyundai (South Korea)	Mitsubishi Samsung	Renault	Mitsubishi		Mitsubishi Renault	

Mercedes-Benz (Germany)	Ssangyong	GM
		Mitsubishi
		Renault
		Volkswagen
			Mitsubishi
			Ssangyong
			Volkswagen
				Cycle & Carriage
				  Bintang
				Ssangyong
					Fiat
					Mazda
					Mitsubishi
					Ssangyong
					Toyota
					Volkswagen
						Cycle & Carriage
						  Bintang
						Honda
						Mitsubishi
						Ssangyong

Figure 1.5 *(cont.)*

Company	Equity arrangement	Joint venture	Supplies or buys major components	Marketing/ distribution arrangement	Technology arrangement	Manufacturing /assembly arrangement
BMW (Germany)		Chrysler Peugeot	Chrysler FSO GM Honda Peugeot Volkswagen		Chrysler Honda	Ford Peugeot
Suzuki (Japan)	GM	GM Mitsubishi Peugeot	Daewoo First Auto Works GM Mazda	Ford	Daewoo First Auto Works	Ford Fuji Heavy GM Mazda
Volvo (Sweden)		Ford GM Mitsubishi	Fuji Heavy GM Mitsubishi Renault Volkswagen	Daewoo Fuji Heavy Mitsubishi	Fuji Heavy Isuzu Mitsubishi	Fuji Heavy
Fuji Heavy (Subaru) (Japan)	Nissan	Isuzu	Daihatsu Fiat Nissan Volvo	Nissan Volvo	Volvo	Nissan Suzuki Volvo
FSM (Poland)	Fiat		Fiat		Fiat	Fiat

Company						
FSO (Poland)			BMW Daewoo		Daewoo	Daewoo
Daihatsu (Japan)		Peugeot Toyota	Fuji Heavy Kia Toyota		Kia Peugeot Toyota	Toyota
Isuzu (Japan)	GM	Fuji Heavy GM Mazda Mitsubishi	Daewoo GM Honda Mazda Nissan Toyota	GM Volvo	Daewoo GM Nissan Toyota Volvo	GM Honda Nissan Mitsubishi Renault
SKODA (Czechoslovakia)	Volkswagen		BAZ Volkswagen	Volkswagen	BAZ Volkswagen	
Daewoo Group (South Korea)	FSO	GM	FSO Honda Isuzu Nissan Suzuki	Nissan	FSO Honda Isuzu Nissan Suzuki	FSO
Kia (South Korea) (Includes Asia Motors	Ford Mazda	Ford	Daihatsu Mazda	Ford Mazda	Daihatsu Mazda	Ford]z0

Figure 1.5 *(cont.)*

Company	Equity arrangement	Joint venture	Supplies or buys major components	Marketing/distribution arrangement	Technology arrangement	Manufacturing/assembly arrangement
Ssangyong (South Korea)	Mercedes-Benz		Mercedes-Benz	Mercedes-Benz	Mercedes-Benz	Mercedes-Benz
SAAB-Scania (Sweden)		GM	GM	GM		
Proton (Malaysia)	Lotus Mitsubishi		Mitsubishi		Mitsubishi Peugeot	
Yulon (Taiwan)	Nissan		Nissan			Nissan
Porsche (Germany)		First Auto Works				BMW
Bertone (Italy)						Fiat GM
Pininfarina (Italy)			Fiat			Fiat Mitsubishi Peugeot
Steyr-Daimler-Puch (Austria)	Chrysler		Chrysler Fiat Peugeot		Chrysler	Chrysler

China Motors (Taiwan)	Mitsubishi		Mitsubishi	Honda
Cycle & Carriage Bintang (Malaysia)		Mazda Mercedes-Benz		Mazda Mercedes-Benz
Beijing Auto Works (China)	Chrysler	Chrysler	Chrysler	
First Auto Works (China)	Porsche Volkswagen	Suzuki Volkswagen	Suzuki Volkswagen	Volkswagen
Dongfeng (China)	Peugeot	Nissan	Nissan Peugeot	

Figure 1.5 *(cont.)*

semiconductor research (dozens of companies for varying lengths of time over a 10-year period) (Anonymous, 1997; Corey, 1997; Hilts, 1997; Morrison, 1997; Puttre, 1997; Zink, 1997).

The last alliance type noted in Figure 1.4 is *dissolution*. Shell Italia, a wholly-owned subsidiary of Royal Dutch/Shell Group, the Anglo/Dutch energy firm, in the mid-1990s dissolved two alliances with the Italian conglomerate MonteEdison. Shell wanted to invest heavily in upgrading and expanding operations, while Monte-Edison was unable to because of its heavy debt. British Airways had unsuccessful strategic alliances with United Airlines and USAir, along with many successful ones, prior to its proposed alliance with American Airlines (Carnevali, 1997). An estimated two-thirds of the airline alliances formed between 1991 and 1996 were dissolved because of changing situational circumstances.

TYPES OF ALLIANCE: OTHER PERSPECTIVES

In addition to types of structures, other perspectives exist from which to view multinational strategic alliances.

First, different *functions* or *operations* can be involved, and these functions will affect all aspects of alliance development. British Steel, in order to supply an iron product to their joint venture mill in Decatur, Alabama in the US (owned by LTV Corp. of Cleveland, British Steel plc and Japan's Sumitomo Metal Industries Ltd), dismantled its mill in Hunterston, Scotland. The mill was cut into 27 000 pieces, loaded onto eight ships and carried across the Atlantic and reassembled on a small island in Alabama. The British Airways and American Airlines alliance, in contrast, focused on linking computerized customer service and marketing functions.

In another service industry situation, Penske Logistics Europe, which is 79% owned by General Electric and 21% by the Penske Corporation, both US firms, plans to offer European-wide logistics services. These include distribution and warehousing tasks involving sophisticated information technology capabilities to track shipments, bill customers and replenish stocks. The operation also will involve ownership of its customers' inventories, subassembly of components, inbound materials scheduling, debt collection, tax representation and product testing. The new firm's target areas are the

UK, Italy, Germany, France, Belgium, the Netherlands and Luxembourg. Its primary market segments are automotive, fast-moving consumer goods, food, pharmaceutical/healthcare and specialty chemicals (Gresser, 1997).

Second, the *partners* involved can affect all aspects of the alliance process. The requirements of state-owned partners protecting other aspects of their national economy in controlled markets can be quite different from those of privately-owned companies working for profit in free markets.

Third, the *size* of a venture is another characteristic that will affect strategic alliance development and management. In small ventures the personalities of the individual partners are important influencing factors. In larger alliances, the character, culture, experiences with alliances and capabilities of the partner companies, as well as of their managers and owners, will be controlling factors.

Fourth, the *relative competitive position of partners* is another perspective from which to view alliances. Today, alliances among competitors and potential competitors are quite common (Zutshi, 1998). Airlines often use them (British Airways and American Airlines, Alitalia and Air France), as do oil companies in selected regions (Mobil and British Petroleum in Europe), jet engine makers (GE and Rolls-Royce) and automakers (Toyota and General Motors).

Fifth, the *country* and *culture* involved represent and affect choices in multinational strategic alliances. For example, the characteristics of the country involved may affect the choice of which country to choose for venturing. In turn, the culture and customs of the selected country can influence all aspects of the alliance process, from how negotiations are conducted, the partners selected, the alliance structured, and the leadership and management exercised.

Sixth, others consider *equity* investment a criteria for classifying an alliance as strategic. Peter Pekar considers *non-equity* alliances, such as the one proposed between British Airways and American Airlines, as 'transactional', not 'strategic', alliances (Pekar and Harbison, 1998). On the other hand, Pekar would classify the Northwest/Continental Airlines alliance as 'strategic' because Northwest purchased 14% of Continental in addition to integrating marketing operations.

When thinking about type of alliance, then, multiple dimensions need to be considered at all phases of the strategic alliance process.

These dimensions are discussed from varying perspectives in the following chapters.

MULTINATIONAL STRATEGIC ALLIANCES: A DIVERSE AND OFTEN RISKY MULTINATIONAL STRATEGIC MANAGEMENT ENABLER

The wide range of multinational strategic alliances types makes it difficult to develop generalities applicable to all of them, or to fully cover the topic in one chapter. This chapter, therefore, has presented only a highlight summary of the topic.

Entrepreneurial skills, such as those outlined in Figure 1.1, on p. 9, are important to alliance management. Managing multinational strategic alliances is a complex and difficult process for many reasons. Such alliances involve diverse partners, some of whom are competitors or potential competitors with different strategic goals. They function in a multicultural environment and break new ground in many areas: distribution, contract law, cultural and change management and free-market economy development. These alliances are found most often in rapidly changing, highly competitive, uncertain, and risky multinational contexts. For these reasons, managing them requires adaptability, innovation, balance, creativity, grit, dedication, persistence, hard work, and some luck.

The risks involved in multinational strategic alliances were illustrated in the experiences of McDonnell Douglas Corporation in late 1996 and early 1997. McDonnell had announced a $1.6 billion 'deal' to build 40 airplanes, 20 in California and 20 in Shanghai (Gerth and Sanger, 1996). As part of the contract, McDonnell agreed to sell China $5 million worth of machine tools – provided that they were not used for military purposes. The Chinese apparently diverted the tools to a military plant to be used in missile production. A federal grand jury in Washington, DC, subpoenaed thousands of documents from McDonnell and other parties in the case in an effort to determine whether American export-control laws had been criminally violated. Because the machine tools had been shipped prior to the start of the alliance and had been used illegally by China, it appeared that the alliance might be cancelled. In late 1997, China admitted the violation and pledged to correct the problem (Sanger, 1997). Such experiences dictate that extreme care is needed before entering into alliances, especially those in developing countries.

INSTITUTIONALIZING (IMBEDDING) STRATEGIC ALLIANCE SKILLS

The benefits of alliances are obvious, as evidenced by the number of them. Since 1930, for example, General Electric has participated in more than 30 joint ventures and contractual linkages. General Motors has undertaken dozens of equity and non-equity alliances, while the auto industry has engaged in more than a thousand in the areas of manufacturing, marketing and distribution, parts and components, technology and research and development.

The potential usefulness of strategic alliances, though not for every firm in every situation, is clearly documented. The problem then is making them work effectively in appropriate situations – a complex task due to the geographical distances, differing personalities and strategic needs, the time needed to negotiate details and develop trust among partners, the unforeseen competitive moves and international crises that occur, and many other influencing factors.

Experience with forming strategic alliances is one key to success, as seen from UPS's experiences and the Booz-Allen & Hamilton survey results cited on pp. 1–2 (Harbison, 1997a,b; Kelly, 1997). As the Booz-Allen & Hamilton study also pointed out, systematically institutionalizing or imbedding an alliance capability within the corporation and following a disciplined, systematic approach to alliance development and management are equally important. This book deals with these two aspects by presenting a systematic process for developing and managing strategic alliances and by providing 'Best Practice' guidelines and situational analysis checklists at the end of each chapter and in Appendix A.

REFERENCES

Anonymous (1997). Israel In, *Electronic Business Today*, April, pp. 87–88.
Badaracco, J. (1991). *The Knowledge Link: How Firms Compete Through Strategic Alliances*, Boston, MA, Harvard Business School Press.

Bloomberg Business News (1997). Raisio to build plant in Carolina. *The New York Times*, August 29, p. D2.

Brandenburger, A.M. and Nalebuff, B.J. *Co-opetition.* New York, Doubleday Currency.

Bransletter, L. and Sakakibara, M. (1997). Japanese Research Consortia: A microeconometric analysis of industrial policy. *Presentation/Paper*, Annual Conference, Strategic Management Research Society, Barcelona, Spain, October 8.

Bryant, A. (1996). American Airlines expects to sign British Airways pact. *The New York Times*, June 10, p. D2.

Brzezinski, M. (1997a). Daewoo boldly invades old soviet bear. *The Wall Street Journal*, May 7, p. A14.

Brzezinski, M. (1997b). Politics will steer Ukraine's decision on auto partner. *The Wall Street Journal Europe*, January 24–25, p. 4.

Burt, T. and Willman, J. (1998). Test results for Unilever spread hit Raisio shares. *Financial Times*, March 17, p. 17.

Carnevali, N. (1997). An Application Study of Multinational Strategic Alliance Type and Structure Decisions From a Contingency Perspective, master's thesis written under the supervision of Dr. R.J. Mockler. New York, St. John's University.

CE Roundtable (1997). The virtual organization. *Chief Executive*, July, pp. 58–66.

CEO Brief (1997a). Leaps of faith, and the best of both worlds. *Chief Executive*, June (Suppl.), pp. 8–11, 12–15.

CEO Brief (1997b). Side by side. *Chief Executive*, June (Suppl.), pp. 2–7.

Corey, E.R. (1997). *Technology Fountainheads: The Management Challenge of R&D Consortia.* Boston, MA, Harvard Business School Press.

Davenport, T.H. and Prusak, L. (1998). *Working Knowledge.* Boston, MA, Harvard Business School Press.

de Keijzer, A.J. (1995). Identifying potentially effective joint venture partners. Global Market Conference on China, New York. *The Journal of Commerce*, Baruch College, November 8.

Echikson, W. (1997). From Finland, one for the heart. *Business Week*, May 5, p. 8.

Gerth, J. and Sanger, D.E. Aircraft deal with Chinese questioned. *The New York Times*, October 30, A1, A10.

Gomes-Casseres, B. and McQuade, K. (1991). *Xerox and Fuji Xerox*, Case # 9–391–156. Boston, MA: Harvard Business School Press (Revised 12/8/92).

Gregoriou, E. (1996). *Method of Entry of the Russian Menatep Bank and Arab Bank in Cyprus.* Research Working Paper, New York, Strategic Management Research Group.

Gresser, C. (1997). GE to set up Europe-wide logistics venture. *Financial Times*, August 26, p. 14.

Hilts, P.J. (1997). Companies forge gene research link. *The New York Times*, April 30, p. D8.

Harbison, J.R. and Pekar, P. (1997a). *Cross-Border Alliances in the Age of Collaboration.* New York, Booz-Allen & Hamilton.

Harbison, J.R. and Pekar, P. (1997b). *Institionalizing Alliance Skills: Secrets of Repeatable Success.* New York, Booz-Allen & Hamilton.

Ibrahim, Y.M. (1996). Village in Finland faces a gold rush fed by margarine. *The New York Times*, July 23, pp. A1, D6.

Ipsen, E. (1997). Finnish firm redefines health food. *International Herald Tribune*, January 9, pp. 1, 15.

Jacobson, G. and Hillkirk, J. (1986). *Xerox: American Samurai.* New York, Macmillan.

Kelly, J. (1997). All together now, *Chief Executive,* November, pp. 61–63.

Kobayashi, K. (1991). *The Rise of NEC,* Cambridge, MA, Blackwell, pp. xvii–xx.

Kraar, L. (1996). Daewoo's daring drive into Europe. *Fortune,* May 13, pp. 145–152.

Lynch, R.P. (1993). *Business Alliances Guide.* New York, John Wiley.

Molvor, G. (1997). US License deal boosts Raisio. *Financial Times,* July 16, pp. 15, 18.

Morrison, G.B. (1997). On to decade two. *Electronic News,* August 25, p. 1.

Nakamota, M. (1997). NTT shuns global alliances. *Financial Times,* January 7, p. 13.

Naughton, K., Engardio, P. and Roberts, D. (1995). How GM got the inside track in China: a relentless push and clever strategy seem to have won the auto maker a huge joint venture. *Business Week,* November 6, pp. 56–57.

Overseas Projects (1997). *Corporate Publication,* Seoul, Korea, Daewoo Group.

Pekar, P. and Harbison, J.R. (1998). (of Booz-Allen & Hamilton). Implementing alliances and acquisitions. *The 1998 Strategic Alliances Conference.* New York: The Conference Board, April 30–May 1.

Pollack, A. (1995). Chrysler to buy control of Japanese chain. *The New York Times,* June 27, pp. D1, D5.

Porter, M.E. (1990). *Competitive Advantage of Nations.* New York, Free Press.

Puttre, M. (1997). Russian–American consortium fuel cell research. *Design News,* March 24, p. 10.

Reed, J. (1997). Foreigners transform Hungary's banks. *The Wall Street Journal,* September 24, p. A18.

REFRAC Technology Development Corporation (1996). *Annual Report for 1995,* New York.

Roos, J., Roos, G., Dragonetti, G. and Edvinsson, L. (1997). *Intellectual Capital: Navigating in the New Business Landscape.* London, Macmillan.

Sanger, D.E. (1997). China to return computer it had diverted to military. *The New York Times,* September 12, p. A10.

Stern, G. (1995). GM executive's ties to native country help auto maker clinch deal in China. *The Wall Street Journal,* November 2, p. B5.

Thornhill, J. (1997). Estonian banks thrive in a new economy, *Financial Times,* September 24, p. 3.

Updike, E. and Nakarmi, L. (1995). A movable feast for Mitsubishi. *Business Week,* August 28, pp. 50, 51.

Wong, W., Lee, S.T., Thoo, K.F. and Tang, Y.Q. (1996). The choice of relevant investment forms in China: Wholly foreign-owned versus joint venture enterprises. In *Business Opportunities in Sichuan Province, China* (Tech Meng Tan, ed.). New York, Prentice Hall, pp. 115–124.

Zink, J.C. (1997). Competition may encourage collaborative research. *Power Engineering,* May, p. 6.

Zutshi, R. (1998). *Strategic Alliances: Cooperation and Competition.* Woburn, MA, Butterworth-Heineman.

2
Strategic Management Fit: The Enabling Role of Alliances for an Individual Firm

Each company, industry and country has individual strategic needs which dictate the role of alliances in a multinational company. The strategic role, or fit, can range from significant, enterprise-wide strategic use, as was the case with News Corporation, Toshiba and Motorola, to an important enabling role as at Gillette as it expanded worldwide. In addition, that strategic role can vary over time as circumstances change.

DETERMINING THE STRATEGIC FIT: DIFFERENT STRATEGIC NEEDS DICTATE DIFFERENT ALLIANCE STRATEGIES

Rupert Murdoch, chairman and owner of a 30% controlling interest in the Australian-based News Corporation, used alliances to achieve his corporation's objective:

> to own every major form of programming – news, sports, films, and children's shows – and bring them via satellite or TV stations to homes in the United States, Europe, Asia and South America.

Murdoch has formed dozens of alliances to achieve this objective over a relatively short time period. For example, News Corporation, which owns two satellite services, Star TV in Asia and B Sky B in the UK, announced in 1995 the formation of a direct broadcast service in Latin America with three partners: Globo, the leading media company in Brazil; Grupo Televisa, a giant Mexican broadcaster; and Tele-Communications Inc., the US's largest cable operator. The new service was expected to have only one million subscribers initially in May 1996, but Murdoch felt that the service had a potential audience of more than 400 million in Central and South America. The partners planned to invest $500 million in the service, which would transmit 150 entertainment, news and sports programming channels to homes equipped with satellite dishes and digital receivers. From 1995 through 1997, Murdoch entered into other partnerships worth billions of dollars, in the US, Europe, Latin America and Asia. In no instance has his company worked alone.

Even though he has experienced setbacks, Murdoch is given a good chance of succeeding. Observers describe him as an entrepreneurial opportunist who is willing to act quickly, ignore naysayers and spend heavily to enhance his strategy. His management and leadership style is described as 'well suited to an era of rapidly changing technologies and multicountry alliances' (Fabrikant 1996). If successful, Murdoch's worldwide media operation will substantially contribute to the growing globalization trend he is responding to and taking advantage of.

Toshiba Corp., the oldest and third largest of Japan's electronics giants (after Hitachi and Matsushita), has also made strategic alliances a key element of its corporate strategy (Schendler, 1993). Since the early 1900s when it contracted to make light bulb filaments for General Electric (essentially a co-production agreement), Toshiba has entered into partnerships, technology licensing agreements and joint ventures to complement its substantial marketing, manufacturing and research and development skills. Strategic alliances have enabled Toshiba to become a leading worldwide manufacturer of electronics products – from large power plant equipment to complex memory chips.

Toshiba has strategic alliances with many companies: Apple Computer, Asahi Chemical Industry, Ericsson, GEC Alstholm, General Electric, LSI Logic of Canada, Motorola, National Semiconductor, Olivetti, Rhone-Poulenc, Samsung, SGS-Thomson, Sun Microsystems, Telic Alcatel, Thomson Consumer Electronics, Time Warner and United Technologies. Some of these alliances have involved billion-dollar investments and have made major strategic differences for Toshiba. Its alliance with Motorola

(Tohoku Semiconductor) helped make Toshiba a world leader in the production of memory chips. Its alliance with IBM enabled Toshiba starting from scratch to become the world's second-largest supplier of color flat-panel displays for portable computers. Other partnerships produce nuclear and steam power generating equipment, computers, fax machines and copiers, advanced semiconductors, rechargeable batteries and fuel cells, medical equipment and home appliances.

Fumio Sato, Toshiba's president and CEO, believes strategic alliances are the only strategy for a high-tech company with global ambitions: 'It is no longer an era in which a single company can dominate any technology or business by itself. The technology has become so advanced, and the markets so complex, that you simply can't expect to be the best at the whole process any longer.' For example, in the future, new-generation random-access memory chips are expected to cost over a billion dollars to develop; because of the cost, Toshiba has entered into alliances with nine other chipmakers.

Toshiba constructs its alliances so that the roles and rights of each partner are clearly defined. Each pact includes the corporate equivalent of a prenuptial agreement, so both sides know who gets what if the partnership does not work out. Another reason its alliances work so well is that senior management plays an active role in each relationship and so is able to develop trust and personal chemistry. This enables resolving inevitable conflicts along the way. According to Jack Welch, CEO of GE: 'I've dealt with Toshiba for 15 years, and it's always been a very easy relationship. When things go awry, a call to Sato-san will take care of the problem within 24 hours.' In the view of Toshiba's CEO, carefully chosen partners are essential to moving quickly and marshalling the company resources needed to keep up with the high-tech race in all phases of its businesses, from product design and development to manufacturing and distribution.

The mixed joint venture/wholly-owned subsidiary strategy of Mitsubishi Motors Corp. in Asia, described in Chapter 1, arose from country and market requirements as well from corporate enterprise-wide strategic and other company needs. During the early 1980s, Mitsubishi Motors Corp., Japan's youngest automaker, faced heavy competition in Japan (its primary business area). When considering expanding (market diversification) into

Europe and the USA, Mitsubishi also faced severe competition
from experienced companies such as Honda and Toyota. Necessity
dictated that the company diversify into a newly emerging market
where competition was less severe at the time – Asia. A strategy, a
major component of which was strategic alliances, that was born
out of necessity turned into great good fortune.

Auto sales throughout Asia were booming as fast as local economies in mid-1995. Since 1989, South Korea's gross domestic product
had soared 300% and car ownership had jumped 500% to 74
million. More than 500 new cars were hitting Bangkok's traffic-
choked streets daily. The Asian market was expected eventually to
surpass in size the combined European and North American markets (Updike and Nakarmi, 1995). Few companies were as well-
situated to ride the surge as Mitsubishi, which had established a
huge network of relationships in Asia both through building
wholly-owned subsidiary facilities, as well as by establishing joint
venture strategic alliances. The firm also had a wide mix of products
designed to match the varied tastes of Asian car buyers, a major core
competency tailored to meet market needs and help the firm
weather periodic downturns.

Problems arose for Mitsubishi during the Asian currency crisis in
early 1998 and Mitsubishi reported losses, but the situation was
expected to turn around over the long run (Nakamoto 1998). Mitsubishi's eventual move into the US was predictably not successful
since the company lacked an appropriate mix of products and
partners there.

Banco Bilbao Vizcaya faced a maturing, highly competitive banking and investment services market in Spain, as did banks in other
European countries in the mid-1990s. Banco Bilbao's solution was
to move into culturally compatible, developing markets in South
America using joint ventures and wholly-owned subsidiaries. This
successful strategic move led to a 3-year turnaround for the bank by
late 1997 (Uriarte, 1997).

As evident from these experiences and the ones described below,
developing alliance strategies is a decision highly dependent on
specific situation factors – both internal company and external
competitive market and industry factors.

AS NEEDS CHANGE, SO DOES ALLIANCE STRATEGY: AN EVOLVING STRATEGIC FIT DECISION

The role of strategic alliances within a firm's strategic framework depends on a number of factors. For example, strategic alliances played an integral role in Motorola's enterprise-wide strategic framework. This framework emerged over a 20-year period as the company attempted to formulate a strategic response to changing competitive market conditions in its industry, a response that was limited by scarce resources. From its inception in 1928 through 1975, Motorola focused on consumer electronics products such as radios and TVs, and on semiconductors. Global competition in the mid-1970s, especially from Japanese manufacturers, threatened its two-core businesses, semiconductors and radio/communications products, and led Motorola to revise its enterprise-wide strategy. First, it decided to become a global company, like its competitors. Second, Motorola decided to move into the application (user) areas served by semiconductor core business.

Motorola's major competitors were diversified and worldwide – Philips (Netherlands), Siemens (Germany) and NEC, Toshiba and Hitachi (Japan) in semiconductors; and NEC, Matsushita and Fujitsu (Japan) and L.M. Ericsson (Sweden) in communications. Motorola was at a disadvantage because these companies already had established significant overseas operations and could sell to their own diversified divisions. These competitors also had the resources to develop new technologies that could make Motorola's technologies obsolete. In addition, the market for sophisticated, high-tech products had shifted to the Far East, so Motorola needed to establish a presence there, among major users of its products. These market shifts especially threatened Motorola's growing line of microprocessors (a category of semiconductors).

Given Motorola's limited resources, the solution to these competitive disadvantages in design, research, development and user access was for Motorola to form closer ties with users. The need to move quickly, resource limitations, the high cost of high-tech development and the need to gain access to the Japanese manufacturers who were major markets for microprocessor and other semiconductor products suggested that alliances would be a key strategy for survival. Motorola provides an integrated example of a multinational company using alliances for resource leveraging, speed of entry, access to customer markets, legal compliance and access to advanced technology.

Motorola has used a variety of alliances in Japan. In the following discussions, the alliance type and entry method are given in *italics*. In the late 1970s, Motorola had a *licensing agreement* that permitted NEC and Hitachi to build low-end microprocessors using Motorola's technology (Business Week, 1991, p. 96). This alliance was seen as a way to enter the microprocessor market in Japan without a large capital investment at a time when Motorola lacked the resources that it has today. The Japanese partners later used Motorola's technology to become direct competitors, an ever-present danger in strategic alliances. This was an expensive learning experience about the need to protect technology from competitors' cannibalization.

In Japan there exists an alliance system called keiretsu. *Keiretsus* may involve formal and informal relationships with suppliers or marketing channels which have developed over the years (such as Toyota has with its suppliers in Japan) or other interfirm links (for example, among manufacturers and supporting financial institutions). What is difficult for some Western business executives to grasp is that these interfirm links often are built not on contracts but on relationships developed over years, creating obligations that the Japanese feel must be honored – a cultural basis. These links can have important benefits, for example, when companies in an industry (often with government regulatory support) act in unison to exclude foreign competitors from the Japanese market (Gerlach 1992).

Because Japan's keiretsu system promoted favoritism among domestic companies and often locked out foreign companies (Dawkins, 1997; Neff, 1997), Motorola entered into several *joint ventures* with Japanese firms. This gave Motorola access to markets that it might otherwise have had trouble entering effectively. Its most significant joint venture, begun with Toshiba in 1986, was a joint manufacturing company called Tokoku Semiconductor Corporation. This deal allowed Toshiba and Motorola to share technologies as well as the investment burden (Business Week, 1991, p. 98). More importantly, Motorola gained access to the Japanese manufacturers that used its semiconductors, a market previously dominated by Japanese producers. In 1994, the two firms announced plans to build a plant to produce the next generation of semiconductors (Japan 21st, 1994, p. 95). Although this venture has had several problems with technology transfers, Motorola has remained committed to it.

Motorola's joint ventures were not limited to single-partner deals. In 1993, DDI Corp., the main competitor of Japan's Nippon Telegraph and Telephone, agreed to invest along with Motorola in the Iridium project, a noncompetitive venture involving a satellite-based communications system. DDI also formed a $1 billion *consortium* named Iridium Japan with other Japanese companies, including Mitsubishi, Mitsui and Sony (Elstrom 1997). Motorola had been reluctant to develop this project alone because of the project's size and complexity. Motorola subsequently announced a *joint venture* in the satellite communications area, which involved fewer partners and a larger $6.1 billion network of 72 low-orbit satellites capable of worldwide voice, video and high-speed data links that aimed to serve international corporations (Brzezinski, 1997; Hardy 1996; Schine et al, 1997).

Motorola also *exports* to Japan, a market-entry strategy that does not necessarily involve strategic alliances. Motorola, the world's largest producer of cellular phones, manufactures these phones in the USA and exports them to many countries, including Japan. Success in the direct export market was slowed by government regulation and by the fact that the technology of the Japanese telephone company (Nippon Telegraph and Telephone) was less advanced than Motorola's. For this reason, Motorola was unable to fully adapt its products to the market needs and telecommunication infrastructures in Japan.

Motorola also established in Japan a *wholly-owned subsidiary*, named Nippon Motorola Ltd. Through this subsidiary, Motorola built a wafer fabrication plant and planned to build a factory to produce logic integrated circuits. Production was due to commence in 1998 (Mobile Phone News, 1995).

Motorola's decision to enter China, another major Asian market, was based in part on the expectation that China's 1.2 billion population will be one of the largest markets for its products in the 21st century. Motorola has used a variety of alliance entry/operating strategies tailored specifically to the requirements of the Chinese market, one of the world's fastest-growing economies (Schoenberger, 1996).

Motorola entered the Chinese market in 1992, after the Tiananmen Square riots led the Chinese government to permit Motorola to establish a *wholly-owned subsidiary*. Previously, the government had run or controlled most major businesses in China. The government, which tightly regulated the economy, restricted the amount of ownership and participation a foreign company could have in Chinese enterprises. However, because of the explosive growth of China's economy in the past several years and its unstable political conditions, these laws have constantly changed. By entering the venture at that time, Motorola was able to establish facilities in the southern city of Tianjin, located in one of China's economic zones, on very favorable terms. The Tianjin plant manufactures cellular phones, pagers and semiconductors. Some of the production of semiconductors and cellular phones was to be exported. However, demand for pagers was so great in China that the Chinese government purchased all of the pager production. Motorola has also taken advantage of low-cost labor and good supporting infrastructure in Tianjin and has worked to involve the local labor force in all aspects of manufacturing, from design to engineering (Engardio, 1993, p. 58). Through these efforts, Motorola substantially raised the quality of its production in China.

In October 1995, Motorola announced plans to enlarge its relationship with the Chinese government and construct a *wholly-owned* wafer manufacturing facility in Tianjin. Construction of the facility was expected to begin in 1996 and the plant was targeted to become operational in 1998 (Hardie, 1995, p. 60), a move that would increase Motorola's China investment to $1.2 billion (Schoenberger, 1996).

In 1996, Motorola was planning a *joint venture equity investment in an existing company*, Panda Electronics Group, which was state-owned until it began listing its shares on the Hong Kong stock exchange. The Chinese government, which is constantly looking for technology and capital to help its economy, encouraged Motorola to undertake the venture. The venture was planned to produce Power PCs and, eventually, pagers and cellular phones (Schoenberger 1996).

China's demand for electronics was so great that Motorola also *exported* goods directly to China (close to $1 billion annually in recent years). In addition, many of the materials China needs for its manufacturing facilities are imported.

Motorola also was involved in developing China's cellular phone infrastructure – through a *joint venture* with two state-owned firms. Motorola supplied equipment and related support services to enable the licensed manufacture of cellular phone equipment at one of these firms, Hangzou Communications Equipment. This was Motorola's only *licensed* cellular manufacturing facility in China.

Motorola joined with LM Ericsson, also a supplier of cellular systems in parts of China, to sign a *contractual agreement* with the Chinese government to interlink the country's cellular phone networks. This contract gave Motorola access to areas of the country that it had not previously penetrated. Including this contract, Motorola had cellular service contracts in areas encompassing over 1 billion of China's population in 1997.

Motorola's success in China in the 1990s was due largely to its superior products and services, which the Chinese government seemed to trust. Motorola was thus able to reap major benefits from its relationship with the Chinese government. Other political factors – in particular, China's human rights policies – have kept Motorola from expanding its local operations more rapidly until the political situation stabilizes.

At the same time, Motorola initiated alliances in the USA with Apple Computer, Hewlett-Packard, Unisys and NCR. These domestic and overseas alliances gave Motorola versatility in creating product designs, spreading risks and expanding the scope and volume of its business to degrees not possible without alliances. Alliances have become a key element of Motorola's enterprise-wide strategic framework and benefited the company in many ways.

STRATEGIC ALLIANCES IN THE AIRLINE INDUSTRY: A DRAMATICALLY DIFFERENT KIND OF STRATEGIC FIT

Strategic alliances are increasingly found in the airline industry because of:

- The needs of business and leisure travelers (worldwide transportation by air to any chosen destination).
- Government regulations (governing landing rights, cross-ownership, route structures).
- The nature of airline route structures (often hub or centralized-base).
- Promotion and selling requirements (most often done by telephone, through independent agents, or on the Internet).

- Capital investment required (for example, the 1997 joint equity investment by Sabena, Swissair and Austrian Airlines in jet aircraft).

As the airline industry makes the transition from national regulation to freer international competition, consolidations are increasing in the industry, often through strategic alliances. The number of airline alliances increased from 324 in 1995 to 389 in 1996 (The Economist, 1996).

Because of the nature of the industry, airline alliances are distinct. They involve open skies agreements, codesharing in order to share flight reservations, shared terminals, shared marketing and other types of contractual and franchising partnerships – often in conjunction with equity joint ventures. Special technology requirements and capabilities have, for example, led to the development of cooperative alliance computer reservations systems, such as the Galileo Computer Reservations System which is operated under the guidance of British Airways and several airline partners. It consists of a massive central data base which is accessed through user terminals in travel agencies and airline reservation offices around the world. The data base offers a comprehensive array of travel information and services, including schedules and availability of air services, international fare quotes, worldwide hotel reservations and car rental facilities, and other travel-related services, including currency conversion and theater/event tickets.

CONTRASTING EXPERIENCES AT OTHER FIRMS

Less rethinking and reformulating of strategic frameworks was needed at Gillette, as its strategic thrust gradually became worldwide during the 1980s. Gillette was a strategically well-focused company, although it did expand for a time beyond shaving and personal care products (and pens). Gillette's strengths were its leading technology, its superior resources and its worldwide brand leadership. Alliances were important to Gillette for several reasons. First, countries such as China generally required joint ventures for overseas companies to operate there. Second, joint ventures were necessary for marketing and distribution in many places – the European Economic Union countries, for example. Third, in controlled emerging economies, such as China, adequate free market infrastructures for distribution, sales and promotion did not exist; they had not been needed in the past because the government generally purchased all products.

Industry, company and market situation factors led Gillette to use alliances in a more limited way than did Motorola – as an enabler to grow in China, for example. Gillette's Shanghai joint venture plant, like many of its other plants worldwide, uses local cooperative distributor alliances to ensure mass distribution of Gillette's products. Alliances were essential for Gillette to prosper at the business unit level, and not as important at the enterprise-wide level as at Motorola. Like Motorola, Gillette learned through experience. On at least one occasion, Gillette had to restructure a joint venture operation because of changing circumstances.

Microsoft, the US software giant, has sales offices and wholly owned subsidiaries in nearly 60 countries. Each country's managers, almost all of whom are locals who know their home markets, create partnerships with small local companies that sell Microsoft products. To support these networks of partnerships, Microsoft offers joint management and sales training and development programs and enters into various kinds of contractual alliances with independent local software distributors, as well as works with software developers and resellers who develop, manufacture and sell Microsoft and Microsoft-related products. It also brings promising people from key resellers and software developers to come to work for Microsoft for up to a year. Some observers debate whether Microsoft delegates too much responsibility to its partner companies around the globe, many of which are small, new businesses. This model, however, has worked well in Japan, Europe and the USA and so appears to be workable elsewhere (Schendler, 1997). Microsoft also uses alliances in other ways. For example, in August 1997 it announced that it was entering an alliance with Apple Computer, a major competitor, and investing in the company.

Oracle, another US worldwide software developer, has a similar partnership program. Oracle enters into formal associations governed by contracts with local companies that make capital investments in the partnership program. These relationships are continuing ones, which give partners access to Oracle's latest technology and serve as beta (prototype testing) sites of Oracle's latest software (Survey, 1997).

These and other companies' experiences show how the strategic role of alliances can vary with situation circumstances. Alliances were essential elements of Motorola's, Airbus', and The News Corporation's enterprise-wide strategy, but in a different way for each company. Alliances for Gillette were, in contrast, effective and essential business unit enablers (for organizing, marketing and managing) in selected geographic areas. In planning an alliance strategy, therefore, each company must reexamine its strategic framework to determine the exact role of alliances, especially in relation to different market-entry/ operating approaches available.

ALLIANCES OR OTHER ENTRY/OPERATING APPROACHES? A MAJOR STRATEGIC FIT DECISION

While alliances are useful in many situations, they are only one of many available approaches. Amersham International, a UK healthcare and life sciences group chose to grow through *mergers* with Norway's Nicomed and Sweden's Pharmacia Biotech (Green, 1997; Taylor, 1997). BAA, the UK's airports retail and management group, *purchased* Duty Free International of the US (Skapinker, 1997). In contrast, Blockbuster Video has used a *mixed strategy*, forming *joint venture* alliances in non-English-speaking countries, such as Italy, and establishing *wholly-owned* stores in the UK.

British Petroleum's Decision

British Petroleum (BP) also uses a mixed strategy (Carasol-Volpe, 1997). When BP considered substantially strenghtening its position in Europe, the company analyzed the following options in the mid-1990s.

BP considered the possibility of *buying existing oil distribution companies in European countries* to increase the number of its outlets and gain market share rapidly. BP sought local/national oil companies with a large number of retail outlets that could be integrated with its logistics and production systems. BP especially needed to strengthen its positions in Italy, Belgium, France, Spain and Germany. BP also sought to expand in Turkey and Eastern European countries. The expense involved in such country-by-country purchases, especially when the overall European market was maturing, as well as the difficulties involved in assimilating different cultures and satisfying varying strategic needs, argued against this approach.

The alternative of *internal growth* was feasible, but BP estimated that constructing its own retail outlets in targeted areas would take at least 8 years, an unacceptable timetable. The options of pursuing *joint ventures (equity investments) with local firms* or *starting new joint ventures with local partners* were rejected because of the difficulty of meshing multiple differing corporate cultures and strategic fits.

BP also considered a *strategic alliance with a major European partner* operating in many European countries. Four possibilities existed: Exxon, Shell, Mobil and ENI (Agip). With more than 10% of the market apiece, market leaders Exxon and Shell were considered too large to entertain such an alliance. ENI, an Italian firm, had most of its refining facilities in Italy and so did not fully complement BP's. Mobil had complementary facilities and a union with BP could create a market share comparable to that of Exxon and Shell. BP and Mobil eventually negotiated a *newly created joint venture*, limited to retail station networks, logistic infrastructures and production plants. Both companies expected to benefit from the sound strategic and operational fit that would enable the new entity to compete against Exxon and Shell, while at the same time preserving and protecting each partner's other businesses. The limited scope of this well-defined alliance was also considered best because BP and Mobil previously had attempted a broader collaborative venture in 1990 which had failed.

Other Company Experiences

General Motors Corp. also has used a mixed strategy in expanding overseas operations to a point where 50% of its capacity is expected to eventually be overseas. The company owns many of its overseas plants and enters into joint ventures where required (as in China). British Telecommunications (BT), which in 1996 proposed a $22 billion merger with MCI that never was completed, also uses a mixed strategy, as described in Chapter 1.

Contingency Decision Situations

Figure 2.1 outlines the basic contingency process involved in deciding whether to use alliances instead of other entry/operation strategies – such as exporting or creating a wholly-owned subsidiary – in
an overseas location. This outline was developed from studying the
experiences of the many companies discussed in this book.

As the situation factors listed at the top of Figure 2.1 are evaluated in a decision situation, an initial strategy will begin to emerge
and be formulated. For this illustrative introductory discussion, the
possible decisions have been limited to three alternative strategies: a
wholly-owned subsidiary; joint ventures/contractual partnership
agreements; and exporting.

To successfully pursue a *wholly-owned subsidiary* strategy, either
through starting one's own subsidiary or buying an existing facility,
a firm must have adequate financial resources. Regardless of other
favorable factors – for example, strong sales potential, a low level of
political risk, the availability of technically skilled workers, or recep-
tiveness of the foreign government involved – inadequate financial
resources will limit the use of this entry strategy. In 1995, Siemens of
Germany used this strategy to locate a new $1.7 billion semiconduc-
tor plant in Northern England. Favorable factors included Siemens'
strong financial resources, the area's low labor rates and high unemployment levels, lack of political barriers, political stability, availability of skilled non-militant labor, and infrastructure with technical schools and electronics component manufacturers which could
support companies in the computer industry. Due to reduced worldwide demand, however, Siemens was forced to close the plant in
1999.

In the early 1990s, Menatep Bank, the 10th largest bank in Russia,
was considering ways to create an operation through which it could
perform overseas banking unencumbered by heavy government
regulations, such as those in Russia (Gregoriou, 1996). The Jor-
danian Arab Bank Ltd, one of the largest banks in the Arab world,
faced the same decision in the late 1980s. Both banks tentatively
selected the island of Cyprus, located centrally in the Mediterra-
nean, for serving Europe, Asia and Africa. Cyprus had modern
business services, a favorable tax structure, a good climate and
ample skilled labor.

In addition, Menatep chose Cyprus because more than 7000

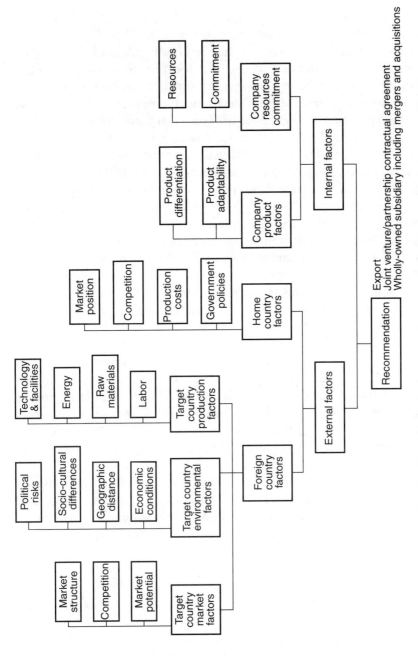

Figure 2.1 Decision Situation Diagram: Entry/Operating Strategy – International Market Overview Diagram

Russian businesses had registered offshore companies in Cyprus and used locally registered international banks there to avoid problems in Russia and yet get full international banking services. Menatep also intended to use this location to expand its international operations by serving non-Cypriot customers in Cyprus customers in other overseas locations. Its marketing focus was on the corporate customer segment. The Arab Bank, which was larger than Menatep, had a much more extensive international operation to service, was larger than Menatep, and focused on individual, corporate and institutional customers. The Arab Bank wanted to establish a more comprehensive banking operation in Cyprus.

Menatep chose to form a *wholly-owned branch*, since it was easier to form and subject to less regulation. The branch was restricted to doing business with non-Cypriot customers in Cyprus and with overseas customers, something which fit Menatep's strategic objective. The Arab Bank, in contrast, opened a *wholly-owned subsidiary*. Since its objective was to open a full-service operation for Cypriot and overseas customers, meeting the additional regulatory requirements was worth the effort.

The availablity of financial resources does not necessarily mean that the wholly-owned subsidiary approach is recommended. The market may be difficult to penetrate, legal restraints may be difficult to overcome, or wholly-owned foreign investments may not be allowed. In these situations, if a firm finds an overseas market attractive, a *joint venture* might be considered. The Daewoo Group used this approach when investing in Central Europe and Russia to take advantage of the market potential for automobile sales.

Contractual partnership agreements are a viable alternative if management is unsure of the target market's sales potential, product adaptation is high, political conditions are unstable, a firm's level of international expertise is limited, or the business requires them. Contractual partnership agreements often are used to limit a company's exposure to risk when entering a new and unfamiliar market. Partnerships are especially popular among airlines, where they enable partners to function as a single carrier while remaining separate companies.

An *exporting* strategy is a minimum-risk approach. In a joint venture partnership agreement, a company may have to fund part of the project and/or relinquish a substantial portion of the venture's ownership. Exporting eliminates these costs and associated risks. If the sales potential for the target market is high or uncertain, the estimated production and distribution costs are lower at home than in the foreign location, product adaptability requirements are low, import and export restrictions are favorable, raw materials are relatively more expensive abroad, the political climate abroad is unstable and the firm has limited financial resources, then exporting is a recommended strategy. Based on these factors, it is not surprising that many small companies make use of exporting.

US mail-order companies have used exporting extensively to penetrate the Japanese market. They have succeeded because they are extremely adept at doing business by mail, it is the least complicated way to penetrate the market, distribution costs through mail-order are much cheaper than through retail channels in Japan and Japanese tastes and buying habits are similar to those of Americans. In 1994, L.L. Bean's mail-order sales in Japan reached $100 million, up 66% from 1993. Total US mail-order sales to Japan were approximately $750 million in 1995 – about 2–3% of total retail sales in Japan. In response to complaints about size and fabric differences, several companies, including Eddie Bauer and L.L. Bean, opened retail outlets in Japan where customers can examine and try on products before ordering them by mail, in effect creating a mixed strategy appropriate for their specific situation (WuDunn, 1995).

Barilla Pasta was the top-selling pasta in Italy in the 1980s when it considered entering the French market (Ruggiero, 1996). Previously, it had exported successfully to Sweden, where there was a receptive market and fragmented competition. France, in contrast, had a major competitor, Panzani, and a slow population growth rate, which indicated an uncertain market. France's strong culinary traditions were favorable to Italian traditions, since Italy was the original source of major elements of French cuisine, but France also had a poorer transportation system and higher labor costs than Italy, and it lacked local energy sources, which increased the cost of energy. These external factors, which indicated a risky market, combined with Barilla's excess capacity in Italy, prior exporting experience and modest financial resources, dictated that exporting was a sensible way to test the strength of Barilla's Italian reputation in the French market and to determine whether adequate demand could be generated to support a manufacturing facility there.

Decisions involving alternative worldwide market entry/operating approaches usually are more complex than the above discussion indicates. This discussion is designed only to introduce the basic contingency process at work when deciding whether and how to use alliances as opposed to other options, such as exporting or forming wholly-owned subsidiaries.

A WIDE RANGE OF STRATEGIC REASONS TO USE ALLIANCES

Strategically, alliances can add value to a firm's product line or products by adding items or features to a line, bringing new or existing items to market more quickly, expanding overseas markets, increasing service availability, and enhancing research and development. In the distribution area, alliances can provide new marketing channels, better control over channels and improved supply. Alliances can help in operations by creating capacity in new locations, improving efficiency, adding new technologies and developing new processes. They also can provide additional financial resources, penetrate new overseas markets more quickly, create synergies, decrease market risks, provide knowledge that expands a company's skill base, overcome market barriers and reduce competition (Lewis, 1990).

To maximize these benefits companies need to take steps to anticipate and avoid problems through careful planning and effective administration.

PREPARING FOR PROBLEMS AND FAILURES INVOLVED IN TRANSLATING THE STRATEGIC ALLIANCE CONCEPT INTO ACTION

In 1985, CdF, the chemical division of state-owned Charbonnages de France, originally the nation's coal mining company, had a large but rundown plant in Chimie, France – the French Villers St Sepulcre plant. The plant produced acrylonitrile butadiene styrene (ABS), an engineering thermoplastic used to manufacture such goods as computer housings, automotive dashboards, household appliances and telephones. Even though the market for ABS was large and growing rapidly, CdF had no funds to invest in the plant. Without an outside investor, the plant would close and many people would lose their jobs (Parker and Burdet-Taylor, 1990).

At that time, Borg-Warner Chemicals (BWC), a Dutch division of Borg-Warner in the USA, was a major supplier of the material and wanted to expand rapidly in Europe. While the Chimie plant was in disrepair, CdF had superior ABS technology capabilities and its R&D team had spent years working on a new generation of related products. From a strategic fit perspective, therefore, a joint venture seemed to make sense for Borg-Warner.

There were potential problems, however. Absenteeism in the plant was high, workers mistrusted management and there was little dialogue between them. The five unions were strong and anti-management. Safety was lax and quality standards were low in an industry where these factors are important to success. There was also a cultural gap between the Netherlands-based employees of Borg-Warner's chemical division and CdF's French workers. Borg-Warner management decided that the potential benefits of an alliance could outweigh the risks, since having this plant would give them one-third of the ABS European market.

Borg-Warner felt that the risks associated with the deal could be reduced by careful planning. To increase the venture's chances of success, Borg-Warner identified potential problems and formulated plans for handling them, then discussed these plans with the potential partners prior to signing the final venture agreement. The negotiations and structuring which followed this initial strategic decision are described in Chapter 3.

Potential rivalry can be a difficult-to-prevent threat in many situations. For example, Durawool Inc. (a US firm) entered into a joint manufacturing venture in the late 1980s with China Metallurgical Zuhai Sez United. In the 1990s, a key employee left to start a similar venture. Under Chinese law, this step was legal, since the venture contract set limitations on such competitive actions only for the partners (Holusha, 1996). In this instance, the original venture contract could have extended the penalty and participation clauses to cover more employees. Participative profit sharing and other employee benefits might also have been added to the original contract.

In situations where potential for misuses of proprietary technology exist and the partners are not well-acquainted, other steps can be taken to protect partner interests. One chemical company protected its proprietary technology by using older but adequate technology in its new venture in China. Similarly, Gillette often protects its technological competitive advantage by manufacturing only standard razor and blade models in the alliance country, while importing its newest Sensor products.

The following chapters discuss many of the ways to anticipate and avoid problems during negotiations and partner selection, when developing alliance structure and type, and when managing and leading it.

Not all problems can be anticipated. The 10-year joint venture begun in New Zealand in 1986–87 between Ford and Mazda was closed in 1996 because import tariffs had declined from 55% to 15%. This meant that cars from neighboring countries could be made and imported more cheaply than cars could be made in New Zealand. In addition, the factory in New Zealand needed major capital improvements (Nakamoto, 1997). Problems also were encountered by Ford in South America where Ford's joint venture with Volkswagen (VW) was dissolved in part because of consumers' growing preference for VW's smaller cars.

Ultimately, every joint venture is susceptible to changing circumstances in rapidly changing multinational environments and a firm using alliances must be ready to deal with these unforeseen circumstances.

CRAFTING A WORKABLE STRATEGIC ALLIANCE STRATEGY: BEST PRACTICES GUIDELINES

The initial phase of determining strategic fit described so far in this chapter is simple in concept:

- Identify a firm's enterprise-wide strategies and define strategic needs precisely
- Explore ways, or conditions under which, strategic alliances might help to meet these needs
- Identify potential strategic alliance partners

British Telephone's strategy, for example, was to become a leading global telecommunications company principally by either purchasing or forming alliances with second-tier overseas telephone firms which were rivals of a country's existing or former monopoly. In this way, BT hoped to capitalize on its experience with privatizing and deregulating telecommunications in the UK. They initially focused on such firms in Europe.

Borg-Warner Chemicals identified the strategy (expand quickly in Europe in a key chemical area) and the preferred alliance partner with which to do it – a major French company which had relevant advanced technology. British Petroleum moved to strengthen its position in the international oil industry (its enterprise-wide strategic objective) by identifying four potential European alliance partners and then analyzing the strategic fit of each with BP's existing core strengths in marketing, distribution and production.

This is only a preliminary phase, however. It is necessary for companies to craft a detailed alliance strategy that will translate overall strategies into action. This can be done by studying an enterprise's operations from different detailed viewpoints:

- Analyze and evaluate the key activities of the value chain involved in implementing the firm's stated enterprise-wide strategy. This component-by-component analysis determines which activities can be done safely by, or shared with, other firms. In the News Corporation situation, both the programming and broadcasting activities were of value, but could be shared effectively with alliance partners in a way that each partner learned from the other.
- Determine which of the activities might be done separately, either by different alliances with different partners or in stages over time. This incremental approach allows time for partners to develop an effective working relationship. Both Toshiba and Motorola used this approach over the years with different partners. The Finnish company, Raisio, used the incremental approach to reduce the risks arising from their unfamiliarity with strategic alliances and the markets for their new cholesterol-reducing product.
- Specify which activities can be done through alliances while protecting core competencies and technologies that are competitive advantages. Develop scenarios of how partners might misuse your core competencies. In Gillette's situation, distribution activities and the manufacture of cheaper older model razors and blades could be shared. The manufacturing technologies involved in producing Sensor razors and blades were substantial competitive advantages and so these were manufactured outside of China and imported for sale.
- Study ways to leverage each firm's resources synergistically, that

is, ways to maximize each partner's strengths. The capital and specific manufacturing capabilities of four major companies and government influence were required initially for Airbus to perform the research and development needed to design and manufacture competitive commercial aircraft.

- Do not focus so exclusively on the possible synergies that insufficient attention is given to studying the operational fit. Borg-Warner avoided this problem by making detailed operating plans and then openly discussing them with its potential partner prior to signing the final venture contract. In other words, strategic alliance success does not just happen because the strategic fit is favorable; success is made to happen.
- Keep lawyers informed and consult them for guidance, but where possible be careful not to introduce them into the negotiations before relationships have been developed and basic strategic issues settled. This was not possible in the British Airways/ American Airlines situation, however, because the industry was highly regulated.
- Prepare contingency plans that allow for forming new alliances that will not be limited by existing alliances. For example, Microsoft and Motorola crafted each alliance in a way that enabled it to move into different product and geographic areas in different ways as circumstances unfolded.
- The alliance must add value, that is, it must be worth more to each partner to enter the alliance than to go it alone, and each partner must learn something from the alliance. This was the case with both British Petroleum and Mobil in their 15-country alliance, as their 43-part alliance meshed joint operations by combining the strengths of both companies.

The above best practices guidelines have been developed from actual company experiences. They provide a useful framework for formulating enterprise-wide and business unit strategies, for using strategic alliances and for setting parameters for making more detailed strategic choices. In strategically managing and implementing alliances at all levels – from the enterprise-wise rethinking, through crafting an alliance business strategy, negotiations, selecting partners, creating the specific structure of the alliance, staffing, operational planning and management and leadership – situation background studies are needed to extend this framework.

For this reason, the situation factor analysis continues as negotiations progress and partner fit is evaluated.

To supplement the above best practices guidelines from another perspective, Appendix A at the end of this book provides a summary checklist of key questions to ask and answer when performing the situation analyses involved in the strategic fit phase of multinational strategic alliance development and implementation.

AN EMERGING CONTINUING PROCESS

The following chapters provide additional examples of how situation factors can affect strategic alliance decisions and actions, beginning with negotiation and partner selection, and continuing through

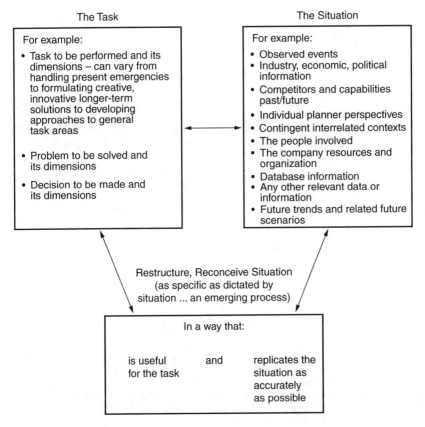

Figure 2.2   A Basic Emergent Entrepreneurial Contingency Process

formulating the type and structure of an alliance, and effectively managing and leading it. Throughout the processs, the entrepreneurial process outlined in Figure 2.2 is at work continually.

As a tentative decision is made to pursue an alliance of some sort, crafting a more detailed alliance strategy, and determining the type and structure of the alliance continues. For example, further definition is given to the details of the alliance, including: percent ownership; mix of financing; different kinds of material, technology and machinery contributions by each partner; division of activities and sharing of activities; staffing; location; autonomy; controls not just for operations but also for measuring and controlling each partners contributions over time; and guidelines for management after inception of the alliance. These activities are discussed in the following chapters.

REFERENCES

Brzezinski, M. (1997). Bill Gates may tap Soviet arsenal to launch an 'internet in the sky'. *The Wall Street Journal*, February 20, p. 3.
Business Week (1991). Making deals – without giving away the store. *Business Week*, June 17, pp. 96–98.
Carosol-Volpi, M. (1997). *Strategic Alliances in the European Downstream Oil Industry: BP and Mobil*, Research Working Paper. New York and Rome, Strategic Management Research Group.
Dawkins, W. (1997). When the mask cracks: Wide-ranging reforms of the way business and finance is carried out is changing the face of Japan. *Financial Times*, May 28, p. 15.
The Economist (1997). British American Airlines? *The Economist*, May 25, p. 72.
Elstrom, P. (1997). Iridium is looking a little star-crossed. *Business Week*, April 14, p. 40.
Engardio, P. (1993). Motorola in China: A great leap. *Business Week*, May 17, pp. 58–59.
Fabrikant, G. (1996). Murdoch bets heavily on a global vision: media magnate seeks to own and broadcast every form of programming. *The New York Times*, July 29, pp. D1, D8, D9.
Gerlach, M.L. (1992). *Alliance Capitalism: The Social Organization of Japanese Business*, Berkeley, CA, University of California Press.
Green, D. (1997). A symptom of bad timing. *Financial Times*, July 3, p. 20.
Gregoriou, E. (1996). *Method of Entry of the Russian Menatep Bank and the Arab Bank in Cyprus*, Research Working Paper. New York and Rome, Strategic Management Research Group, December.
Hardie, C. (1995). Construction pace quickens. *Electronic News*, October 2, p. 60.
Hardy, Q. (1996). Motorola is plotting new satellite project: M-Star would be faster than Iridium system, pitched to global firms. *The Wall Street Journal*, October 14, p. B4.

Holusha, J. (1996). For steel-wool maker, Chinese lessons. *The New York Times,* May 28, p. D10.

Japan 21st (1994). Toshiba–Motorola joint venture in Sendai. *Japan 21st,* September, pp. 95–96.

Lewis, J.D. (1990). *Partnerships for Profit.* New York, The Free Press.

Mobile Phone News (1995). Motorola subsidiary prepares for new factory in Japan. *Mobile Phone News,* July 17, p. 6.

Nakamoto, M. (1997). Mazda, Ford to share parts. *Financial Times,* April 18, p. 17.

Nakamoto, M. (1998). Mitsubishi chooses the open road to industrial recovery. *Financial Times,* March 12, p. 15.

Neff, R. (1997). Unlocking Japan – at last. *Business Week,* April 14, pp. 56–57.

Parker, C. and Burdet-Taylor, J. (1990). *Borg-Warner Chemicals (A),* a case study. Lausanne, Switzerland, IMEDE.

Ruggiero, R. (1996). *Determining the Best Strategy of Entry For Barilla Pasta (Italy) Into France,* Research Working Paper. New York and Rome, Strategic Management Research Group.

Schoenberger, K. (1996). Motorola bets big on China: The US high-tech company is doubling its stake in what could become the world's largest electronics market. *Fortune,* May 27, pp. 40–45.

Schine, E., Estrom, P., Barrett, A., Edmonson, G. and Shari, M. (1997). The satellite biz blasts off. *Business Week,* January 27, pp. 62–70.

Schendler, B. (1993). 'How Toshiba makes alliances work. *Fortune,* October 4, pp. 116–119.

Schendler, B. (1997). Microsoft: First America, now the World. *Fortune,* August 18, pp. 214–217.

Skapinker, M. (1997). DFI deal places UK group second in duty-free market. *Financial Times,* July 4, p. 1.

Survey (1997). Partnerships essential for getting a market lead. *Sunday Business Times* (Cape Town, South Africa), June 8, p. 18.

Taylor, R. (1997). Deal long in the making. *Financial Times,* July 3, p. 20.

Updike, E. and Nakarmi, L. (1995). A movable feast for Mitsubishi. *Business Week,* August 28, pp. 50, 51.

Uriarte, P.L. (1997). BBV's 1000 Day Program. Presentation/paper, SMS International Conference, Barcelona, Spain, Strategic Management Society (SMS), October 6.

WuDunn, S. (1995). Japanese do buy American: By mail and a lot cheaper. *The New York Times,* July 3, pp. 1, 43.

3

Negotiation and Partner Selection

As alliance strategies are developed and implemented, negotiation is necessary in every phase of the process:

- Exploring and developing details of the alliance at both the strategic and operating levels
- Identifying and selecting compatible partners
- Determining alliance type and structure
- Managing and leading alliances
- Revising alliance strategies

This chapter examines a variety of alliance situations and describes negotiation and partner selection activities involved in them.

HUMAN FACTORS

While it is important to focus on the strategic and organizational fit of strategic alliances, it is equally important to consider the human aspects (Slowinski, 1992). People and personal chemistry are what ultimately make alliances work. Al Zeien, CEO at Gillette, refers to people as the grease and glue that make alliances work.

Human factors are important early in the alliance negotiation process. In the first three company experiences discussed in this chapter – General Motors (USA) in China, Studds-Nolan (an Italian/Indian joint venture), and Tambrands (USA) in Russia – human factors, though not the only controlling factor, were critical to success in different ways. While people factors were less important during the British Airways/American Airlines negotiations with government regulatory bodies, the CEOs personalities were still a pivotal factor.

People are a prime focus of the partner selection activities discussed in this chapter. Multinational alliances generally involve multiple cultures. Appendix B at the end of this book discusses the impact of cultural factors on strategic alliance and provides frameworks for dealing with cultural differences.

Several aspects of human factors are focused on in this book:

- The competencies or skills of the people involved and their appropriateness for a specific alliance
- The confidence or trust and personal chemistry needed for success and ways to nurture it, given multinational alliances across borders are difficult to monitor and manage because of cultural and geographic gaps
- The dimensions of any cultural gaps and ways to create synergies and bridge gaps effectively
- The compatibility of partners not only in terms of strategic and operational fits, but also in terms of compatibility of basic values, leadership/management/operating styles and corporate cultures
- The commitment to making the alliance work
- The leadership and management interpersonal skills needed to carry out the alliance's strategic objectives

The impact of human factors on an alliance depends on the alliance's type and structure, size, the functions performed, and the partners and countries/cultures involved. Human factors are discussed in this chapter because they are extremely important in negotiating and partner selection. They are, however, also relevant in the other alliance activities covered in the following chapters.

GENERAL MOTORS' EXPERIENCES IN CHINA

The negotiation process General Motors (GM) went through in trying to put together a billion-dollar joint venture in China in the mid-1990s was long and complex (Naughton et al, 1995; Stern, 1995). GM's strategy for China, which evolved over several years, was to make itself a major presence in the 1.2 billion population Chinese market. This was part of its overall strategy to develop a major global presence (Meredith, 1997).

In the mid-1990s GM was considering a Shanghai joint venture plant to produce 300 000 midsize cars and minivans annually. Negotiations began in earnest in 1994 with GM's CEO John F. Smith Jr's visit to China and a visit by Chinese officials to GM's operations in Brazil, which are linked by computer to the company's worldwide automotive and technology businesses. This link allows cars and factories to be designed in concert with GM technical centers around the world. GM promised that the Shanghai facility would have the same leading edge capabilities. A 40-person Chinese delegation also visited Detroit in late 1995 to learn about operations there. Rudolph A. Schlais Jr, a GM employee who had earlier negotiated GM's China parts making venture in 1992/93, was chosen to head the venture.

By 1996, GM appeared able to conclude the billion-dollar deal with Shanghai Motors, because it agreed to share its technology in automobile manufacturing, as well as in electronics (through its Hughes Electronics Division) and in computer technology (at that time its Electronic Data Systems Unit). Such a technology sharing approach had been used successfully by Motorola, AT&T and Daimler Benz.

To enhance its position further, GM established two GM-China Technology Institutes to teach Chinese college graduates how to design car parts, engines and transmissions. At least three more were planned, at a total cost of $40 million. GM brought Chinese engineers to Detroit to learn computer-aided design and other aspects of vehicle development. GM calculated that China would acquire the technology anyway, so why not get it from GM. Such an approach appealed to the technology-hungry Chinese.

GM officials hoped that China would become a stepping stone for selling to all of Asia. As a regional source of auto parts, low-cost vehicles, and even engineering expertise, China would be linked to design centers in the US, Brazil, Europe and Japan. It was expected to be many years, however, before GM's investment in China in 1998 paid off because of overcapacity – current capacity in China overall was double the current market demand (Smith, 1998).

Not all of GM's previous ventures in China had been trouble-free. GM's joint venture factory in Northeastern China was about to begin pickup truck production in 1995, when GM's partner, Jinbei Automotive Co., was acquired by First Auto Works of Changchun. The new owner wanted to renegotiate the deal, putting everything on hold for a time.

With such problems in mind, GM included a high level female Chinese executive, Shirley Young, in the Shanghai Motors negotiations. Ms. Young was born in Shanghai, had relatives there and spoke Chinese. Her father was well known in China; he had been killed by the Japanese when he was China's consul general to the Philippines during World War II. Her stepfather had been China's ambassador to the US, UK, and France. She and others from the 1000-strong Chinese-American employees at GM formed a committee to advise GM on Chinese relations. Ms. Young's extensive cultural contacts in China helped considerably during negotiations. She even joined the board of the Shanghai Symphony Orchestra, after which GM donated $125 000 to the group.

Ms. Young coached GM employees on how business is carried out in China. For example, in the US negotiators normally talk business first and then, if things are going well, sit down to a meal together. In contrast, the Chinese dine together first, then transact business. GM felt that awareness of such subtle human differences was a necessary step in successful negotiations. Again, Ms. Young's role shows what a critical success factor people can be in strategic alliance success.

Even with concessions and connections, success in the Shanghai Motors alliance was still uncertain in early 1998. For example, GM encountered problems with its pickup truck operation when its Chinese partners decided to renegotiate the deal after the plant was completed and operations were about to begin. In addition, in 1998 GM subsequently lost out to Honda in its efforts to take over a joint venture plant abandoned by Peugeot in Southern China. In practice, therefore, while human factors are important, negotiation can be an emerging process during which the importance of key factors shifts with changing market conditions and perceived partner needs.

TAMBRANDS INC.'S (FORMERLY KNOWN AS TAMPAX INC.) EXPERIENCES IN RUSSIA

Tambrands Inc., which makes Tampax, the world's leading feminine hygiene napkins (tampons), during the 1980s explored entering the

Soviet Union. It formed joint ventures first in Kiev (Ukraine) and second in St. Petersburg (Russia). In late 1997, Tambrands was acquired by Procter & Gamble (De Muth, 1992; Emmons, 1990, 1993; Haslech, 1991; Knobel, 1993; Lewis, 1997; Tambrands, 1988–95, 1996).

The period of negotiation and partner selection for the proposed Soviet joint venture, which was named Femtech, was long and complex. After studies indicated a substantial potential Soviet market existed for Tambrands' product, Tambrands participated in a medical products trade exhibition in Moscow in 1985. The company also engaged a medical businessman with experience in the Soviet Union. Visits to local businesses and retail outlets developed contacts and confirmed that product demand was high in the USSR. Tambrands' Russian-language brochure on menstruation was widely distributed and used in the Soviet Union as a result of this initial effort.

Tambrands took its first steps towards finding a joint venture partner in 1987, after the Soviet Union began allowing foreign joint ventures and after it was learned that use of tampons instead of cotton pads by women in the Soviet Union would reduce cotton usage substantially and so significantly help decrease imports of cotton (a major drain on Soviet reserves). Tambrands enlisted the help of British prime minister Margaret Thatcher in promoting a Tampax venture in the USSR. Through her efforts Soviet interest in the project was stimulated and Evgeni Chasov, Director of the Ministry of Health for the USSR, was asked to assist with negotiations.

Tambrands participated in additional trade exhibits, educational lectures and presentations at health institutes around the USSR and advertised in Russian-language publications. Eventually, a preliminary agreement was reached between Tambrands and Techsnabexport, the trading company responsible for all foreign trading operations of the Ministry of Health whose Director General was Yuri Saakov. This agreement outlined general principles which would guide any future joint venture contract and structure.

Finding a joint venture partner involved considerable work by Tambrands' vice president-international, Constantin Ohanian, who had been developing the project to this point. He talked with potential partners from different Soviet states, but the most enthusiastic ones were small. At a 1987 health products exhibit in Moscow,

Ohanian met Dr Dmitrij Volukh, head of the Central Pharmacy Department (GAPU) of the Ukraine. The two hit it off immediately – the personal chemistry seemed very good. At Volukh's invitation, Ohanian and Yuri Saakov, Director General of the Ministry of Health, visited Kiev in the Ukraine to discuss a possible joint venture with the Ukrainian GAPU. The Ukraine's population of more than 50 million made it an attractive market. The GAPU operations were impressive and a half-completed building in Borispol (50 kilometers from Kiev) was available and could be adapted to Tambrands' specifications.

They also studied the availability of cotton, the basic raw material of Tampons. All of the needed raw material could be obtained from a nearby government plant (200 miles from Kiev). Since Tampons used 80% less cotton than the hygiene pads then used by Russian women, the savings in cotton usage would be enormous, enabling Russia to considerably reduce cotton imports. Everyone agreed that the likelihood of obtaining the cotton needed for tampon manufacturing was high. Overall, the project appeared to benefit the Russians in other ways: it would provide a safe product that had government approval and would serve as a model for other joint ventures.

A last step in the negotiating process was to visit the Ukrainian Ministry of Health, GAPU's supervisory body. The Ministry's First Deputy, Andrej Serdyuk, was enthusiastic about the project and supported signing an agreement following the general principles outlined earlier. At a subsequent meeting with the Ukranian Minister of Health, Anatolij Romanenko, who also supported the agreement, it was proposed that a final clearance be obtained from Evgeni Chasov, the Minister of Health for the USSR. Chasov, who had been interested in the project since talking with Margaret Thatcher, was delighted with the proposal and urged that it be pursued. Negotiations to this point had taken almost 2 years.

A series of meetings was then arranged to work out the details of the joint venture contract. The discussion of this process is continued on pp. 102–105 in Chapter 4, as the type and structure of the strategic alliance were worked out once a partner was tentatively selected.

THE PROPOSED BRITISH AIRWAYS/AMERICAN AIRLINES STRATEGIC ALLIANCE

During the mid-1990s, British Airways (BA) was looking to strengthen its North American presence (Mockler 1997). At the same time, American Airlines (AA) was looking to form an alliance with a European airline located in a country that allowed an open skies agreement. Negotiations with France reached a standstill when the French government was unwilling to enter such an agreement.

After almost 2 years of negotiations, AA and BA worked out an agreement to coordinate passenger and cargo services through a codesharing agreement – the two airlines' flights would have BA/AA codes. Even though some observers argued that the alliance bordered on being a merger (Staff Reporter, 1998), it did not involve an exchange of equity or board seats. Even though routes would be shared, both carriers would retain their individual brand identities. The alliance would simply enable the airlines to grow together and reap the synergistic benefits. To negotiate the contract details, which are described on p. 119 in Chapter 4, and eventually create and implement a structure for the alliance, the two carriers established a joint alliance team led by senior executives nominated by each company.

This was only the first phase of negotiations. Government agencies in both countries were involved in the decision and the subsequent detailed structuring of the alliance. Although it was not the first US–European airline alliance, the BA/AA alliance was the first alliance of its kind in terms of size of companies and terms of agreement. Because it involved two of the world's leading airlines and it came in the wake of three other big alliances, the BA/AA proposal received extra scrutiny.

The BA/AA alliance proposal was aggressively criticized by other airlines and transportation companies, and by the European Commission. As of 1998 it remained to be seen whether the alliance would benefit customers in the long term, or whether it would squash competition and create a monopoly. Strong arguments were continually being advanced that codesharing alliances did not benefit consumers (McCartney, 1998).

USAir (renamed US Airways) filed suit in a US federal court against both BA and AA for 'seeking to undermine USAir's competitive position and limit overall competition in the US–UK markets.' USAir alleged that BA and AA had violated antitrust law and that BA had 'breached its fiduciary duty' to USAir as an alliance partner (Air Transport World, 1996).

During an exchange of testimony before the House of Commons Transport Select Committee (which in fact had no direct jurisdiction over the alliance), the CEOs of rivals BA and Virgin Atlantic expressed opposing views. Virgin's CEO, Richard Branson, argued that the alliance would mean less choice and higher prices for passengers since it would give the two carriers a large share of the US–UK market (Morrocco, 1996). Robert Ayling, BA's CEO, disagreed, stating that competition would in fact increase because there would be more carriers at Heathrow as a result of the US–UK open skies agreement.

Critics argued that the alliance would result in AA and BA dominating transatlantic competition, particularly in the lucrative New York–London market frequented by high-paying business travelers. Critics also claimed that the two carriers would dominate US–UK air travel unless other airlines were able to gain substantial additional rights at London's Heathrow Airport. This placed pressure on the UK government and the British Airport Authority to surrender gate slots at Heathrow.

Competing US airlines criticized the conditions laid down by Britain's trade minister as inadequate. Delta Air Lines and UAL Corp.'s United Airlines argued that the concessions demanded by the UK failed to ensure a competitive balance at Heathrow. United Airlines, which had an alliance with Lufthansa and SAS, claimed that the BA/AA alliance was anti-competitive because the carriers would control more than 60% of the US–UK market and 87% of the Chicago–London market. United Airlines quantified its demands for the surrender of slots in London, New York and Chicago, requesting that the BA/AA alliance give up 30 slots at Heathrow Airport, 12 at John F. Kennedy Airport and six at O'Hare Airport.

The US Justice Department consequently opened an antitrust investigation of the alliance to determine if it would unfairly dominate Heathrow, the main airborne gateway to England and Europe. Heathrow is valuable because it is a major hub for travelers headed to many European cities.

In late 1997, BA decided that it would be at least a year before all of the negotiating problems could be resolved and the alliance could take place, if at all.

A SMALL BUT COMPLEX INDIAN/ITALIAN STRATEGIC ALLIANCE

Studds-Nolan, an Italian–Indian joint venture, is an example of a much smaller joint venture, where the personalities and cultures of the people involved, the distance between partners and their unfamiliarity with each other, and the inexperience of the partners in working with alliances had a significant impact on the negotiation, partner selection, structure and management of a strategic alliance (Anand and Delios, 1996).

In small ventures, the individuals involved can be a significant factor. Two Indian brothers, Ravi and Madhu Khurana, owned and managed two sports helmet companies in India: Gadgets (which manufactured helmets for motorcycling, bicycling, horseback-riding, canoeing, rollerskating and skateboarding) and Studds Accessories (which marketed the helmets). Its brand was well-known and its helmets competed at both the high and low ends of the market, since its quality was high (its bicycle helmets, for example, met quality standards in all European and North American countries). In an effort to expand, Studds exported 20% of its production, mostly to South America and South East Asia where the main competitors were from Taiwan and South Korea. The main competitors in developed countries were from Italy and Japan. The worldwide market was an estimated $1 billion. Studds' annual sales were approximately $5 million with little promotion or dealer support.

Gadgets had 380 employees (including 60 supervisors) and Studds Accessories had 25 employees. The organization culture at Gadgetsand Studds was described in this way:

> Managers, responsible for a specific functional area, did not have much cross-communication. Where responsibilities overlapped and conflicts developed, resolution was sought through discussion with either Ravi or Madhu Khurana. Managers were reluctant to assume responsibility for decisions, and the general managers were reluctant to release such responsibility to managers. Consequently, both Ravi and Madhu were intimately involved with the day-to-day operations.

Gadgets and Studds were heavily unionized and the unions had considerable bargaining power because of the Indian government's 'no-fire' policy. This policy stated that once an employee had been hired, a company was obligated to employ this individual for the lifetime of the company or employee. Dismissals were rare and often were accompanied by a considerable payoff. Union activities, strikes by truckers and port workers and internal union activities frequently disrupted production and consumed substantial management time.

Union strength also made changes in manufacturing processes difficult. For example, in 1992 an injection-molding machine was purchased to manufacture plastic molded helmets for the low-end market segment. The injection molding process used less labor than was used in the production of fiberglass helmets, a premium product. However, the unions resisted implementing this process and the injection molding machine remained idle, inhibiting growth of Studds helmets in lower-end market segments.

In an effort to expand both manufacturing and overseas sales, Studds decided to search for an overseas partner. They identified 10 potential partners and finally selected two, Nolan and Bieffe, who visited India and were visited by a team of Studds' executives in early 1994. Nolan, an Italian company, was receptive to the deal because it needed increased capacity, low-cost manufacturing, and to a lesser degree access to the Indian market. Studds selected Nolan because of Nolan's leadership, well-known worldwide brand, size ($26 million in sales), research and development capabilities, wide distribution network, heavy promotional efforts and well-defined policies.

A letter of intent for a joint venture, Studds–Nolan Ltd, was drawn up in July 1994. It called for adding manufacturing capabilities to Studds Accessories, which would be owned equally by the two partners (20% each) with 60% to be sold to the public. Gadget would remain in control of the Khurana brothers. In September 1994, Nolan representatives visited Studds in India for a second time to discuss operational, management and control issues. As negotiations continued (focusing mainly on operating decisions) and early implementation steps were carried out, major disagreements arose. For example, the actual cost of land for the proposed manufacturing facilities exceeded budget; some of the expenditures were informal payoffs that could not be receipted. Nolan objected to this and gradually began to insist on more operational control. Considerable suspicion and distrust arose between the partners.

Further disagreements arose when Studds management visited Nolan in Italy in February 1995. For example, Nolan insisted that joint venture disagreements be adjudicated in London or Paris, while Studds insisted on India. At this point, both parties considered terminating the agreement.

The problems arose for many reasons:

- *Adds mutual strategic value* – Mutual strategic goals were not specified in detail. For example, the agreement did not specify the distribution Nolan would be committed to for selling Studds–Nolan branded products worldwide and the transfer pricing policies. Nor did the agreement specify how potential competition with each partner's existing lines would be handled. For instance, it was especially unclear as to how the production of Gadgets' products under the Studds' brand name would be handled by Nolan distribution systems worldwide, if at all, even though this was a major Studds' objective. Nor was it clear how Nolan helmets would be competing with Studds' in the Indian market, even though one of Nolan's objectives was to expand its Indian market. At the same time, there were few assurances as to how the obvious production problems arising from Indian labor unions would be handled.
- *Enables learning* – No organizational structures were put in place to provide for the continuing exchange of information about marketing by Nolan and production by Studds. Nor was any structure developed for overcoming cultural gaps and re-solving conflicts, for example, like the one arising over the closed and informal way that payments were handled within the Indian culture.
- *Protects and enhances core competencies* – No provision was made for the transfer of technology on a continuing basis, es-pecially from Nolan's research efforts and Gadgets' development work.
- *Enables flexibility* – No mechanism was set up to insure that management in India might evolve, since it would be run solely by existing managers. In addition, neither party was prohibited from undertaking competing operations, resulting in unlimited and uncontrolled flexibility.

In addition to failing to create a framework for success, the alliance had many human problems: insufficient personal involve-ment of senior partners, which led to cultural gaps and potential operating problems not being identified; insufficient time devoted to resolving potential personality and cultural problems and to build-ing a base for trust, commitment and resolution of future conflicts; and lack of personal chemistry nurturing. Further, there was no

Analytic framework	Studds	Negotiation questions/recommendations	Nolan
Strategic fit	*Strategic goals – what they want*	*Strategic fit*	*Strategic goals – what they want*
• Access to markets/distribution	• Immediate distribution worldwide	• Is Nolan willing to provide worldwide distribution of Studds' brand?	• Low cost per unit production
• Technology transfer	• Under Studds' name?	• Will Studds distribute the Nolan brand in India?	• Expand capacity with low capital investment
• Production costs/capacity	• Access to new technology at low cost	• What are the ways that Nolan will provide technology transfer?	• Access to broader product line – under Nolan name?
• Product line/new products	• Access to additional capacity	• Can Studds deliver low-cost production of both high and low-end products?	• Minor interest in expansion in Indian market, but under Nolan name?
• Brand use/protection	• Broad product line/high-low	• Reliability of meeting delivery deadlines and priorities?	
• Other		• What are the ways brands will be used? For example, will the Studds–Nolan brand be sold everywhere, even in markets with existing Nolan and Studds products?	*Negotiation and partner selection*
Negotiation and partner selection	*Negotiation and partner selection*	• What will be the branding strategy for existing and new high- and low-end products?	• Partner characteristics —Italian, vocal, expressive —apparently little trust in partner
• Partner characteristics —values —culture —compatibility —personal chemistry	• Partner characteristics —Indian, less open —caste system, hierarchical, culture —family business	• How are transfer prices, terms, etc. to be worked out?	• Partner resources —has worldwide distribution —has worldwide brand name, and wide product line —has technology and technology r&d capabilities
• Partner resources —distribution —production facilities —brands/product line —technology	• Partner resources —distribution only in India —low cost production facilities but only for high-end items? —many production problems in India —brand well-known in India and select foreign countries, such as Canada —extremely busy running their own businesses	*Negotiation and partner selection*	• Negotiating style —formal, business focus
• Negotiation process —timing —involvement	• Negotiation process —not ready to spend time to get to know each other —formal, business focus	• Essentially requires restarting the process to see if the strategic alliance relationship can be rebuilt	*Type and structure*
Type and structure			• Type —worldwide, larger company, not family owned
• Type —joint venture (JV) —contract/partnerships			
• Structure —operational fit —location			

—finance
—accounting
—organization
—board composition
—alliance team to solve ongoing problems

Management: making it work
• Who runs? how run?
• How is control exercised
• Reporting responsibilities
• Distribution, transport, delivery priorities
• Production, union, automation, cost control, government regulations
• Conflict resolution mechanisms

Type and structure
• Type
—family owned and operated
• Structure
—family managed, rigid, hierarchical

Management: making it work
• Autocratic, non-participative
• Strong restrictive unions and labor regulations
• Frequent operation disruptions
• Highly regulated business environment
• Greatest interest is in new technologies and worldwide distribution, but little attention paid to how to achieve these goals

• Do both parties have the time required to develop a better understanding of each other and a working relationship?
• Does each partner have the interest and commitment to do this?

Type and structure
• Type
—possible to avoid JV problems by moving incrementally in small steps?
—possible to decompose in some way into separate contracts?
—co-distribution
—co-production
—technology transfer
• Structure
—possible to change composition of Board to provide closer operating control by Nolan?
—possible to have some shared management?
—a termination agreement will be needed

Management: making it work
• Can liaison manager be assigned?
• Are the cultural and strategic fit differences too great to allow bridging the gap between the two partners?

• Structure
—less rigid, less hierarchical

Management: making it work
• Substantial geographic distance from JV partner makes control difficult
• Has a variety of other interests worldwide
• Greatest strategic interest in low cost production, but little attention paid to ensuring goal is achieved

Figure 3.1 Strategic Framework for Renegotiation: Studds–Nolan Situation

specific ongoing mechanism for allocating senior partners' time for working out details as they arose on a proactive, rather than reactive basis.

An initial effort to reconcile the differences is shown in the negotiating framework outline in Figure 3.1. This framework identifies strategic areas which needed defining and specifies the questions which need to be resolved to avoid the problems which arose during the initial phases of the strategic alliance development. This framework also suggests some tentative ways to make the alliance work.

Problems were created at all phases of the alliance formulation process in this situation. The *strategic fit* for each party was not clearly defined nor did it control plan development. *Negotiations* were limited and allowed little time for the parties to get to know each other and their differing cultures. The *partner selection* process was cursory and not used to develop a basis for trust by encouraging greater interaction among the partners or to test whether sufficient personal chemistry, commitment and trust existed to resolve future conflicts and make the alliance work. When *structuring* the deal, time was not taken to explore possible operating fit problems and their impact on the way the alliance was set up. As a result, no provision was made for interactive learning, for overcoming known problems in production, for satisfying the strategic goals of each partner in marketing, or for enabling effective shared *management and control* of the operation to deal with future unanticipated situations. These problems are addressed in the negotiating framework outlined in Figure 3.1.

Several steps were advised to salvage what appeared to be a hopelessly deteriorating situation. First the situation was decomposed, that is, broken into several strategic components; an alliance partnership was developed and proposed. This was in essence an operational fit study leading to a component-by-component alliance proposal.

- A co-production agreement would specify equipment and technology contributions, as well as guidelines for the amount of brand and type of helmet production and guidelines for allocation of production to each partner and distribution channel. A joint production management control and coordinating team of Nolan and Studds executives could be created to work out these details and resolve disputes.

- A distribution partnership/contract would be in three parts: *worldwide* through existing Nolan channels, *in India* through Studds' channels, and *in developing countries* where neither partner currently had distribution.

A joint group would also be set up to develop these proposals. Negotiation on these 'operational fit' aspects could be expected to involve considerable travel between the two partners and the extensive participation of executives in both firms. A detailed termination agreement would be created prior to these negotiations so that an amicable separation could be worked out should the negotiations not be productive. In light of what had happened to date, there was some doubt that the alliance could be salvaged, even if both parties agreed to try.

United Parcel Service (UPS) used a similar decomposition approach when its alliance in one country gradually moved away from UPS's core business of small package delivery and became a large mover of cemetery gravestones, mattresses and other large freight. This part of the business began to drain the efficiencies of the alliance's operations network, which was designed for small-package shipments. The solution was to form a second alliance with Danzas, a Swiss freight-forwarding company, to handle larger shipments (such as palletized shipments). This enabled UPS to profit from this business, without hurting its small package business (Kelly, 1997).

CELLULAR PHONE VENTURE IN TASHKENT

When a group of investors from the state of Georgia in the USA first explored taking advantage of their successful experiences with cellular telephone networks in the USA, the six partners (an accountant, doctor, dentist, stockbroker, engineer and insurance man) developed a strategy of finding a major city with poor phone service in one of the countries that had been part of the former USSR, which some of the partners had visited (Guyon, 1996). At first they investigated Moscow, but found little interest in their small venture there. At the suggestion of those with whom they had negotiated in Russia during an exploratory visit in 1990, they next investigated Tashkent in Uzbekistan. Tashkent, the fourth-largest Soviet city, fitted their desired strategic market profile with its 2.2 million population and very poor phone service.

The US partners in the new venture, named International Communications Group (ICG), invited Uzbekistan's minister of communications to visit Georgia and see the South Carolina cellular systems they had developed. They convinced a neighbor, former President Jimmy Carter, to take time to chat with their Soviet visitor. Another critical success factor was that large companies were not interested in Tashkent and the new venture was the first to trust and believe in Tashkent's future.

On August 19, 1991, ICG formed a joint venture with the Soviet Republic of Uzbekistan, with ownership split 45% for ICG and 55% for the Uzbeks. The Americans agreed to finance construction of the system, which was named Uzdunrobita. Several days later, Uzbekistan declared its independence from the Soviet Republic. The Americans hastily persuaded the Uzbeks to re-register the venture from Moscow to Tashkent because of the legal uncertainties.

Another problem was that Uzdunrobita had no working capital nor had the Americans raised money to buy equipment. Up to this time, ICG had spent $500 000 on travel, translation and documents. To raise money, ICG sold more than 50% of its equity to a group of Pakistanis, for which the Americans got $2 million and a stake in a Pakistani pay-phone company. The Uzbeks also raised money by persuading Uzbek Air, the nation's airline, to buy $160 000 worth of phones and give Uzdunrobita an office in Tashkent, as well as a desk, a car and several employees. The Uzbek government also contributed, loaning the venture a dozen of its best engineers and computer software designers, as well as its best government expediters. Using $10 million in loans and equipment from Northern Telecom, Uzdunrobita expanded to eight Uzbek cities and planned to expand country-wide eventually.

There were problems which had to be overcome to make the venture successful. These are discussed in Chapter 6.

OTHER PERSPECTIVES ON NEGOTIATION

While the qualitative factors discussed thus far are important, financial and production aspects of the negotiations can require considerable work. These may involve financing, as in the Tashkent phone venture discussed above and in the Rally Dawson venture discussed in Chapter 4 (pp. 108–109). The negotiations will also involve financial projections of profitability. The task of projecting sales and costs accurately can be difficult.

In 1991 Fiat (Italy) and Peugeot (France) were considering forming a new joint venture, named SEVELNORD, which would be an extension of their existing joint venture, SEVEL, a large auto industry alliance which was formed in Italy to make commercial vans (Bidault and Schweinsberg, 1996; Herrera and Mainiero, 1997). The new joint venture under study in 1991, SEVELNORD, would involve production of minivans and was scheduled to begin in 1994.

The SEVEL venture had started producing commercial vans in 1981. The vans were marketed under different brands (Fiat, Peugeot, Citroen, Talbot and Alfa Romeo) through each partner's distribution channels. A new factory had been built in Italy specifically for the venture. The venture was a huge success, with sales doubling the original estimates. Both partners contributed equally in terms of research and development, engineering and investment. Fiat managed the plant within its production system. While the plant was legally a separate company, many corporate functions (such as accounting and purchasing) were carried out by the parent partner companies.

Fiat appointed the director of the venture, while Peugeot appointed the deputy directors for quality control, product coordination (logistics) and administration and management/accounting control. This gave Peugeot a measure of control to balance Fiat's. Joint planning and decision making were handled by several committees, all of which had an equal number of representatives from both partners:

- A formal *Board of Directors* issued directives based on decisions by the lower level committees or by the executive committees of each partner in case of high-level disagreements.
- A *Directors Committee*, a second-level committee, studied broader issues, including new product development, finance, production volumes, employment levels, investment profitability and budgeting.
- A *Steering Committee*, a third committee level, was responsible for styling and bringing a product to market, as well as for operational planning for both production and marketing.

- A fourth-level, *Joint Committees*, consisted of subcommittees responsible for such specific tasks as technical engineering, product planning, logistics (including marketing) and quality. Unresolved disputes at the fourth level were referred to the Steering Committee.

Negotiations developed guidelines on how pricing would be handled. Each partner's purchase price of a vehicle off the assembly line was based on costs and invoiced in Italian lire. A cost-plus system was negotiated in 1978 in the original alliance agreement. The 'cost' was based on variable costs, budgeted fixed costs and capacity fixed costs (mainly amortization). The allocation of production was based on the number of units ordered by each company and production planning decisions by the Steering and Joint Committees.

During the 1980s Fiat and Peugeot began studying the potential of the personal minivan market in Europe. Their projections were for more that 400 000 annual unit sales by the year 2000, but these projections varied considerably by country. In light of projected market growth, both partners began exploring the personal minivan market. Both decided that they would need a partner and so negotiations began for a joint venture between Fiat and Peugeot for the production of minivans.

The alliance, named SEVELNORD, was scheduled to begin in 1994. In 1991, the major open negotiation questions involved the production capacity needed, the creation of a 10-year production plan and the handling of potential competition between the two partners. A team of executives from each partner was assigned the task of developing proposals. The first step was to review the successful SEVEL alliance to see what might be learned from it that would help in crafting the new alliance. Next, extensive Return on Investment (ROI) analyses were done at different projected sales levels. Overall, the project looked promising, but risky, in light of potential competition.

A new plant was to be built in Valenciennes, France. The venture structure would be the reverse of SEVEL, with the director appointed by Peugeot, the deputy directors by Fiat. There would be the same managing committees, equally staffed by the two partners. The financing and pricing were to be handled in the same way.

There were, however, differences to be negotiated in the marketing area. In the first alliance, engines for each brand were manufactured by the respective partner and shipped to SEVEL, giving a distinct attribute to each brand vehicle. In addition, demand exceeded supply. This relieved any competitive pressures between brands. With the personal minivan, the only distinctions between brands besides the name plate were the taillights and grill. Since the brands would be marketed across Europe, they would be in direct competition, even though each brand would be distributed through different channels. Peugeot, for example, would be competing with Fiat in Germany, France and Italy. The partners agreed that this was acceptable. After having worked together for more than a decade in the past, the two partners felt that they knew each other well enough to overcome and resolve differences and disputes encountered along the way.

As seen from this experience, negotiations inevitably involve alliance details beyond partner selection. Decisions to be made include alliance type and structure, staffing, operational fits, and guidelines for managing the alliance – all topics discussed in the following sections and chapters.

FINDING/MATCHING/SELECTING COMPATIBLE PARTNERS

Both the Tambrands and Tashkent cellular phone venture negotiating experiences describe the partner search and selection process during the development phases of strategic alliance formulation. As seen from the experiences described earlier, finding a partner is not always easy. Sources for finding partners can vary from industry associations and trade shows, personal and business contacts, past experiences, customers and suppliers, competitors, related industries, professional consultants, foreign trade missions and governmental agencies, and US agencies, such as those attached to consulates abroad and US Department of Commerce offices.

The Initial Phases of the Partner Selection Process

The process of selecting partners – both individuals and company – can begin during the planning phase, as business strategies and needs are defined and as opportunities are explored. For example, British Airways and American Airlines knew the kinds of companies they wanted as allies and the partners available were a small group with which both partners were well acquainted. Murdoch's News Corp. was in a similar situation as it planned its multinational alliances. The company's business needs were well-defined and the potential telecommunication partners available were well known.

This first level of the partner selection process focuses on strategic fit, core business competencies, business and competitive gaps that need to be filled, and other business needs. This phase was discussed in Chapter 2. The negotiation phase extends the selection process as the parties become better acquainted. As the process continues, the focus shifts to several measures of fit or compatibility that can affect alliance success. These include partners' personalities, values, skills, interpersonal interaction styles, commitment and cultural characteristics, as well as company culture, values, management style, philosophy, commitment and business strengths and weaknesses. Many of these have been documented as critical to building trust and testing personal chemistry, a major alliance success factor that enables coordination, communication and conflict resolution (Bergquist and Betmee, 1995; Mohr and Spekman, 1994).

For example, each company has its own mix of strengths and weaknesses, as well as its own company culture. These factors are critical in partner selection. Although United Airlines was a logical strategic business partner for British Airlines, for instance, it did not turn out to be a perfect match because of the differing cultures and management styles, as well as strategic objectives of the two companies. The same was true of USAir, which for a time had an alliance with British Airways. In both instances, the incompatibility became apparent to both partners only after the alliance had been in effect for some time. Prethinking can help avoid such problems.

Questions about the compatibility of partners also arose in the experiences of Studds–Nolan. The problems were related to the cultural differences of the people (Italian and Indian), differing management styles and the lack of attention paid to getting to know each other, identifying potential differences, and reconciling differences. The solution was to first recognize the differences, between the two companies and between their managers and then determine if the identified gaps could be bridged through renegotiation, increasing interpersonal interaction and careful restructuring of the alliance agreement.

The joint-venture between Corning and CIBA-Geigy was handled differently. Representatives of the two companies spent more than 2 years planning the alliance. While part of this effort focused on establishing groundrules and policies for the alliance, considerable time was spent getting to know each other, learning about the companies involved and continually studying the companies' and their managers values, culture and strategic objectives. Despite this exemplary negotiating process, Corning exited the alliance in 1989 for strategic reasons (it needed more immediate profits and was using the money to invest in the laboratory equipment area) and sold their interest to CIBA-Geigy (Gates, 1993, p. 18; Lei and Slocum, 1991).

In contrast, an AT&T (USA) and Olivetti (Italy) joint venture designed to produce personal computers, was formed quickly so that the companies could get a jump on the market. Only after committing to the alliance did the partners discover major differences in their management styles, corporate cultures, strategic objectives and core competencies – differences they had failed to explore adequately and reconcile before making the alliance commitment. Eventually the alliance was formally dissolved (Gates, 1993, p. 12; Lei and Slocum, 1991).

Selecting a partner, therefore, involves selecting both the company and the people. The negotiation process described in the preceding section is a key step in the partner selection process. The negotiations provide an opportunity to get to know partners, especially when differences and conflicts are being resolved. Failure to allow time to get to know each other is a common and critical failing in strategic alliance development.

Coca-Cola attributed much of its success in Central Europe to the type of people and firms it had as partners (Nash, 1995). The people were relatively forthright, entrepreneurial, innovative, honest and adaptable to free-market business practices. These partner characteristics have proved effective in many cultural settings (de Keijzer, 1995). Part of Coca-Cola's success was attributable to the fact that Central European countries, such as Hungary, had a relatively free underground economy in the 1980s and the people generally had resisted communist influence.

Cultural differences can make it difficult to evaluate the personality and chemistry of potential partners. The Japanese culture, for example, is insular and patently self-protective. Westerners are routinely warned that Japanese businesses often appropriate technology unless ironclad protection clauses are included in an agreement. Such preconceptions can make it difficult to develop trust when dealing with individuals (who may or may not conform to the preconceptions), and trust is a necessary ingredient of successful alliances.

China's entrepreneurial tradition builds on close family ties, which also often makes nurturing trust a difficult task for foreigners. In addition, years of state control of the economies of China and Central European countries, among others, have nurtured a bureaucratic tradition which discourages entrepreneurial thinking among large segments of the population. For example, in China many state-owned businesses are potential joint venture partners, but their managers cannot be depended on to think entrepreneurially even though the Chinese have a culturally imbedded entrepreneurial tradition. At the same time, some view foreigners as greedy exploiters, or interlopers. Recognizing and then overcoming these problems is a necessary ingredient of success in multinational strategic alliances.

During the partner selection process, therefore, it is important to distinguish among the many personality types and traits in each culture. The mix of those traits within each individual involved should be observed and tested formally (Mockler, 1996), as well as informally.

Negotiations can be used for observing and gaining a feeling for the traits of the potential partners. Where appropriate, personal relations and trust can be cultivated and nurtured at this time. Tambrands followed this approach when negotiating its joint venture in the Ukraine. Several years of extensive interactive meetings and negotiations were used by participating partner personnel for getting to know each other and developing working relationships. These interpersonal exchanges later provided a basis for helping make the alliance work.

The problems discussed so far are less common in developed Western countries, where cultural and business traditions are more established and similar. For example, sources of information are more readily available and more reliable in Western countries, which have services such as Dun and Bradstreet's credit reports. Financial information can be difficult to assess, however, because of the varied accounting approaches and terminology used in different countries. The problem is more severe in developing countries, where accounting systems often are inadequate and credit rating services rarely are available. This lack of basic information makes partner selection more complex and increases reliance on the personal characteristics of the people involved. In addition, even in developed countries, cultural and business practice differences must be explored, as they were in the Borg–Warner venture.

Taking Steps to Develop a Workable Alliance

In some situations the strategic fit is favorable, but available partners involved are not ideal. In these situations, it is important to identify and plan carefully for handling the problems by developing a 'workable' strategic concept. In the Borg–Warner Chemicals Europe situation introduced on p. 53 in Chapter 2, the strategic fit was excellent. Through a joint venture with the CdF Chimie (France), Borg–Warner (Netherlands/USA) would have one-third of the European market for ABS, an engineering thermoplastic – a rapidly growing chemical market. CdF Chimie in turn would be able to participate in this growing market and preserve the jobs of a large number of French workers. The problems with the partner fit were enormous, however. To anticipate and manage the problems identified during the strategic planning phase, Borg–Warner developed operational plans for handling them before the joint venture contract was signed with the French government.

Detailed studies of operational fit on all levels are a significant contributor to alliance success; neglecting this step often leads to failure. For example, many aspects of the operational fit study of the French partner led Borg–Warner to include clauses in the joint venture contract to cover potential problems before they surfaced. Both sides recognized that professional and production workers at the French plant would resist the new venture, even though the workers were aware that without Borg–Warner the plant would have closed and they would have been out of work. The French, as seen from the strikes and labor disruptions during late 1997, have a strong sense of the social responsibility of business and are willing to take action to promote their special brand of socialism.

One of the operational planning tools developed by Borg–Warner during the negotiation and partner selection phases was an analysis of the French social environment. It consisted of four parts. First, the legal environment was analyzed. This covered individual contracts, company agreements, collective agreements and labor laws and regulations. These became the well-defined labor regulatory framework within which the joint venture's management had to work.

Second, the different levels of employees were identified: top management, mid-level management and professional staff, sales representatives, foremen-technicians, clerical and secretarial staff, and operators or workers. Each level had different characteristics' and different laws, regulations and past practices applied to each level. These were identified.

Third, six specific aspects of labor relations were studied:

- *Labor unions.* Labor unions were organized on an industry-wide basis, but less than 20% of the total workforce was unionized, and there was no union shop or closed shop. There were five major unions at the plant.
- *Management employee relations.* Local unions had syndicates representing employees and time was allowed for them to do union work during working hours; they could collect dues, distribute pamphlets, have a meeting place and use company bulletin boards. These unions also had delegates who were allowed company time to do union work and present individual worker grievances. Additional committees also represented workers and discussed working conditions.
- *Committee on health, safety and working conditions.* This was a permanent task force of union and company representatives for monitoring causes of accidents and advising on working conditions.
- *Individual rights to expression.* Rights to expression usually involved issues such as job content, organization and working conditions issues.
- *Labor disputes.* These were resolved through the various committees already identified above.
- *Trends.* More negotiations took place at the company level than nationwide. Union power grew and waned periodically over the years.

Fourth, the French Villers St-Sepulcre plant, which was to continue operating with its existing work force and facilities under the joint venture, were examined within the historical context of past practices. Workers come from a farming background, so they are traditionally hardworking. The plant had had many owners, each unsuccessful, so the workers had low expectations in regard to compensation and benefits. The workforce was aging and stable.

In this situation, the cultural differences between the Dutch and French partners were significant, especially in the areas of work ethic and management practices. For example, considerable resistance to change and to the systematic management practices of the Dutch management was expected at the middle management and professional levels. Both the French and the Dutch partners were aware of the differences, discussed them openly, and realized that recognizing and taking steps to resolve problems was the only way to make what appeared to be a strategically ideal alliance work. Understanding the dimensions of this cultural gap and taking steps to bridge it in a planned way in this situation is an example of how careful planning and development can increase the chances for success. It illustrates how conflict resolution during negotiations can be effective in developing working relationships among partners and providing a forum for the partners to get to know each other.

Because of the complexities discussed above, months of negotiations were required as lawyers from the USA and several European countries thrashed out terms of the agreement. Twelve countries, many with different local laws, were involved since different Borg–Warner divisions handled the products. The newly formed Borg–Warner Chemicals Europe B.V. joint venture would be run from Amsterdam, Borg–Warner's European headquarters, and be 70% owned by Borg–Warner and 30% by CdF, the same proportion as their asset contribution. The new joint venture company (controlled by the Dutch Borg–Warner chemical division) would manage the French operation (Beaumar), the Dutch operation (Holmar) and the Scottish operation (Grangemar). Forty separate documents had to be reviewed and signed to finalize the joint venture. The deal was not finalized for several months after the partners reached their agreement since French government approval, the final phase of negotiation, was required. Under terms of the alliance contract, Borg–Warner named the president and Cdf named the executive vice president.

Before the deal was finalized, an integration plan specifying operating details and completion dates was developed. The plan covered human resources, marketing and sales, technology, operations and finance. The following gives the highlights of the human resources plan, which was prepared by Mr. Wim Broekhuysen, Director, Human Resources of Borg–Warner Chemicals (Company Records; Parker and Burdet-Taylor 1990).

As a first step, both partners agreed in 1986 that a number of planned actions would be undertaken to start the integration of the two companies, ensuring the establishment of good working relationships.

Areas of attention in these plans were identified:

1. Harmonization of conditions of employment
2. Structure of organizations to obtain consistent authority and responsibility levels and communication process.
3. Human resources review to ensure that the rights of wo(man) were on the right track.
4. Integration of personnel policies so that they reflect Borg-Warner's philosophy, while respecting the cultural practices to reassure the French organization.
5. Familiarization with the industrial relations (unions and works council).
6. The extension of the internal communications program.

The action plans to be prepared during 1986, which would be included as part of the alliance agreement, would cover:

1. *Conditions of Employment*
   All contracts governing employees at the new plant will be reviewed, and any differences between those contracts and the ones at Borg Warner will be reconciled. Any special individual contract will be reviewed and integrated.
2. *Organization Structure*
   A preliminary orgainzation structure for the new venture will be developed and used as a basis for discussions with the unions, French managers, and the French government as a final organization structure is developed.
3. *Human Resources Review*
   The assignment of individuals within the new structure will be handled by a small committee consisting of representatives of both partners. The comittee will function to resolve individual assignment problems.

4. *Personnel Policies and Procedures*
    Existing policies and procedures at both partners will be studied
    and reconciled. They will cover such topics as:
    Job evaluation; compensation level; performance review;
    merit increases; training and educational assistance; human
    resources planning; management performance bonus; re-
    cruiting and selection; international transfers; company cars;
    service recognition; etc.
    Care will be taken to make sure they comply with local govern-
    ment regulations and existing union contracts. Those that are
    governed or influenced by local or national practices pertain
    to:
    Secondary benefits (including complementary benefits to so-
    cial security); employees' representation (Work Council);
    union contracts and negotiations; pensions; retirement age;
    vacation entitlement.
5. *Industrial Relations*
    In France, industrial relations are largely determined by gov-
    ernment policy and by the dialogue between employees' associ-
    ations and trade unions. There is legislation that regulates the
    rights of the union branches which function within the organiz-
    ation separately from the Works Council. In addition, there are
    elected employee representatives who have the right to meet
    with the chief executitve once per month.
    All these regulations will be specifically identified and special
    training programs introduced for all non-French managers so
    that they are aware of them.
6. *Internal Communications*
    Several pages were devoted to all aspects of this area, with special
    attention being paid to how to handle cultural differences.

Where appropriate special personal training programs will be
developed at all levels to insure problems can be resolved on a
continuing basis.
Appendix B at the end of this book provides general information
on cultural differences. This information is useful not only in negotiating and in selecting partners, but also in managing, leading and
generally making multinational strategic alliances work in both
developing and developed countries.

CRAFTING A WORKABLE NEGOTIATING STYLE AND PARTNER RELATIONSHIP: BEST PRACTICES GUIDELINES

This chapter focused on the human and other factors involved in the early phases of the strategic alliance development process: negotiation and partner selection. This process begins with the planning activities.

Negotiations involve many steps, most often with and through people, either from the partner enterprises involved or from interested outside parties, such as government regulatory agencies and competitors. Compatible partner selection involves planning considerations about the companies involved and the alignment of their competencies in the planned joint venture. In addition to the companies involved, the people involved are a factor in the partner selection process, especially in smaller joint ventures and contractual partnerships.

Best practices guidelines useful in this phase of alliance development have been developed based on the company experiences described in this and the preceding chapters. These include:

- Allow ample time during negotiations for partners to get to know each other and to test and develop personal chemistry, especially through reconciling anticipated areas of possible conflict. This approach was used by Tambrands and by Borg–Warner.
- During negotiations, face and resolve as many critical issues as possible before the venture contract is signed. This can lengthen the duration of negotiations but saves time and hard feelings later. This was done at Toshiba and Borg–Warner.
- Make an effort to anticipate and resolve possible problems through operational planning in key areas. This was done at Borg–Warner and Fiat to enable planning for implementation problems, and at General Motors to allow its Chinese partners to experience the ways technology could help the Chinese venture prosper.
- Allow time to move from suspicious bargaining to mutual concern. Find practical ways to cooperate that help assure the economic soundness of the new venture. This was done at Tambrands and Borg–Warner.
- During negotiations and partner selection, make certain partners share values, have high standards, and have a spirited

commitment to the venture, something which was not done in the Studds–Nolan venture.

- Identify potential champions and nurture them during the early phases of the strategic alliance formulation process, as was done in the Tambrands alliance.
- Make an effort to understand and adapt to cultural differences, such as those discussed in Appendix B at the end of the book since ignoring them can create communication and partner selection problems. This was done in the Borg-Warner and Tashkent cellular phone venture.
- Expect crises to occur. Use the early phases of strategy planning, deal negotiation and partner selection both to anticipate potential crises and to provide contractual and interpersonal bases for resolving them. These elements were missing in the Studds–Nolan alliance.
- Maintain flexibility as alliances are developed in order to reshape the alliance strategy and its implementation as the process evolves. It is important not to be overly reliant on any one partner. This was done at Toshiba and British Airways.
- During the negotiation and partner selection processes, as in subsequent strategic alliance processes, it is useful to make written records of informal oral commitments and agreements to be referred to at a later date to refresh memories of earlier commitments. Tambrands', Borg-Warners' and British Airways' use of such documents were effective examples.
- Resist promising more than you can deliver in sales, costs, profits, or project completion dates in order to control expectations and avoid over-optimism and disappointments.
- Be frank and open during negotiations, but avoid being blunt. Check that language differences do not lead to misunderstanding. For example, in Asia, 'yes' often only means 'I heard you'; it does not necessarily mean 'I understand you or agree with you'.
- Have a profile of the qualities wanted in a partner to use as a benchmark during negotiations. Perfection cannot be expected, but the strengths and weaknesses identified will provide a basis for staffing decisions later.

As in Chapter 2, the above best practices guidelines are reviewed from another perspective in Appendix A at the end of the book, where a summary checklist of key questions that might be asked and answered when doing the situation analysis involved in the negotiation and partner selection phase of multinational strategic alliance development and implementation is given.

REFERENCES

Air Transport World (1996). AAlienation of affection. *Air Transport World*, September, p. 9.

Anand, J. and Delios, A. (1996). *Studds Nolan Joint Venture*. London, Ontario, The University of Western Ontario.

Bergquist, W., Betwee, J. and Muel, D. (1995). *Building Strategic Relationships*. San Francisco, Josey-Bass Publishers.

Bidault, F. and Schweinsberg, M. (1996). *Fiat and Peugeot's Sevelnord Venture (A)* *(B1) (B2) (C)*, a case study. Lausanne, Switzerland, International Institute for Management Development (IMD).

de Keijzer, A.J. (1995). Identifying potentially effective joint venture partners. *Global Market Conference on China*. New York, *The Journal of Commerce/* Baruch College, November 8.

De Muth, J. (1992). The East is (in the) red. *World Trade*, November, pp. 44–46.

Emmons, W. (1990). *Tambrands Inc.: The Femtech Soviet Venture*. Boston, MA, Harvard Business School Publishing Division.

Emmons, W. (1993). *Tambrands Inc.: The Femtech Soviet Venture*. Boston, MA, Harvard Business School Publishing Division.

Gates, S. (1993). *Strategic Alliances: Guidelines for Successful Management*. New York, The Conference Board. pp. 12, 18.

Guyon, J. (1996). Some good old boys make lots of money phoning up Tashkent. *The Wall Street Journal*, June 21, pp. A1, A6.

Haslech, R. (1991). Whither free enterprise? The difficulties for Western investors in the Soviet Union. *Europe*, April, pp. 15–18.

Herrera, M. and Mainiero, A. (1997). *Fiat Drives to China*, a case study. New York and Rome, Strategic Management Research Group (St. John's University).

Kelly, J. (1997). All together now. *Chief Executive*, November, pp. 61–63.

Knobel, B. (1993). On the waterfront Russian-style. *International Business*, December, pp. 43–45.

Lei, D. and Slocum, J. (1991). Global strategic alliances: Payoffs and pitfalls. *Organizational Dynamics*, Winter, pp. 42–54.

Lewis, D.E. (1997). Returning to market as undisputed leader, Tambrands buy would give P&G 50% of tampon market,' *Boston Globe*, April 11, pp. D1, D6.

McCartney, S. (1998). Airline alliances take toll on travellers. *The Wall Street Journal*, February 18, pp. B1, B6.

Meredith, R. (1997). The brave new world of General Motors. *The New York Times* (Money and Business Section), October 16, pp. 1, 12, 13.

Mockler, R.J. (1996). Chinese and American entrepreneurs: Common frameworks for managing cross-cultural differences. *Proceedings of the International Conference on Cross-Cultural Management*, Hong Kong Baptist University, Hong Kong, August 26–28.

Mockler, R.J. and Carnevali, N. (1997). Type and structure of multinational strategic alliances: The airline industry. *Journal of Strategic Change*, Fall, pp. 249–260.

Mohr, J. and Spekman, R. (1994). Characteristics of partnership success: Partnership attributes, communication behavior, and conflict resolution techniques. *Strategic Management Journal*, **15**, 135–152.

Morrocco, J. (1996). BA defends pact with American. *Aviation Week and Space Technology*, July 15, pp. 44–45.

Nash, N.C. (1995). Coke's great Romanian adventure. *The New York Times* (Business Section), February 26, pp. 1, 10.

Naughton, K., Engardio, P. and Roberts, D. (1995). How GM got the inside track in China: a relentless push and clever strategy seem to have won the auto maker a huge joint venture. *Business Week*, November 6, pp. 56–57.

Parker, C. and Burdet-Taylor, J. (1990). Borg-Warner Chemicals (A), a case study. Lausanne, Switzerland IMEDE.

Slowinski, G. (1992). The human touch in successful strategic alliances. *Mergers & Acquisitions*, July/August, pp. 44–47.

Smith, C.S. (1998). In China, GM bets billions on a market strewn with casualties. *The Wall Street Journal*, February 11, pp. A1, A8.

Staff Reporter (1998). Alliance? Open skies?. *Barron's*, January 12, pp. 49–50.

Stern, G. (1995). GM executive's ties to native country help auto maker clinch deal in China. *The Wall Street Journal*, November 2, p. B5.

Tambrands (1988–95). *Annual Reports*. White Plains, NY.

Tambrands (1996). Letter to Shareholders. White Plains, NY.

4
Determining Type and Structure of Strategic Alliances: Operational Fit

This chapter discusses the impact that factors discussed in the preceding chapters (strategic fit, negotiating and partner selection factors), as well as other situation factors, can have on determining the type and structure of a strategic alliance.

ALLIANCE TYPES AND STRUCTURES

Strategic alliance types, which were identified in Chapter 1, are outlined in Figure 4.1. Many examples of these alliance types have been discussed in earlier chapters. For example, REFRAC Technology Development's alliances involved continuing licenses of its technology, while Microsoft entered into a vast number of distribution alliances with small overseas independent software distributors. Gillette, Daewoo, Coca-Cola and Mitsubishi all made equity investments in multinational joint ventures.

A wide range of alliance types have been used in the automobile industry, as shown in Figure 1.5 on pp. 20–27. These include equity investments, multi-partner joint ventures, and non-equity contractual and cooperative arrangements in such areas as marketing and distribution, technology, vending/purchasing and manufacturing/assembly. Since auto industry alliances, like other alliances, are often among competitors or potential competitors, they can be complex and require considerable effort to formulate.

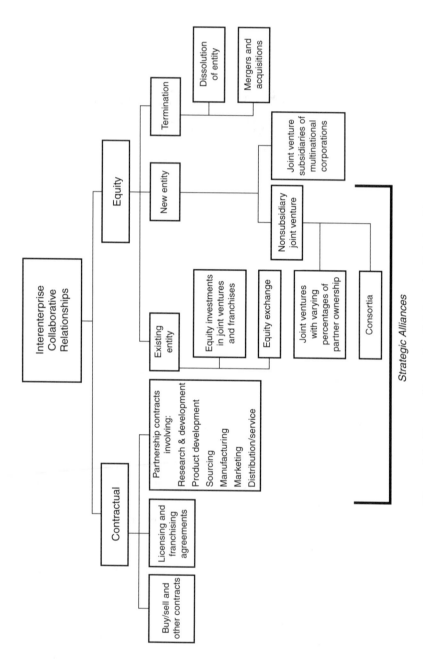

Figure 4.1 Types of Interprise Collaborative Relationships

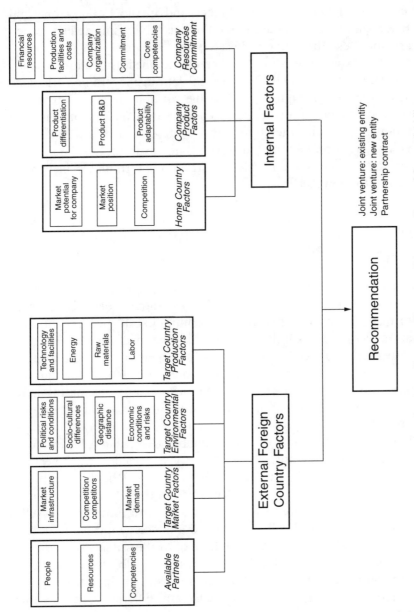

Figure 4.2 Decision Situation Overview Diagram: Type of Strategic Alliance

Even where alliances are fairly straightforward strategically, their structure can be complex. This was the case in the British Petroleum/Mobil Oil European alliance and in the Foote, Cone and Belding alliance with the French Publicis advertising agency, which are both described later in this chapter.

These experiences show that there is no one formula for structuring strategic alliances beyond general contingency frameworks such as that shown in Figure 4.2. Possible variables in situation factors are too numerous for detailed generalized formula solutions. The following sections, therefore, not only describe the impact of individual situation factors, but also provide examples of different alliance types chosen and alliance structures formulated in light of these situation factors.

OPERATIONAL FIT: IMPACT OF SITUATION FACTORS ON ALLIANCE TYPE AND STRUCTURE

During the strategic alliance development process, information about how the alliance might ideally operate is normally gathered through the analyses involved in determining strategic fit, negotiating and selecting compatible partners. This general information has to be translated into specific alliance structures which depend on: strategic needs; each partner's size, location, core competencies, operational strengths and weaknesses, personalities of the participating managers and corporate culture; competitive pressures; and major operating requirements. There must be a significant operational fit or hope of an operational fit developing before an alliance is formed.

A detailed study of how the alliance is expected to work needs to be done before a deal is signed. For example, British Petroleum's and Mobil Oil's complementary assets in their European alliance affected the structure of their proposed venture in the mid-1990s (Carasol-Volpi, 1997). The proposed alliance would combine $3.4 billion of BP's assets with $1.4 billion of Mobil's assets. These assets consisted of retail networks of petrol stations, logistic systems and production and refinery plants – all downstream operations.

The BP/Mobil alliance involved many different joint ventures. For example, their fuel joint venture would run refining, commercial manufacturing and retail networks. Since BP's retail network was almost twice the size of Mobil's and BP's refinery capacity was more than double Mobil's, BP had a 70% interest in this fuel joint venture. All retail branches were to carry BP's logo, since BP's name was widely known in Europe. Mobil, in turn, had a 51% interest in the lubricants joint venture, which managed both lubricant brands (Mobil and BP), marketed lubricants and special products and ran the related blending plants. The alliance package excluded upstream operations (such as exploration), international sales and trading, international aviation and marine fuel, gas marketing and research and development facilities.

While the strategic concept was simple, alliance details were not. The alliance consisted of a variety of different alliance types and structures for fuel and lubricants in each country where the companies were established. The alliance agreements involved 43 countries, including 15 European Union countries, plus Switzerland, Turkey, Cyprus, all of Eastern Europe, and Russia west of the Ural Mountains. The alliance's commercial and financial areas were coordinated by a supervisory committee comprised of an equal number of representatives from each company.

The alliance yielded significant gains on the logistics side. Prior to the alliance, BP and Mobil relied on exchanges with other companies to supply a significant portion of their sites. The alliance made direct supply possible in most areas, notably in the UK, France and Germany. Compared with their main competitors, Exxon and Shell, the new alliance had better located refineries and a superior supply/sales system. The new alliance's stronger marketing position was expected to lead to increased market share.

Overall, the alliance became the second largest-fuel marketer (with a 12.5% market share) in Europe and the third-largest in terms of refinery capacity there. The alliance was the leader in the European lubricants market, with an 18% share, ahead of Shell's 14% and Exxon's 10%. This new positioning strength was expected to lead to stronger sales growth.

In addition, its large size and resulting efficiencies were expected to yield savings of $400–490 million a year:

- Economies of scale in manufacturing and supply were expected to result in annual savings of $130–180 million. These would arise from reduced labor costs, fewer offices and lube oil plants, as well as cost savings in distribution originating from the integrated network.

- Annual corporate expenses were predicted to decrease by $140 million.
- The operation of fewer fuel business offices would yield $130–170 million in savings annually.

One-time conversion costs included $180–220 million for workforce reductions, and $200–250 million for rebranding stations with BP logos and colors.

In another situation, a large international US chemical company had as a joint venture partner an established chemical manufacturer in China. The Chinese partner provided the venture with manufacturing facilities which were part of its existing chemical complex and was designated the local raw material supplier for the new venture. To meet these requirements, the venture was structured as a jointly-owned manufacturing facility (formerly owned by the Chinese partner, but equipped by the US partner and managed by it), with supply contracts and technical support agreements between the US and Chinese partners.

The structure and type of Motorola's and Mitsubishi's many alliances varied depending on the different businesses and partner companies involved. As discussed in Chapter 2, pp. 39–43, Motorola used different alliance types over the years to balance, supplement and integrate their existing and needed core competencies. In many instances, companies move in incremental stages through research and development, distribution and marketing, co-production contractual relationships and eventually equity joint ventures to gain experience in a market and develop relationships with partners (Chow et al, 1997, pp. 387–393).

The alliance's strategic importance to each party is another key factor that affects alliance type and structure. For example, in one venture in Shanghai, the Chinese partner (a municipality) was interested in the business mainly as a source of income – not as a means of increasing market position of related businesses. It therefore offered its American partner, a global leader in its field, a two-thirds interest in the venture and allowed it to assume operating control. The municipality believed that the American company knew the business better and so would be able to make it more profitable if left in control.

The people involved can affect an alliance's type and structure, as well as its development and management. For example, the cultures of the people involved in Borg–Warner Chemicals strategic alliance in Europe had a major impact on the steps involved in structuring and implementing the alliance. Especially in small ventures, people can have a significant impact on success, as seen in the Studds–Nolan and Tashkent experiences described in Chapter 3.

Where the potential for misuse of proprietary technology exists and the partners are not well-acquainted, the situation may require a much more restrictive alliance structure. Many companies protect their proprietary technology from partners who are potential rivals by using older but adequate technology, as did Gillette through importing its newer Sensor products and making only traditional razors and blades locally. Duracel failed to protect its technology from cannibalization in its joint venture agreement in China – an expensive mistake. The contingency nature of multinational strategic management requires negotiation of protective alliance structures that are at the same time appropriate for the market, partners and products involved.

Potential conflicts with other business areas of partners can affect an alliance's structure and type. For example, the benefits of the learning potential in a General Motors/Toyota alliance in Fremont, California, apparently outweighed the fact that the autos produced were to be sold competitively under both the GM and Toyota brands. The deal was structured to terminate once the shared learning had reached a logical time limit.

CHANGING CIRCUMSTANCES AND STRUCTURAL ADAPTATION

Changing circumstances are a significant reason why strategic management is an emerging process. When rethinking enterprise-wide strategic frameworks and formulating business unit strategies, a specific vision of what is desired and needed often emerges in stages. This is the first activity described in the strategic management process outlined in Figure 4.3: knowing exactly what kind of company is envisioned without knowing precisely what it will look like. As structures and deals are negotiated and defined in detail, precise definitions of strategies often emerge over time, through implementation experiences.

The assessment of an alliance, therefore, continues as circumstan-

The Focus: An Emergent Entrepreneurial Leadership Process
The Process
1. *Strategic vision/mission:*
   'I knew exactly what kind of company I envisioned; I Just didn't know precisely what it would look like.' Precise definitions, in other words, often emerge over time, through the experiences involved in doing it.
2. *Strategic guidelines:*
   This is the map, the path, the planned steps. The secret here is KISS – 'Keep It Short and Simple.' That means one page written, five minutes oral, maximum length.
3. *Implementation:*
   'Doing whatever was necessary to get the job done, within well-defined general moral, legal, ethical and policy guidelines.' This often involves reconciling and balancing diverse, conflicting and often paradoxical forces, on a continuing basis, in a complex and rapidly changing competitive market environment.

The Activities
- Creating an overall vision (values, mission, strategic focus on core competencies, opportunities in future) and strategic framework (the guidelines or map). Specific strategies and strategic plans (enterprise-wide and in business units and functional areas) often emerge over time, through the enabling systems and processes.
- Activating, energizing, putting into place and monitoring enabling systems and processes, such as: functional area operations; telecommunications/information systems; accounting and finance systems; organization and business structures, processes and cultures; and strategic alliances.
- Nurturing enabling human resources and processes through: organization development; understanding cultural diversity, staffing, training, and communicating; and effective flexible leadership and integrative management at all levels.
- Ensuring that a core management staff (with appropriate interpersonal, communication, entrepreneurial and management skills and potential) is in place and functioning.
- Communicating and implementing the strategic framework, as well as the cultural benchmarks that are needed to enable the core management staff to translate the desired vision into action. The actual process involves superior visionary and pragmatic leadership appropriate for both the managers and people/groups involved in the situation.
- Leaving managers relatively free to manage, and pushing decision making as close to the customer as possible, but intervening where appropriate to make certain integrative activities are operating efficiently and effectively to achieve the company's strategic short- and long-term objectives.

Figure 4.3 Strategic Management: Multinational and Domestic

ces change. Shell bought out its partner's interest in two alliances, Montell and MonteShell, when the businesses needed additional capital investments and its partner, MonteEdison, was unable to make those investments. Lower import tariffs and aging facilities led to the 1996 termination of the Ford/Mazda alliance in New Zealand.

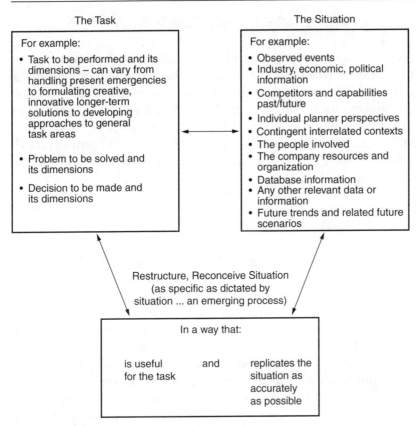

Figure 4.4 A Basic Entrepreneurial Contingency Process

The best structure is whatever organizational arrangement is accepted through negotiation by all the parties and enables managers to improve their chances of getting what they want from necessarily ambiguous relationships in the existing and anticipated competitive market. Above all, the alliance must fulfill four basic criteria: add value, enable learning, protect and enhance core competencies and competitive advantages, and enable the operational flexibility needed for alliance success.

While planning is useful, it does not insure success, because many factors affect success. Since planning involves the future – that is, uncertainty and risks – all contingencies cannot be anticipated (Park and Ungson, 1997). Entrepreneurial adaptability, crisis management, flexibility and contingency thinking as outlined in Figure 4.4 are, therefore, major contributors to success.

DEVELOPING DETAILED STRUCTURES

As the process of developing an alliance structure continues, further definition is given to the details of the alliance, including: percentage of ownership; mix of financing; kinds of material, technology and machinery contributions by each partner; division and sharing of activities; staffing; location; autonomy; controls not just for operations but also for measuring and controlling each partners contributions over time; and guidelines for management after alliance inception.

Tambrands Inc.

The early negotiations which led to selecting a potential partner for Tambrands' Femtech joint venture in Russia were described in Chapter 3 (De Muth, 1992; Emmons, 1990, 1993; Haslech, 1991; Knobel, 1993; Lewis, 1997; Tambrands, 1988–95, 1996). This section describes the negotiations involved in developing the specific type and structure of the venture and the details of the venture contract.

As negotiations progressed, a team of operational experts at Tambrands worked on the operating details of the joint venture. These team members later served as a source of experienced managers to staff the alliance once it was formed. As they worked the legal department was consulted to begin drafting the joint venture agreement; an experienced outside international law firm helped draft the agreement. The objective was to have an agreement which covered the major points in principle, but did not cover every last detail, since the joint venture was expected to be able to respond to change over time.

Control was a key concern for Tambrands. However, Soviet regulations permitted foreigners to have only 49% of the venture's equity and required that the chairman of the board and the general director (president) be Soviet citizens. Tambrands, therefore, specified in the contract that consensus would be required on all key management decisions, a condition of many successful multinational joint ventures.

Tambrands also wanted to make its major capital investment through a loan, in order to:

• Enable repatriation of the bulk of their investment

- Guarantee some return on the investment
- Protect most of the investment from exchange rate fluctuations

In addition, Tambrands wanted both partners' investments to be equity investments in order to avoid arguments over in-kind valuations of building, equipment, access to distribution channels and the like. These points were covered in the summary outline of contract conditions discussed in Chapter 3 pp. 88–90.

Tambrands planned to have the plant produce Tampax products for sale in former Russian territories only, as well as processed cotton fiber for export. The plan called for starting with a $16 million pilot plant which would be expanded if the venture was successful. Initially, it would have a fiber processing production line and four tampon manufacturing lines. Tambrands would finance its 49% share with $1 million in cash and $7 million in loans, part of which would be from outside sources. Capacity expansion would be financed over a 5-year period through retained earnings. The export earnings from bleached cotton sales would be used for equipment purchases, royalties and interest payments but would not be used to pay dividends to Tambrands.

The joint venture contract also covered sourcing questions. The venture was to have the ability to buy raw materials from abroad when domestic supplies were below acceptable quality standards or were more costly than comparable materials purchased abroad. In addition, the contract also provided protection against changes in Soviet law that would affect the joint venture's profitability or ability to fulfill contract obligations.

These operational details needed definition to provide a basis for structuring the joint venture. In every strategic alliance, it is necessary to review and specify the operational aspects of the ventures to determine if there will be an operational fit among the partners, as well as a strategic fit. If not done in adequate detail, this phase can be a major cause of problems after a venture is begun. These items are general in nature, but at the same time they target specific strategic issues which, if unresolved early, can have a significant impact on the venture's success. This is a crucial phase of alliance development, and Tambrands is a good example of how it was done effectively.

Constantin Ohanian, Tambrands' chief negotiator, made an additional trip to the Ukraine in late 1987 to clarify issues raised by the conditions in the proposed contract draft being prepared by Tambrands' strategic alliance development team. Ohanian used this opportunity to become better acquainted with the partners involved, to clarify undecided issues and to acquire additional information about the venture's expected future operations. This important step helped anticipate and avoid misunderstandings about strategic and operational issues.

Key strategic issues were initially included in a letter of intent. This was used as a basis for a feasibility study – the study of operations which translated the strategic intents into operational realities. As part of this operational feasibility study, financial analyses and projections were made for the initial 5-year period. Subsequently, an outline was made of the key provisions of the proposed Femtech joint venture agreement and a proposed agreement was prepared. The feasibility study and the agreement were explicitly based on overall mission statements and strategic objectives:

> to make available an effective internal means of menstrual protection to Soviet women in tampons, reduce the need for absorbent fibers for this menstrual protection and in this way reduce foreign currency spending for such fibers, and produce adequate financial returns for investors with limited risks achieved by following carefully structured investment and growth plans.

These documents, translated into Russian, were the basis for the negotiations which followed in March 1988. Constantin Ohanian was the sole negotiator for Tambrands; the Russians had three: lead negotiator Saakov (Deputy Director General, Techsnabexport, a trading company responsible for all trading operations of the USSR Ministry of Health), Volukh (Head, Ukrainian GAPU) and Serdyuk (First Deputy, Ukranian Ministry of Health). The four negotiators (with their four interpreters) read through the proposed agreement line by line to make sure each understood it. No one else was in the negotiating room. Consultations with legal or financial advisors, when necessary, took place outside the room.

The negotiations were intense but fruitful, with the parties insisting on full explanations of the implications of key points. Each side agreed to modify many aspects of the draft agreement by reaching a consensus, not a compromise, on what was best for the joint venture. A major sticking point was the equity investment, which the Russians finally agreed to (cash, instead of in-kind contributions by each partner). Ohanian also finally yielded on one point: he agreed to accept 5% of Tambrands' dividend payments from the joint venture in finished tampon products, which in all likelihood would be exported.

Between May and June, additional revisions were made to the joint venture documents. Conditions specified in addition to those already mentioned above included: composition of the Board of Directors; a 2-year non-competitive agreement; arbitration of irre-solvable issues would be settled by arbitration in Stockholm, Sweden; dividend policies; and a termination agreement. All of the key clauses were contained in the two-page typed document which outlined contract conditions.

The final contract was then sent to Tambrands' president, Ed Shutt and Evgeni Chasov, Director of the Ministry of Health for the USSR. The agreement was signed in mid-June 1988.

In compliance with Soviet law, Femtech's board of directors consisted of: Dr Dmitrij Volukh (chairman), general director of the Ukranian GAPU; Constantin Ohanian, Tambrands vice-president international; Andrej Serdyuk, Deputy Minister of Health of the Ukraine; and Dustin Allred, Tambrands group vice-president. Yuri Saakov, a Soviet foreign trade specialist who spoke fluent English and had been associated with the venture from the beginning, was appointed general director of Femtech, and Ross Dineen, the experi-enced general manager of Tambrands Canadian subsidiary, became deputy general director. In addition, two experienced Tambrands' manufacturing and product development executives were involved: Chris Curry was responsible for managing the design and installa-tion of manufacturing lines and hiring and training key production personnel; Tony Butterworth was responsible for raw material supply and quality assurance. Ohanian intended to spend a signifi-cant part of his management time overseeing the success of the venture he had taken to this point.

Foote, Cone and Belding (FCB) and Publicis SA

By 1991, Foote, Cone and Belding (FCB) had built a network of 173 advertising agencies in 43 countries worldwide. One of their most innovative partnerships was with Paris-based Publicis SA's wholly-owned subsidiary Publicis Conseil, one of France's premier adver-tising agencies. The alliance was called Publicis/FCB European

Communications Group (Applbaum and Yatsko, 1993; Kanter et al, 1993).

The globalization of multinational companies had led to pressures to globalize advertising agencies so that they could respond to multinational corporations' needs. A strategic alliance approach was preferred by Publicis, since it was strong in Europe and had considered and then rejected, mergers and acquisitions as a way to serve its international clients beyond Europe. Publicis was under considerable pressure from clients (some of which were threatening to leave Publicis if it did not go global) and from competitors. After several abortive attempts to form alliances, Publicis began talks with FCB.

FCB had established a complex web of acquisitions and alliances throughout the world, including Europe. Founded in 1873, FCB had grown steadily over the years. While the company was widely admired for its account management capabilities, it was not as known for its creativity. This changed during the 1980s under the leadership of a new president, Norman Brown, who also expanded substantially FCB's international operations. By 1987, FCB had offices in North America (31), Europe (27), Latin America (17), Asia (7) and the Pacific Rim (11). From its clients' perspective, however, FCB was not expanding fast enough internationally. This led Brown to explore forming additional major strategic alliances, especially in Europe and Japan, one of which was with Publicis.

In early 1988, representatives of FCB and Publicis met to negotiate a possible alliance. The strategic fit seemed good. The two agencies shared many clients. Publicis was strong in Europe, but was weak in the Asian, North American, Latin American and Asian/Pacific Rim areas – areas of strength for FCB. The alliance would also produce an enterprise with the size and worldwide scope to compete for client accounts such as Nestle, who had declared that it was consolidating its worldwide advertising with a limited number of large worldwide agencies. Management at FCB and Publicis also believed that the two companies shared basic creative and operating philosophies. They took time to work out detailed policies to govern their new alliance operation.

The structure that evolved was extremely complex, as shown in Figure 4.5. The structure took into account the operational fit required by two advertising services companies serving a wide range of clients with differing geographic and creative needs, some of whom were competitors.

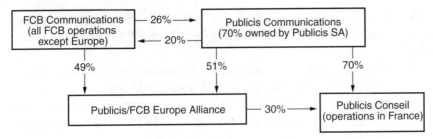

Figure 4.5 Publicis/FCB Structure

Under terms of the deal, which was announced in May 1988 and became effective in January 1989, the two partners agreed that (Applbaum and Yatsko, 1993, pp. 8–9):

- Publicis SA would set up a company, Publicis Communications, which would hold 100% of the Publicis advertising and media buying networks (called Publicis Conseil in France and Publicis International for all units outside France). Publicis SA's drugstores, real estate holdings, radio and print media operations were excluded.
- FCB would acquire a 26% share in Publicis Communication. In exchange, Publicis Communication would acquire 20% of FCB Communications, which consisted of all existing FCB advertising operations (except those in Europe).
- The two companies would exchange board members. Norman Brown would sit on the Publicis Communications board and Maurice Levy, chairman of Publicis SA, would sit on the FCB Communications board.
- An alliance entity called Publicis/FCB European Communications Group (Publicis/FCB Europe) would be established in Europe. Publicis Communication would hold 51% and FCB Communications 49%. The joint operation would contain all of FCB's European operations and all of Publicis' international offices, and would own up to 20% of Publicis Conseil initially, with an option to buy 10% more.
- The Board of Directors of Publicis/FCB Europe alliance would be composed of an equal number of members from its two parent companies. Craig Wiggins, the chairman of FCB/Europe, would serve as alliance chairman/CEO; Gerald Pedraglio, executive vice president of Publicis, would serve as its vice chairman/COO.

- Publicis New York agency, owned by Publicis Communications, would report to and receive support from FCB/Leber Katz New York.
- The organization would continue with two worldwide management groups. FCB Communications would manage operations in the Americas and Asia. Publicis Communications, under the auspices of Publicis/FCB Europe, would manage the alliance's European operations.

There were several reasons for structuring the alliance this way. The different equity exchanges were designed to document the firms' commitment to a comprehensive global alliance, not just a European alliance. At the same time, it verified that the firms would remain independent entities. Making the Publicis/FCB alliance's stake in Europe roughly equal demonstrated to clients that each firm had an equally strong commitment to Europe. Publicis Conseil's independence from the alliance preserved the French integrity of the long-established Publicis operation in France and demonstrated that Publicis had not sold out to American interests, an important cultural consideration.

The deal was structured so that neither company would buy the other, but so that each would have a meaningful share in the other. An American was appointed head of the alliance so that FCB clients would see that FCB had retained a meaningful presence in its European operations rather than then turning them over to Publicis. This was important in the advertising services business since client perception is a crucial success factor. In this way, the complex structure accommodated a wide range of cultural, operational and customer/client business relationship factors.

Considerable leadership and management skills were required to make such an alliance work. Some of the problems encountered are discussed in Chapter 6, pp. 163–165. The complexity of the alliance structure was a major contributing factor in this alliance's eventual failure (Melcher, 1997).

Rally Dawson Sports in Pakistan

In 1990, Rally Dawson Sports ($29 million in sales) was making a decision about opening a manufacturing plant in Pakistan and marketing its sports products (tennis, cricket, golf, soccer, baseball, skiing, football, badminton and field hockey equipment) from that part of the world (Springate, 1990). Labor and material costs were low in Pakistan and the government encouraged foreign investments. Initially, Rally wanted to create a wholly-owned subsidiary, as it had done in other countries. Eventually, Rally decided to take on a joint venture partner to overcome local political, supply, distribution and marketing problems. Rally obtained its potential joint venture partner, Hamid Sports of Pakistan, through the Pakistani Trade Office in Washington, DC.

As negotiations progressed, it was decided that Rally would own 60% of the $4 million joint venture, called Ampak International Ltd, purchasing its interest with machinery and funds borrowed internationally. Rally relied on funds borrowed from non-Pakistani sources to finance the purchase for several reasons. The Pakistani government did not want to dip into foreign exchange reserves and Rally had cheaper financing sources outside of Pakistan. Local banks were to be used for working capital borrowing. In addition, the government limited profits which could be taken out of the country to the amount originally invested ($2.4 million) plus half the cumulative profits.

The needs of Ampak and its local competitive environment, the financial resources and structure of the two joint venture partners, and the availability of funds worldwide were all considered in creating the structure of the venture. For example, an *allocation* problem arose when Rally's subsidiary in Spain needed additional capital investment. This forced the company to secure an external source of financing – the Export–Import Bank – and to structure the Pakistan Ampak venture in a way that kept cash investment low so that funds would be available for Spain. Rally's financial management assisted in making the investment decision by preparing detailed forecasts of costs, profits and losses, cash flows and return on investment.

Financial forecasts, profit and loss projections and pricing/costs relationships were used even more extensively in the Fiat/Peugeot alliance discussed in Chapter 3.

Airbus Industrie: A Major Successful Consortium

Airbus Industrie was a strategic alliance created by four countries – England, France, Germany and Spain. Initially, Airbus was a marketing and research and development consortium of four companies whose percentage of participation was dictated by their contribution to airplane manufacturing. Airbus also coordinated the four manufacturing operations. In early 1996, Airbus captured 40.2% worldwide plane orders, Boeing 56.4%, and McDonnell-Douglas 3.4%. Dramatic organization changes at Airbus helped increase Airbus' market penetration to more than 50% in 1998. Airbus' competitive advantage was that its planes were more fuel efficient and had lower operating costs than Boeing's.

However, heavy competitive pressures were increasing from Boeing, which had introduced new models, cut lead times, and pared prices (Tagliabue, 1996). Airbus was encountering many other problems: huge amounts of money were needed for new plane development, high costs resulted in non-competitive pricing and a cumbersome corporate structure which led to long product development lead times. In addition, the inability to raise directly the money needed to develop new models, tightening government budgets and heavy losses at Aerospatiale (France) and Daimler-Benz (Germany) were other factors adversely affecting the consortium. These pressures, and the merger of McDonnell-Douglas and Boeing, forced Airbus to make strategic and structural changes in 1996 and 1997 (Bryant, 1997).

To carry out strategies that would alleviate the cost, capital and lead time problems, Airbus President Jean Pierson proposed an enterprise-wide reorganization to centralize control in May 1996. This arrangement, formalized in early 1997, would unify functions like design (then done at four locations), eliminate white-collar bureaucracies such as market forecasting, and assign work on a competitive bid basis, even to the point of using lower-cost outside contractors (Tagliabue, 1997).

Under the proposed restructuring, Airbus would be a stand-alone marketing and sales company which coordinated manufacturing and design and in which the four partners would have equity participation. In addition, Airbus would either be (1) vertically integrated, that is it would have its own manufacturing and design assets (now held by the partners), or (2) be a virtual-type organization which would not own the manufacturing and design assets, but rather, would contract them out on a bid basis, or (3) some combination of (2) and (3). In either form, Airbus would raise its own financing and be responsible for its own debts in the future (Haycocks, 1997;

Reed, 1996). Negotiating the new strategy among the four partners was expected to be a lengthy process (Owens et al, 1998).

Consortia-type alliances have been used extensively in the research and development area. Japanese companies were involved in many of them in the 1980s and studies have documented their success (Bransletter and Sakakibara, 1997). More recently, multi-million dollar alliances have been formed to do fuel cell research, advanced network technology development, gene research, and semiconductor research (Anonymous, 1997; Corey, 1997; Hilts, 1997; Morrison, 1997; Puttre, 1997; Zink, 1997).

Incremental Approaches

An incremental approach is sometimes used in structuring alliances. For example, a group of small European paint manufacturers (from Spain, UK, France, and Germany) explored joining together to meet pressures from customers seeking single international sources, just-in-time delivery, volume discounts and greater quality control over suppliers. They felt the joint venture would give them an international reach and access to advanced technologies and new markets (Renart and Oares, 1991). During negotiations, it was suggested that the alliance begin simply, with coordinated raw material purchasing used to obtain lower prices. Partners could use this step to become better acquainted and develop working relationships, prior to formulating a broader joint venture. Through coordinated buying the partners were able to obtain discounts of up to 30%, establishing a verifiable success story that enabled them to move to the next level of more formal cooperation.

AIRLINE INDUSTRY ALLIANCES

Considerable time may be required to develop the type and structure of an alliance, and the structure itself is often not a simple one. For example, the unique nature of the airline business dictates that alliances be structured around diverse requirements. The type and structure options in the airline industry are shown in Figure 4.6(a) (Mockler and Carnevali, 1997). Factors that affect these decisions are outlined in Figure 4.6(b).

American Airlines (AA) and British Airways plc (BA) announced in late 1996 their intention to enter into a strategic alliance (BA Press Release, 1996). Their experiences illustrate some of the complex types and structures of alliances used in a major service industry.

AA had expanded substantially in the 1980s through traditional equity purchases. Beginning in 1982, AA targeted a number of foreign areas for expansion in its drive to become a worldwide airline. In 1982, AA purchased bankrupt Braniff Airline's routes to Latin America; in 1989 and 1990 it purchased TransWorld Airlines' (TWA's) European routes; in 1991 it purchased Continental Airlines' San Jose/Dallas/Seattle/Tokyo route, and in 1992 it purchased bankrupt Eastern Airlines' Latin American routes and Miami/Madrid route. In addition to equity investments in routes, AA had codesharing arrangements with Philippine Airlines, Lone Star, LAPSA, LOT Polish Airlines, Canadian Airlines and South African Airways; it also had frequent flyer reciprocation agreements with BA, Qantas Airways, Lufthansa and Japan Airlines. When the proposed BA alliance was announced in 1996, AA had had considerable experience in linkages with other airlines.

BA also had pursued many airline linkages in its drive to become a dominant global airline. Robert Ayling, BA's CEO, defined BA's goal: to be the world's favorite airline; to be the best-managed airline; to be pre-eminent in customer service (which means maintaining standards of service which are above its competitors at costs which are competitive); and to be truly global, that is, build a global network with a presence in all major markets.

BA has used alliances to advance these goals in a variety of ways. While the industry factors cited earlier favor alliances, another reason that BA used them was the considerable use of alliances by competitors such as: United Airlines/Lufthansa/SAS; KLM/Northwest; and Delta/Sabena/Swissair/Austrian Airlines.

One of BA's earliest agreements with another airline was with UAL Corp.'s United Airlines in the early 1980s. The two carriers planned to codeshare London flights, but the agreement was ultimately unsuccessful. The BA/United service partnership contract did not stipulate that United give up its London routes outside the codesharing agreement. United subsequently bought PanAm's London routes and severed its alliance with BA. When BA subsequently invested $400 million to purchase a 24.6% stake in USAir in

1993, one of the conditions of the contract was that USAir would relinquish its London routes.

One of BA's early experiences with equity investments in a franchise alliance was with TAT European Airlines of France. In September 1992, BA signed an agreement to acquire 49.9% of TAT with an option to purchase the remaining shares on or before April 1997. All of TAT's scheduled international flights were relaunched under the BA name using BA flight designators and all aircraft were painted in BA livery. Brymon Airways and British Asia Airways, also wholly-owned subsidiaries with small regional routes, owned by BA, are operated as franchises.

BA invested 440 million French francs in another French airline, Air Liberté, in 1996, to purchase a 67% stake in the airline. The investment in Air Liberté, coupled with the successful investment in TAT, provided BA with well-connected French partners who had the potential to compete more effectively in the market. When BA acquired 49% of German regional carrier Delta Air in 1992, the company was renamed Deutsche BA. Like BA's agreement with Air Liberté, the agreement between BA and Deutsche BA was an equity investment in conjunction with a franchise agreement. BA acts as a general sales agent for Deutsche BA and TAT. In early 1997, Deutsche BA was relaunched with improved service on board, increased flights, and an image closely integrated with that of BA.

British Airways has a number of franchise agreements with no equity investment, where the franchisee acts as a separate, independent company. An example is Comair of South Africa, with whom BA signed a franchise agreement in 1996. This was BA's first franchise agreement with a company based in Africa. Comair remained a separate, independent company, but Comair cabin crew and customer service staff wear BA uniforms and Comair's aircraft interiors were done in BA's style. BA has a similar agreement with Sun-Air of Scandinavia. In January 1997, Sun-Air began operating as a BA franchise. Sun-Air's hub, Billund, is the second busiest hub in Denmark, and helps give BA a competitive edge in Scandinavia. Other airlines with whom BA has franchise agreements with no equity investment are: Maersk Air (England), Manx Airlines (Europe), CityFlyer Express Ltd (England), Loganair (Scotland) and GB Airways (England). In order to ensure that these franchises, as BA operators, maintain a standard of service and safety that matches

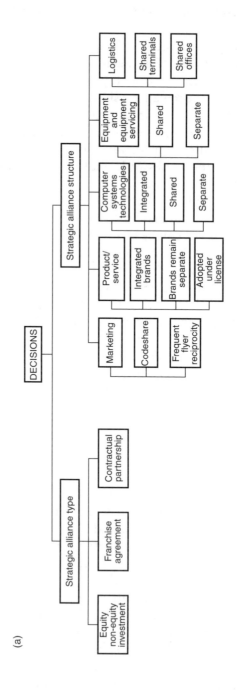

(a)

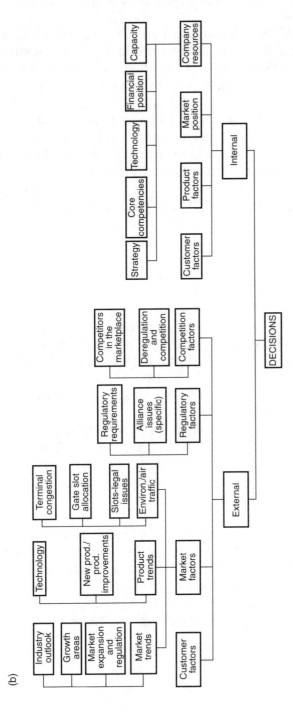

Figure 4.6 (a) Strategic Alliance Type and Structure Decision Situation Diagram: Airline Industry Overview of Decisions to be made; (b) Strategic Alliance Decision Situation Diagram: Airline Industry Overview of Factors Affecting the Decisions

that of BA, customer service and engineering audits are conducted regularly.

Different kinds of alliances are appropriate for different situations. In the case of BA's relationship with Qantas Airways (Australia), for example, an examination of the situation revealed that a franchise agreement was not necessarily the best alternative. British Airways was eager to tap into the Asia Pacific region, and an alliance with Qantas provided BA with a chance to do this. In March 1993, BA invested £304 million to purchase 25% of Qantas. BA's contractual partnership with Qantas is a marketing, joint purchasing and joint service agreement. Financial benefits from the alliances have come from reducing costs through joint purchasing of catering supplies and fuel and shared airport and/or office facilities in Seoul, Melbourne and Tokyo. BA provides ground handling for Qantas in the UK and Germany, and Qantas reciprocates in Australia.

When BA wanted greater access to the North American market, it turned to USAir for a partnership similar to its one with Qantas. BA signed a contractual service partnership agreement with USAir in 1993, buying 24.6% of USAir's stock. The systems of USAir and BA were integrated to the extent that passengers could check in at their point of origination for both USAir and BA flights all the way through to their final destination. Three years after it began, the relationship between USAir and BA ended when USAir ended its codeshare and frequent flyer relationship with BA. In 1997, BA sold its shares in USAir.

BA's only other footholds in North America in 1997 were codesharing agreements with America West and Canadian Airlines. BA's contractual partnerships with these two airlines were non-equity marketing agreements involving codesharing and limited frequent flyer program reciprocation. BA also had entered a contractual marketing partnership with Aeromexico in 1997; the two carriers codeshare certain flights and their frequent flyer programs are partially reciprocal (reciprocation is limited to codeshared flights). BA's relationship with Jet Airways (India) is also a contractual partnership with no exchange of equity. This alliance is unique because it is composed of a marketing agreement involving only frequent flyer program reciprocation – there is no codesharing agreement.

TYPES OF STRATEGIC ALLIANCE IN THE AIRLINE INDUSTRY

The following discussion summarizes the different types of alliances found in the airline industry. As shown in Figure 4.6, these include equity investments and non-equity linkages, in conjunction with contractual agreements. These contractual linkages may be in the form of franchise agreements and/or other kinds of contractual linkages, including service partnerships.

Equity Investments

The airline industry has a wide range of international equity investment alliances. For example, large carriers often purchase other airlines which then become wholly-owned subsidiaries. Wholly-owned subsidiaries are not considered strategic alliances, although they may be operated as franchises.

The use of wholly-owned subsidiaries is limited. For example, in most instances international air laws require that flag carriers have domestic ownership. US law limits a foreign carrier's ownership of a US airline to 25%. European law prohibits a foreign nation from having a majority stake in an EU member state airline. In keeping with this, the European Transport Ministry proposed measures in early 1997 to restrict foreign ownership of Germany's Lufthansa Airlines to 50%.

In many instances, equity investments are partial, involving a wide range of linkages, such as franchise agreements and other contractual partnerships, which can be both equity and non-equity types of strategic alliances.

Franchise Agreements

Franchising involves selling products or delivering services under license. Under a franchise agreement, a smaller (usually regional) carrier is licensed to operate certain routes on behalf of a larger carrier. This alliance form is popular with major carriers because it lets them transfer less profitable routes to smaller airlines to operate as franchises. Successful franchising requires a strong brand identity and a standard of quality and service that consumers recognize.

Some or all of a franchise airline's routes may be franchised. For example, all of Manx Airlines (Europe)'s routes are franchised from BA except for its home-base routes on the Isle of Man–London; crew members on these routes do not wear BA uniforms nor are the aircraft in BA livery.

The routes franchised often are by themselves not profitable to a large carrier; their value to the dominant carrier lies in the feeder service they provide to the dominant carrier (that is, passengers connecting from and to small cities) and the franchise fees paid to the dominant carrier in order to be licensed to fly the designated routes. For example, in 1996 BA's franchises carried 3 million passengers over 130 mainly British and European routes, and provided 200 000 passengers with connections to BA's mainline services (Stevenson, 1996).

Under a franchise agreement a smaller carrier usually uses the larger carrier's colors and its crews wear the larger carrier's uniforms, but the franchisee's logo is usually displayed on the aircraft as the operator. The franchise operator, being small, most often manages to make the small routes profitable. The franchisee may be a wholly-owned subsidiary of a larger carrier, it may be partially owned by a larger carrier, or it may operate as a separate carrier. Flyers benefit from franchise agreements between airlines because they provide flyers with more flight choices on smaller routes and increase accessibility to major cities. Customers also benefit because the product and service offered by the franchisee airline are consistent with the larger carrier's standards.

Franchise arrangements, as seen from this discussion, can involve both equity and non-equity arrangements.

- *Exchange of Equity* (franchisor invests in franchisee airline). BA acquired 49.9% of TAT in 1993 with an agreement to purchase the balance by April 1, 1997. When BA purchased the balance in 1996, TAT became a subsidiary of BA. More recently, BA purchased a 67% stake in Air Liberté.

  When the franchisee is from a different nation than the major carrier, the dominant carrier's percentage of ownership in the franchise airline may be limited by law. For example, BA was allowed only a 49.1% stake in Deutsche BA during the mid-1990s.

  When there is an exchange of equity, the franchisee's assimilation of the franchisor's product is usually more extensive. After

BA's initial 49.9% investment in TAT, for example, all of TAT's scheduled international flights were relaunched under the BA brand name using a BA flight designator and the aircraft were painted in BA livery. In essence TAT was treated as a subsidiary, which it finally became in 1996.

- *No exchange of equity* (operator is separate independent company). For example, BA has non-equity franchise relationships with Sun-Air, Logan Air, Comair, Manx Airlines (Europe), CityFlyer Express, Maersk Air UK, and GB Airways. In some instances the franchisee is licensed to operate BA flights.

Other Kinds of Contractual Partnerships

Once an overall strategic airline alliance structure has been developed, several options are available for the detailed alliance structure. The top half of Figure 4.7 indicates the situation factors to be considered when developing an alliance structure.

Contractual arrangements may or may not be linked with a franchise arrangement and they may or may not involve equity linkages. In general, contractual partnerships (sometimes called 'transactional' alliances (Pekar and Harbison, 1998)) fall into one of five categories, as shown in Figure 4.7.

- *Marketing* – including codesharing and/or frequent flyer programs. Codesharing agreements, also called cooperative-service relationships, allow a carrier to offer passengers service to destinations that it does not itself serve. This enables an airline to expand its route systems without adding planes. In a codesharing arrangement, one airline markets the services of an affiliated airline as its own. Only one airline actually operates the aircraft, but the flight carries the designator code of two airlines. The proceeds from ticket sales on codeshared flights are usually shared by the airlines, based on specified contract terms. Frequent flyer programs are marketed by many airlines to permit customers to accrue miles, or points, and redeem them for upgrade vouchers, free or discounted tickets and other perks. Codesharing arrangements are common today.
- *Product/service* – covering such service elements as price, brand image, quality of service (in-flight and ground), routes, and timing and regularity of flights. By adjusting the service elements,

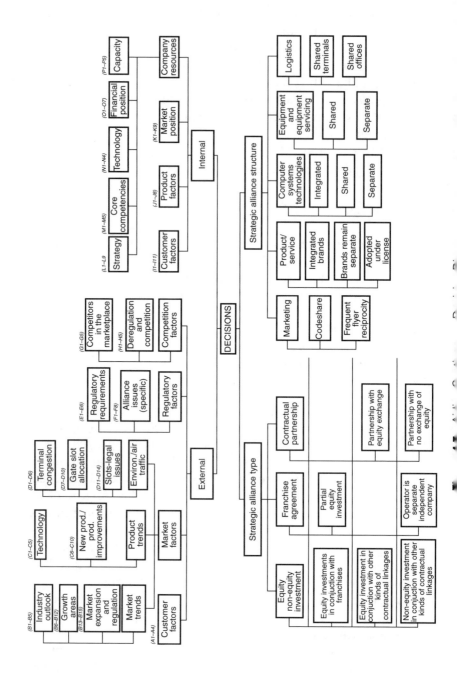

an airline can differentiate its services from those of its competitors.

- *Computer systems technologies* – including reservations, check-in, baggage services and flight information computer systems. These also include crew scheduling, engineering and flight planning systems.
- *Equipment and equipment servicing* – pertaining mainly to aircraft, but also including aircraft parts, fuel and catered meals served on board.
- *Logistics* – including the joint use of offices, terminals for check-in, boarding gates, baggage handling and the landing rights and airport fees involved.

Combinations of these and other service factors within contractual linkages are many. For example, Air Canada, United Airlines and Lufthansa formed a joint venture to handle the purchasing of spare parts for all three airlines. In March 1998, Delta Airlines announced plans to buy 35% of Aeroperu as part of a 10-year marketing alliance designed to help Delta establish a major presence in Latin America. In contrast, the proposed BA/AA alliance did not involve an equity investment. Whether combined with either equity or non-equity strategic alliances, these contractual linkages allow airlines to function as a single carrier while remaining separate companies.

THE PROPOSED BRITISH AIRWAYS/AMERICAN AIRLINES ALLIANCE

The proposed alliance between BA and AA, a unit of AMR, had become a major test of international airline regulation in early 1998. Because both companies are giants in the markets they serve and because the proposed alliance went well beyond a simple marketing agreement, some experts considered it a *de facto* merger (Srodes, 1998).

BA had entered into many types of alliances with other carriers in the past, but in the mid-1990s BA had to re-evaluate its market position to determine how it could grow in the future. In 1995, CEO Robert Ayling determined he had to simultaneously cut costs and grow BA's route network even faster through strategic alliances in order for BA to remain a profitable global airline. According to Ayling, 'BA recognized that the airline industry would consolidate into a handful of global carriers, and to be among the major players it needed to increase its share of the top six air markets' (Stevenson, 1996). One way to increase its share of these markets was to form strategic alliances, such as those with USAir (to gain access to the North American market); Qantas (Pacific/Asia); and TAT and Deutsche BA (Western Europe).

Given its ultimately unsuccessful experience with USAir and its experience with AmericaWest, which was a limited codesharing agreement, BA still wanted to form an alliance with an airline with a strong North American presence. According to Ayling, 'The American economy will continue to be dominant in the western world and for us not to be closely associated with an airline based in that economy I think would be folly' (British Airways News, 1996). BA's management felt that an alliance with another large airline (preferably an American carrier) was necessary to counter alliances that had been created between European and US rivals (KLM/Northwest, Delta/Swissair/Austrian Airlines/Sabena, and Lufthansa/United/SAS). Likewise, AA was looking for a strong European partner and so it appeared to be a perfect strategic fit.

After several years of negotiation, BA and AA reached a tentative agreement on the structure of the alliance. The proposed alliance was basically a coordination of passenger and cargo services between USA and Europe. The alliance did not involve an exchange of equity (AA and BA would not even trade board seats) nor was it a merger. Although routes would be shared, both carriers would retain their individual brand identities. Both carriers already had strong global presences and were financially stable. The alliance would simply enable them to grow together and to reap the synergistic benefits.

The alliance was a codesharing agreement – the two airlines' flights between the USA and Europe, among their most profitable routes, would operate with joint BA/AA codes. The codesharing agreement would extend to as many worldwide BA/AA routes as possible. Where feasible, BA/AA codesharing would also extend to the services of their subsidiary and franchise partners, including American Eagle and BA express regional feeder services.

Under terms of the alliance, both airlines would be able to introduce codesharing on nearly 36 000 city pairs. Codesharing would help both carriers create the industry's broadest global network, offering customers the widest choice of routings and departure times, with seamless connections between the two airlines' services. The BA/AA alliance would make more nonstop flights possible between points in Europe and the USA.

The frequent flyer programs of BA and AA also would be fully reciprocal – the members of both programs would be able to accrue and apply frequent flyer miles on all BA and AA flights (and on any partners the airlines had alliances with). Reciprocity would extend to lounge use (that is, a BA Gold Cardholder could use the AA lounge, even at airports not on a codeshared route). Frequent flyer programs are an important product to consumers and full reciprocity between BA and AA was expected to benefit consumers.

Figure 4.7, which diagrams decision alternatives and factors influencing decisions in these types of alliance situations, is based on BA's and AA's experiences.

CRAFTING A WORKABLE ALLIANCE TYPE AND STRUCTURE: BEST PRACTICES GUIDELINES

As can be seen in Figures 4.6(a)(b) and 4.7, the approach to strategic alliance formulation and implementation is a contingent one – the factors in a situation are studied to formulate a solution. These situational guidelines are not static models, but are revised and refined with experience as new situations are experienced. This process is outlined in Figure 4.8.

The contingent processes, shown in Figures 4.6(a)(b)–4.8 are consistent with the strategic leadership and management process, as outlined in Figure 4.9. Strategic alliances are one subset of that overall process.

Within these contingency frameworks, which present useful overall guidelines, a number of specific guidelines relating to best practices can be drawn from the company experiences described in this chapter.

- Considerable detailed study of how the alliance is expected to work or can be made to work successfully is needed before the deal is signed. This requires in-depth studies of operational fits among the partners and scenario planning to anticipate

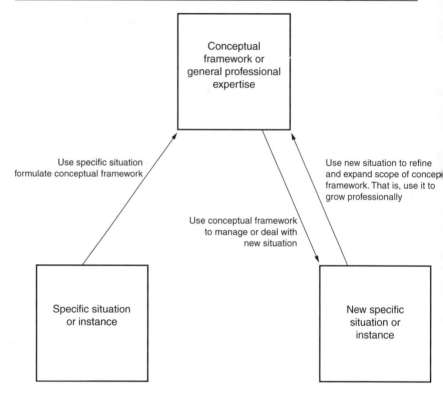

Figure 4.8   Reconceptualization for Professional Growth

possible problems. The successful experiences of such companies as Tambrands and Borg–Warner indicate this.

- Face and resolve as many critical issues as possible before the venture contract is signed instead of deferring them, especially if the potential partners have had little experience working together. This can lengthen the duration of the negotiation but saves time and hard feelings later. This was done at Toshiba, Tambrands and Borg–Warner to enable more detailed contracts to be written.

- Create a structure that will help each partner protect competencies even while interacting with the alliance over a continuing period of time. This was done at Gillette and at the Chinese Chemical company.

- Identify component activities and consider structuring and building the alliance incrementally, starting, for example, with research and development, co-production, or co-marketing agreements, to build a base for more comprehensive joint ven-

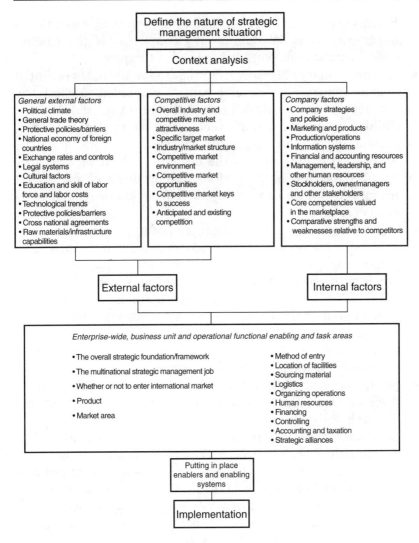

Figure 4.9 The Multinational Strategic Management Process: A Linear Situational Overview

tures. This was done in the European paint manufacturers alliance.

- Be careful when using terms like 'partnership' and 'statement of intent', since they have specific legal meanings. Using these terms informally may create unintended legal obligations which in some instances have led to lawsuits.

- Success depends as much on operational agreements as on legal documents. Borg–Warner is an example, as is the Chong-qing–Yamaha joint venture discussed in Chapter 6.
- Use preliminary alliance structuring studies to enable potential alliance managers to develop experience needed to effectively manage the alliance. Both Tambrands and BA/AA did this.
- Think ahead to possible events affecting management succession and be sure to include any necessary controls in the alliance structure, such as the degree to which each partner controls the appointment of succeeding directors or general managers – which can be anywhere from majority control to right of refusal.
- When structuring the equity division of the alliance, an equal split (50/50) is more likely to work when the two partners have worked together before or have collaborative organizations that are accustomed to consensus management. A control split (40/60) is useful when one partner brings a dominant expertise or contribution to the venture or when two strongly hierarchical organizations are partnering. At times, the equity split may include a third party (40/20/40), which is useful in helping integrate two disparate organization cultures.
- Avoid major capital commitments. Wherever possible strive to defer or avoid them, as was done at Rally Dawson Sports, Femtech, Raiso and major international airlines.
- Be prepared for unanticipated complexities in structure. For example, the British Petroleum/Mobil Oil alliance consisted of a series of different types and structures of alliances for fuel and lubricants in 43 countries. In the FCB/Publicis situation a complex web of interlocking ownership was needed to achieve the strategic objectives of both partners, but it was a step which eventually contributed to the failure of the alliance.
- While it is useful to understand the distinctive types of alliances, in practice each alliance is different and requires situational tailoring to meet specific situation needs. Care must be taken to shape the alliance type selected into a structure which fits the needs of all the partners.
- Prepare for the possibility that an alliance might fail. Mitsubishi, for example, maintained multiple sources of parts supplies so that they were not dependent on any single supplier. Toshiba spelled out the details of alliance termination in their

initial contracts. Like so many 'rules' or 'guidelines', the best practice ultimately will be situational. In many situations it is a good idea not to dwell too much on negatives early in the alliance.

Appendix A at the end of the book provides a checklist of key questions to be asked and answered when doing the operational fit analyses involved in determining the type and structure of multinational strategic alliances.

REFERENCES

Anonymous (1997). Israel in. *Electronic Business Today*, April, pp. 87–88.

Applbaum, K.D. and Yatsko, P.A. (1993). *FCB and Publicis (A): Forming an Alliance*, a case study. Boston, MA, Harvard Business School.

BA Press Release (1996). British Airways and American Airlines to create worldwide alliance. *BA Press Release*. London, June 11.

Bransletter. L. and Sakakibara, M. (1997). Japanese research consortia. *Presentation/Paper*, Annual Conference, Barcelona, Spain. Strategic Management Research Society, October 8.

British Airways News (1996). Airline's future strategy remains global. *British Airways News*, November 8, p. 4.

Bryant, A. (1997). The \$1 trillion dogfight. *The New York Times*, (Money and Business Section), March 23, pp. 1, 14, 15.

Carasol-Volpi, M. (1997). *Strategic Alliances in the European Downstream Oil Industry: BP and Mobil*. Research Monograph, New York, Rome, Strategic Management Research Group.

Chow, I., Holbert, N., Kelley, L. and Yu, J. (1997). *Business Strategy: An Asia-Pacific Focus*. Singapore, Prentice-Hall.

Corey, E.R. (1997). *Technology Fountainheads: The Management Challenge of R&D Consortia*. Boston, MA, Harvard Business School Press.

De Muth, J. (1992). The East is (in the) red. *World Trade*, November, pp. 44–46.

Emmons, W. (1990). *Tambrands Inc.: The Femtech Soviet Venture (A) (B)*, a case study. Boston, MA, Harvard Business School Publishing Division.

Emmons, W. (1993). *Tambrands Inc.: The Femtech Soviet Venture (A) (B)*, a case study. Boston, MA, Harvard Business School Publishing Division.

Haslech, R. (1991). Whither free enterprise? The difficulties for western investors in the Soviet Union. *Europe*, April, pp. 15–18.

Haycocks, R. (1997). Turning Airbus Industrie into a single corporate entity. *Interavia*, April, pp. 13–14.

Hilts, P.J. (1997). Companies forge gene research link. *The New York Times*, April 30, p. D8.

Kanter, R.M., Applbaum, K.D. and Yatsko, P.A. (1993). *FCB and Publicis (B): Managing Client and Country Diversity*. Boston, MA, Harvard Business School.

Knobel, B. (1993). On the waterfront Russian-style. *International Business*, December, pp. 43–45.

Lewis, D.E. (1997). Returning to market as undisputed leader, Tambrands buy would give P&G 50% of tampon market. *Boston Globe*, April 11, pp. D1, D6.

Melcher, R.A. (1997). A marriage made in hell. *Business Week*, December 22, pp. 40–42.

Mockler, R.J. and Carnevali, N. (1997). Type and structure of multinational strategic alliances: the airline industry. *Journal of Strategic Change*, August, pp. 249–260.

Morrison, G.B. (1997). On to decade two. *Electronic News*, August 25, p. 1.

Owen, D., Nicoll, A. and Bowley, G. (1998). Airbus shake-up hit by share dispute. *Financial Times*, December 7, p. 1.

Park, S.H. and Ungson, G.R. (1997). The effect of national culture, organizational complementarity and economic motivation on joint venture dissolution. *The Academy of Management Journal*, April, pp. 279–307.

Pekar, P. and Harbison, J. (1998). (Booz Allen & Hamilton). Implementing alliances and acquisitions. *The 1998 Strategic Alliances Conference*, April 30–May 1. New York, The Conference Board.

Puttre, M. (1997). Russian–American consortium fuel cell research. *Design News*, March 24, p. 10.

Reed, A. (1997). E pluribus unum. *Air Transport World*, August, pp. 26–32.

Renart, L.G. and Oares, F. (1991). *Chemical Labour Grouping, European Economic Interest Grouping*, a case study. Barcelona, Spain, IESE (International Graduate School of Management).

Springate, D.J. (1990). *Ampak International Ltd*. Dallas, TX, The University of Texas at Dallas (revised 1990).

Srodes, J. (1998). Alliance? Open skies? *Barron's*, January 12, pp. 49–50.

Stevenson, P. (1996). Flying the franchises. *Business Life*, July/August, pp. 66–71.

Tagliabue, J. (1996). Airbus tries to fly in a new formation: Consortium's chief hopes at revamping could aid its challenge to Boeing. *The New York Times*, May 2, pp. D1, D9.

Tagliabue, J. (1997). Airbus to be an independent corporation. *The New York Times*, January 14, pp. D1, D4.

Tambrands (1988–95). *Annual Reports*, White Plains, New York.

Tambrands (1996). Letter to Shareholders. White Plains, NY.

Yoshino, M.Y. and Srinivasa Rangan, U. (1995). *Strategic Alliances: An Entrepreneurial Approach to Globalization*. Boston, MA, Harvard Business School Press.

Zink, J.C. (1997). Competition may encourage collaborative research. *Power Engineering*, May, p. 6.

5

Making Multinational Strategic Alliances Work: Management Staffing, Organizing and Leading

While multinational strategic alliances offer obvious benefits, they can be difficult to implement effectively. Multinational alliances may involve sizeable geographic distances, diverse market needs and competition, changing environments and a wide range of unanticipated circumstances. Many people can be involved, as can differing cultures and company objectives. They may also require coordinating diverse business systems.

Essentially, alliance implementation requires doing whatever is necessary to get the job done, within well-defined legal, moral, ethical and business guidelines, a key strategic leadership and management activity as outlined in Figure 5.1. Given the nature of strategic alliances, entrepreneurial skills, such as the basic one outlined in Figure 5.2, are needed. Reviewing successes and failures of others can be helpful, but the experiences of others rarely can be directly transferred to new situations, which often have their own special requirements.

This chapter and Chapter 6 review some common practices and problems encountered in strategic alliance implementation. The concluding sections of both chapters provide best practices guidelines for effective strategic alliance leadership and management. The focus is on contingency guidelines, because the rich variety of

The Focus: An Emergent Entrepreneurial Leadership Process
The Process
1. *Strategic vision/mission:*
   'I knew exactly what kind of company I envisioned; I Just didn't know precisely what it would look like.' Precise definitions, in other words, often emerge over time, through the experiences involved in doing it.
2. *Strategic guidelines:*
   This is the map, the path, the planned steps. The secret here is KISS – 'Keep It Short and Simple.' That means one page written, five minutes oral, maximum length.
3. *Implementation:*
   'Doing whatever was necessary to get the job done, within well-defined general moral, legal, ethical and policy guidelines.' This often involves reconciling and balancing diverse, conflicting and often paradoxical forces, on a continuing basis, in a complex and rapidly changing competitive market environment.

The Activities
- Creating an overall vision (values, mission, strategic focus on core competencies, opportunities in future) and strategic framework (the guidelines or map). Specific strategies and strategic plans (enterprise-wide and in business units and functional areas) often emerge over time, through the enabling systems and processes.
- Activating, energizing, putting into place and monitoring enabling systems and processes, such as: functional area operations; telecommunications/information systems; accounting and finance systems; organization and business structures, processes and cultures; and strategic alliances.
- Nurturing enabling human resources and processes through: organization development; understanding cultural diversity, staffing, training, and communicating; and effective flexible leadership and integrative management at all levels.
- Ensuring that a core management staff (with appropriate interpersonal, communication, entrepreneurial and management skills and potential) is in place and functioning.
- Communicating and implementing the strategic framework, as well as the cultural benchmarks that are needed to enable the core management staff to translate the desired vision into action. The actual process involves superior visionary and pragmatic leadership appropriate for both the managers and people/groups involved in the situation.
- Leaving managers relatively free to manage, and pushing decision making as close to the customer as possible, but intervening where appropriate to make certain integrative activities are operating efficiently and effectively to achieve the company's strategic short- and long-term objectives.

Figure 5.1   Strategic Management: Multinational and Domestic

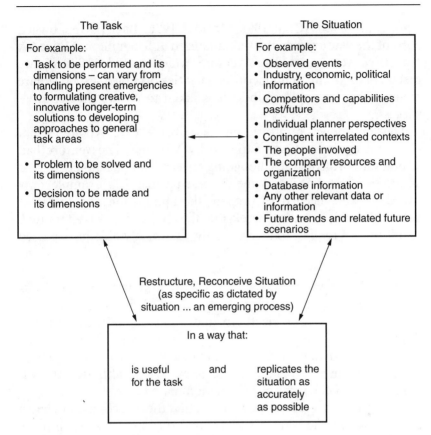

The Task

For example:

- Task to be performed and its dimensions – can vary from handling present emergencies to formulating creative, innovative longer-term solutions to developing approaches to general task areas

- Problem to be solved and its dimensions

- Decision to be made and its dimensions

The Situation

For example:

- Observed events
- Industry, economic, political information
- Competitors and capabilities past/future
- Individual planner perspectives
- Contingent interrelated contexts
- The people involved
- The company resources and organization
- Database information
- Any other relevant data or information
- Future trends and related future scenarios

Restructure, Reconceive Situation
(as specific as dictated by
situation ... an emerging process)

In a way that:

is useful   and   replicates the
for the task   situation as
                                     accurately
                                     as possible

Figure 5.2 A Basic Emergent Entrepreneurial Contingency Process

successful alliances makes it difficult to develop detailed, ready-to-use widely applicable success formulas.

MAKING MULTINATIONAL STRATEGIC ALLIANCES WORK: SUCCESSES AND FAILURES

The following sections describe the practices and problems experienced by several companies in implementing multinational strategic alliances.

Chongqing–Yamaha Ltd.

In the early 1990s, Chongqing Jianshe (China) and Yamaha Co. (Japan) began a joint venture to produce Yamaha motorcycles in

Chongqing, China (Chin, 1996; Mockler, 1996). Each partner owned 50% of the venture, which was capitalized at $75 million. Major tax incentives were granted the venture, which owned 82 000 square meters of land; the manufacturing facilities occupied 40 000 square meters. This section describes steps taken to ensure the venture's success.

The venture was approved on December 9, 1992. About 90% of the plant equipment was supplied by Yamaha. The venture had strong support from the Chongqing government due largely to past connections established by the Chinese partner. For example, only five days were needed to prepare the application and the joint venture was approved one week after the application was submitted. In addition, a request to divert a highway which would have passed through the land owned by the venture was approved by the Chongqing government in only two days.

Plant development was completed in nine months. This was possible because an existing factory of the Chinese partner was being upgraded and so electricity and water were already in place. Sophisticated production technology was contributed by Yamaha, a major worldwide motorcycle manufacturer. The management system combined Japanese and Chinese styles, although the Japanese style of efficiency clearly predominated.

A critical key to success was the fact that the two companies had a decade-long relationship of technology cooperation, so each party knew and trusted the other. The production would take advantage of the cheap labor and manufacturing costs in China and would be exported initially until the Chinese market developed. The venture's long-term goal was to penetrate the Chinese market.

The venture's management was split: the Chairman was Chinese and the General Manager Japanese; there were two deputy general managers, one Chinese and one Japanese. The four manufacturing divisions were each headed by a Japanese and a Chinese manager.

A series of manufacturing and marketing agreements specified how each type of motorcycle would be branded, distributed, priced and sold, which anticipated and resolved competitive conflicts between each partner's line of motorcycles. The extent and cost of any future technology exchanges were also specified by contract.

Language and cultural differences were resolved by the willingness of several key managers to learn their partners' language and to make small behavioral changes to accommodate their foreign partner. It also helped that wages were higher than those paid by competitors in the area and that working conditions were clean and orderly at the venture.

Tambrands Inc.

This section describes the staffing, organization development, management and operational implementation at Tambrands' Russian joint venture, Femtech, through its first year of operations. Its experiences in planning, negotiating and selecting a partner and in developing and structuring the alliance agreement were described in Chapter 3, pp. 64–66 and Chapter 4, pp. 102–105.

The partially completed factory building contributed by GAPU was first rebuilt to Tambrands' specifications. This required considerable interface with Soviet and Ukrainian authorities, which was handled by Femtech's General Director, Yuri Saakov, formerly Director General of the Ministry of Health. During mid-1988, each of the four tampon production lines were assembled and tested in Tambrands' Havant, England, facility and then dismantled and shipped for reassembly and installation at Femtech. During the first year only two of the tampon production lines were scheduled to operate. Fiber processing machinery and two additional tampon lines were scheduled to be installed over the following years.

In the fall of 1988, Soviet citizens were interviewed to be trained as mechanics, operators and supervisors. Four mechanics were sent to Havant for training. Operator training was planned for January 1989. Employees were to increase from 43 the first year to 169 in the fifth year. In November 1988, a team of Tambrands' engineers came to Borispol to assist Soviet construction workers in finishing the plant.

Countless small problems and obstacles had to be overcome because of the many inefficiencies in Soviet working conditions. For example, there was considerable difficulty in getting phone lines installed. Gary West, a Tambrands' executive experienced in start-ups in Latin America, was brought in as manufacturing manager during this period.

The supply and quality problems involved in sourcing cotton fiber were handled by Roman Loochkiv, a GAPU employee who had worked with Tambrands as interpreter during negotiations.

Loochkiv had proved to be knowledgeable about materials, a hard-working self-starter, bright, imaginative and well-connected in Kiev. This again demonstrated that one of the keys to strategic alliance success is finding and nurturing good people.

The first products came off the production line by the scheduled opening day, March 8, 1989 (Women's Day in the USSR). More time was needed, however, to bring the first line up to regular working speed. In addition, during the first year, two buildings were completed: one for administration and tampon production and one for fiber processing. The fiber processing line was installed in late 1989.

Even though Soviet joint venture law was changed in December 1988 to permit foreign ownership to exceed 49% and top management positions to be held by foreign nationals, Tambrands did not press for changes in the venture during the first year. Tambrands retained control over the venture because key decisions had to be agreed to by both partners. Day-to-day operations were handled by Saakov, however, because of the complexities involved in getting things done through the Soviet systems. The post of deputy director was, therefore, eventually eliminated and the venture was run by Saakov and Gary West.

Several key positions in manufacturing were created and filled by March 1990: quality control manager, warehouse/inventory clerk, building and maintenance, tampon production superintendent and fiber processing superintendent. Over the first year, management and administrative personnel rose from 7 to 32 and manufacturing personnel increased from 23 to 102.

Other problems had to be overcome in creating an effective joint venture operation. Soviet regulations made it difficult to hire people already working for other Soviet firms. It was also difficult to find foreign nationals willing to relocate to Kiev where living conditions were relatively primitive. These problems were overcome gradually as highly effective people were added to the staff. For example, Gary West was married in January 1989, his wife Donna joined him in March, and she was eventually employed at Femtech as a quality control inspector. It took several months and considerable effort to persuade the Ukrainian GAPU to allow one of their key employees, Leonid Mikhov, to join Femtech as director of distribution and sales.

Durawool

When the potential for misuses of proprietary technology exists and the partners are not well-acquainted, the alliance should be structured in detail to prevent such misuse. Even when the alliance is structured to protect proprietary knowledge and core company competencies, problems can arise.

For example, Durawool Inc. (USA) entered into a joint manufacturing venture in the late 1980s with China Metallurgical Zuhai Sez United. Using processes developed by Durawool, the Chinese venture manufactured the shards of steel wool that have replaced asbestos fibers in automotive brake pads. The venture's output was sold in both the USA and Asia.

In the early 1990s, the venture's chief engineer, Zhang Ye, who had managed the installation of Durawool's steel-wool fibre manufacturing process and so knew it intimately, left the company and started a competing firm, Sunny Steel Wool Ltd. While the Zuhai venture had signed an agreement that prohibited competitive disclosure and use of the process, Mr Zhang had not. The lawsuit suit brought by Durawool was still pending in 1997; Durawool had obtained a temporary injunction barring the shipment and sale of Sunny products in the USA (Holusha, 1996). This experience illustrates the need for providing adequate equity incentives to key local personnel, in addition to building protections into employment contracts, as well as into the venture agreement.

ANTICIPATING, PLANNING FOR AND HANDLING PROBLEMS

Managers cannot anticipate all events that may occur in a rapidly changing multinational environment. For this reason, entrepreneurial skills are needed to adjust to changing circumstances, to anticipate problems that can be planned for, and to handle unanticipated problems when they arise. As seen in the discussions in Chapters 2–4, many problems can be identified and taken into account when negotiating, selecting partners and formulating the alliance type and structure. Borg–Warner did this. In contrast, Studds–Nolan partners failed to.

In 1992, a European biscuit manufacturer signed a 3-year exclusive distribution contract with an import agent in Seoul, Korea, which was also a national producer and distributor of snacks and biscuits. Instead of going into the Korean distribution channels, however, the first container shipment of the European manufacturer's best-selling biscuits apparently went into the development laboratories of the Korean manufacturer/agent. Within a few months copies of those products were on Korean retail shelves. Four years later, the European firm used a more carefully crafted approach to the Korean market, after successful entries into other Asia markets, such as China, Taiwan, Hong Kong, Malaysia and the Philippines (Agneesseus, 1996).

To avoid these problems, steps should be taken to ensure that the alliance fulfills the four basic criteria for success:

- The alliance must add value, that is, it must be worth more to the company to enter an alliance than to undertake the venture on its own
- The company must learn something from the alliance
- The company must protect competencies even while interacting with the alliance over a continuing period of time
- The firm must retain flexibility, and not be overly reliant on any one partner

The following discussions describe how these criteria can be met when performing alliance development and implementation tasks such as: (1) deciding who will run the alliance and how it will be organized; (2) leadership; and (3) continuing day-to-day management, communication, training and development, and control. This chapter focuses on the staffing, organization and leadership-related activities; Chapter 6 discusses the day-to-day management-related activities.

SELECTING MANAGERS AND ORGANIZING THE ALLIANCE

In staffing a multinational strategic alliance, choices must be made about who will manage the alliance, how the management will be organized and who will manage the liaison among the partners and the alliance. For example, the joint venture itself may be managed by an expatriate or by a local, who may be one of the partner's employees or a third party professional. In addition, each partner often has a liaison manager responsible for managing all interactions between the partner, the alliance and other partners. This section deals with management organization at the alliance. Later sections deal with leadership within the alliance and the liaison management at partner firms.

In an optic fiber venture, the venture's general manager was a newly hired American expatriate who had extensive experience in the technical fields involved and who had worked overseas. Since he was hired by the Dutch conglomerate overseas partner, he had spent considerable time absorbing the perspective of the Dutch partner. His plant manager had worked for the Chinese partner prior to the venture formation. In many situations, the general manager of the joint venture is chosen by the overseas partner and the deputy director (second in command) is chosen by the local partner. The deputy director, who has worked for the local partner prior to the venture, often serves as plant manager.

Other management organization arrangements are also used. For example, Beijing Auto Works (BAW) and American Motors Corporation (AMC) entered into a joint venture named Beijing Jeep Corp. (BJC) to produce jeeps and other four-wheel-drive vehicles in 1984, American middle managers were sent to China to manage day-to-day operations because of their advanced technical knowledge. In this instance, they were not given adequate cultural, language and interpersonal training, and so made many mistakes. The eventual solution was to establish a transition phase in which expatriate managers worked closely with Chinese managers to transfer technical expertise. After this transition period, the Americans returned home (Aiello, 1991).

Volkswagen (VW) entered into a joint venture with China Automotive (CA) during the same period, basing its approach on prior experiences abroad. Volkswagen owned 50% of the venture, Shanghai Tractor and Automobile Co. owned 25%, Shanghai Trust and Consultancy, a subsidiary of the Bank of China, owned 15% and China National Automobile Industry Corp. owned 10%. The venture was capitalized at $67 million, but was expected to expand substantially over the next decade.

There was equal Chinese and German representation on the 10-member board of directors, with a Chinese representative as chairman. A four-person management committee ran the business; this committee reported to the board of directors. China nominated the managing director and head of personnel, and Volkswagen supplied the commercial and financial directors for the committee.

German technicians ran training schools for the Chinese workers in all aspects of assembly work and dispatched experts to help the Chinese to modernize and expand the antiquated existing plant. Over the early years, the plant was equipped with advanced technology and facilities: for example, its engine factory painting workshop and assembly workshop and four production lines met advanced 1980's international standards.

From the outset, host and home country managers were paired and shared decision-making authority. In addition, the German expatriate managers had technical expertise and prior overseas experience, knew the language and culture of the host country and had voluntarily chosen the assignment (Rao et al, 1994).

As seen from company experiences, critical situation factors affecting staffing and organization decisions include: special technical or enterprise business needs, costs, host country business and cultural needs, existing and anticipated competitive market needs, candidate qualifications, the training required, company resources and the urgency of the need. The successful solutions are those tailored to specific situation needs.

Going beyond balancing and accommodating different cultures, it is possible to synergistically combine the best of different cultures to come up with creative staffing and organizing solutions. This was reportedly the case in Hungary after Ameritech Corp. (USA) and Deutsche Telekom AG (Germany) purchased what eventually grew to be a controlling interest in Matav Rt., Hungary's state telephone company. After initial cultural clashes over many operating details, Elek Staub, the newly hired Hungarian manager, skillfully eased tensions with off-site leadership training sessions called 'Vision and Value Training'. He then tapped executive strengths by dividing responsibilities according to corporate and individual culture and experience: the Ameritech executive at Matav was put in charge of marketing and the Deutsche Telekom executive was put in charge of administration. Mr Staub, as representative of the Hungarian state alliance partners, was the liaison between Hungary and the government.

According to the alliance executives, 'everyone in the troika has an equal voice and equal say' and is able to come up with better decisions and actions than when they worked alone. Cultural clashes still occurred, but the enabling leadership and organization structure, processes and culture, enabled going beyond just reconciling differences to creating innovative solutions (Beck, 1996). Such a synergistic approach to cross cultural management has been developed into formal training programs by Dr. Yongming Tang, founder of the Global Synergy Network (Beijing Business, 1996) and by others (Graham, 1997).

While the qualifications of potential managers and the needs of the alliance can at times be balanced, irreconcilable differences can exist at other times. For example, in one situation one partner had the authority to appoint the alliance general manager. That partner's objectives were for the venture to be: (1) a learning mechanism; (2) a provider of synergies; and (3) a new independent venture. Studies have pointed out that each of these objectives require a different manager skill profile. According to the study, the learning objective requires a good technician, someone who is loyal to the company who will not threaten the other partner and a good communicator. Providing synergies requires a good leader who knows the organization well, is loyal to the company and a good leader, and is familiar with subcontracting. Managing a new independent venture requires an independent entrepreneur and an energetic innovator who has experience managing small ventures and is not necessarily overly loyal to any one partner.

Obviously it is hard to find one person who fulfills all of these sometimes contradictory qualifications. In such situations, the strategic objectives must be modified or the combination of skills in the management staff must be balanced in the alliance management organization structure. One problem is often encountered in doing this: shared management has a much higher failure rate than either independent (from the partners) management or management in which one partner dominates the joint venture over the long run, according to several studies (Bidault and Cummings, 1993; Killing, 1988). Shared management apparently works only when the personal chemistry is favorable among the managers sharing authority and decision making.

Generally, the partner with the most expertise in areas critical to success will be given some kind of position in leading and managing the venture. The management organization structure would take into account the needs of the business and partners, as well as the skills of available individuals. Qualifications and needs should guide staffing choices, with as many locals as possible on the staff.

Whatever the final division of management jobs, each alliance partner should have a designated coordinating mechanism. For example, a *coordination team* of representatives from both partners was responsible for preparing the blueprint or feasibility study for the British Airways/USAir alliance in the early 1990s (Forbes et al, 1995a). This same coordination team was preserved and became the first level team responsible for managing the alliance. This team proposed working-group plans, controlled the implementation of plans and workings of the alliance, enabled the communications process, resolved cross-functional and cross-airline issues and reported the status of the alliance's business to the senior officers of each partner. In essence it did a project management job, which involved chasing, cajoling and pressuring individuals and the lower level teams to do the best possible job.

The second level was *steering committees*, staffed with managers and executives from both companies representing several functional areas. These committees created bridges within the alliance and between both partner organizations that enabled moving from visions to action. They facilitated coordination, integration, prioritizing, ensuring that resources were available to carry out working group recommendations and generally overseeing and helping with implementation. Good interpersonal skills were needed for this job.

The third level was *working groups*, also staffed by managers from both partners, which handled specific line responsibilities. These groups identified and clarified possible synergies between partners, recommended specific operating programs (such as frequent flyer programs) and implemented these recommendations after approval by higher level management. The groups were made up of different types of teams: blitz teams, task forces, study groups and joint management teams.

Instead of team liaison, often an alliance liaison manager representing each partner's interests manages the partner/alliance relationships. At a minimum that manager would have access to managers at the alliance and at the partners' firms and to full information about the alliance operations on a continuing basis. The partner/alliance manager(s) would ideally have an appropriate formal position(s) in the alliance management structure.

ALLIANCE LEADERSHIP

The term *leadership*, as used in this book, involves leading or showing the way to some envisioned objective and so involves broader strategic decisions and related actions. Top managers of alliance partners are involved in many of these activities. *Management* involves guiding and controlling a project, person or activity and so involves shorter-term alliance operations.

Leadership and management are exercised in different ways in different situations. In the British Airways/American Airlines situation the alliance team was designed to coordinate the alliance operations while each company performed the activities. At Studds–Nolan, the Indian partners were involved in setting up the alliance and in local management of it. At the fiber optics company in China, the alliance manager ran the alliance unit and represented the top management interests of the Dutch partner, while the plant manager ran the day-to-day operations and represented the Chinese partner's interests.

As the alliance develops and becomes operational top partner management needs to adequately and carefully introduce the nature, scope and importance of the alliance to all involved managers and workers – both at the partner company and at the alliance. It is also important to identify areas of interaction and cooperation among the parties and to provide time and money to introduce all parties involved to the new interactive requirements. This is especially important when additional resources are needed and when major cross-cultural differences exist.

Ambiguities must be clarified so that people at all levels dealing with the alliance can function. For example, a great deal of ambiguity arose during the development and implementation of the alliance between Foote, Cone and Belding and France's Publicis advertising agencies in the late 1980s because of the complexities of the business and of the resulting alliance structures. These ambiguities were lessened for a time by a comprehensive management orientation program which is described in Chapter 6.

While it is not possible to anticipate all events that may arise, an integrative atmosphere of trust and common purpose can be developed which makes solving problems easier. This takes time and leadership. Time may also be needed to readjust the mind-set of each partner's personnel involved in the alliance; a mind-set geared to cooperation and integration, while at the same time balancing that cooperation mind-set with steps required to protect core competencies, is important. The process involves treating problems along the way as learning steps, not as confrontations. Problems will inevitably arise, because of the enormous complexities involved in most alliances.

At all the successful joint ventures visited, the alliance leaders exhibited superior cooperative leadership and management skills and were observed on a daily basis nurturing those integrative learning skills needed for success in today's highly competitive and rapidly changing multinational business environment. Samuel Hearne at MonteShell and John Mumford at British Petroleum provide examples of such leadership in action.

MonteShell

Samuel Hearne faced a challenging leadership situation when he became managing director at Shell Italia, a wholly owned subsidiary of Royal Dutch/Shell Group, the Anglo/Dutch energy firm. Shell Italia managed MonteShell, an Italian joint venture between Edison SpA, the energy division of MontEdison, an Italian conglomerate and Shell Italia. MonteShell was formed in 1987 to combine Shell Italia's retail operations with MontEdison's refinery operations in Italy to create a major retail petroleum sales network (Forbes et al, 1995b).

In order to overcome problems, many of which could be traced to cultural differences between the Italian and Northern European countries, Hearne approached the situation by identifying people in the alliance who could help him learn, who talked about new ideas and solutions and who were committed and wanted to make a difference. Hearne then explored ways to use these individuals without upsetting their bosses. In his mind, traditional hierarchical managers tend to set goals, delegate implementation and then review financial and operating results reports. His approach was to acquire the perspective of either employees or partners and understand how they viewed the world. In his words:

> I certainly made it a point in the early stages of sort of smiling a lot, which I have found to be universally helpful, and trying to make it clear that I wasn't

here just to see one side. I began quickly to meet my partners on their own ground. They weren't interested in going out to dinner with their wives. This has never, ever been part of the culture here. It is just breaking the ice in a business sense and in a personal sense – in the sense that they can trust me. That's the other thing – you know, you said that you would do something – and that you didn't have any other hidden agenda. In the Italian culture, trust is very important, I think. One of the key things is whether, in a one-to-one relationship, you can be trusted or not. I've found it important to register up front that if you said you were going to do something, that you do it.

Hearne felt small success stories could affirm his policies and generate momentum. He had a long list of unresolved issues:

> They were and weren't big things – they were personal in a sense because the Italians, you know, the Italian culture very much is focused on honor. If they thought they had been cheated or undercut – they won't think (in terms of) money, they'll think in terms of gestures and the messages that they send. I ended up moving out one guy that the other people thought was no good, and that broke things open. So, in that sense, it was not difficult to break that log jam. It just takes somebody to break it. It was clear that the mutual gain was in gaining momentum. It just needed a trigger to do it.

Once the momentum had begun and the organization culture was reoriented, Hearne was able to deal with basic business problems. He refocused the firm on the core businesses (liquefied petroleum gas and retail outlets), eliminated many secondary operations and worked on solving the refinery problems.

While Hearne's leadership style improved operational effectiveness, the alliance eventually was terminated because of a mismatch of strategic goals: Shell wanted to invest heavily in upgrading and expanding the retail sales operation; MontEdison was heavily in debt and was unable to. As a result, Shell bought MontEdison's interest in early 1995. It did the same in 1997 with another joint venture with MontEdison – Montell, a plastics joint venture – because of similar strategic differences.

British Petroleum (BP)

At British Petroleum, John Mumford successfully used a cooperative leadership style, a leadership style which is effective in many strategic alliance situations. But he used it in a different way.

In 1992, heavy losses at British Petroleum plc, a stodgy oil giant, forced it to halve its dividend and fire employees. Five years later, after aggressive cost-cutting, restructuring and overseas expansion through mergers/acquisitions and strategic alliances, BP was growing strongly in revenues, pretax profits, and stock market share price.

To achieve such a turnaround, downsizing and cost-cutting were not enough, however. Successful strategic alliances, such as the one with Mobil discussed earlier in Chapters 2 and 4 were needed. In addition, major leadership and organization steps were taken to facilitate the turnaround. For example, the entire organization culture was revamped. First, a reorganization shifted authority to local levels, where middle managers were made accountable for their own results and were given a financial stake in them. Instead of contacting centralized authorities, these managers solved their own problems and created their own opportunities. Traditional rituals such as meetings and memos were replaced by a livelier, more confrontational communications style. This meant freer flow of information among all levels and divisions.

Lofty job titles and confining job descriptions gave way to looser roles where initiative, not conformity, was prized. Performance evaluations were given by peers and subordinates, as well as by supervisors. Perhaps most significantly, the underlying management structure was reordered through the development of networks or groups of employees who did similar work but who were located countries, or even continents, apart. This move severed the chain of command which had stifled BP's rapid response to changing markets.

Cultural changes were also important to BP's revival during the early 1990s. For example (Murray, 1997):

> John Mumford was settling into his new job as head of BP Thailand in Bangkok when the 1992 loss was announced. A vast language and cultural gulf separated the British executive from his 2000 Thai employees, and traditionally his role was one of lord of the manor: 'sketching out solutions and handing them to subordinates, like you were dealing with a maid or gardener', as he put it.
>
> Meanwhile, Mr Mumford faced a serious morale problem. By 1994, BP would slash its worldwide work force nearly in half, to 60 000 from 112 000 in the early 1990s. Though a growth market, Asia was as hard hit as any region by shrinking budgets and organizational turbulence.
>
> Not that Mr Mumford was left stranded. He was soon participating at conferences and teach-ins organized by Pamela Mounter, a BP Oil communications adviser who was an early architect of the company's reconstructed information flow. With her help, he launched a local, Thai-language newsletter and a monthly bag lunch with groups of staffers.

Simple though they sound, both moves threatened the office hierarchy, which was so firmly established that workers followed a complicated etiquette for who left the elevator first. 'One of the most confusing things you can do is treat a Thai subordinate who is manifestly junior to you as a peer', Mr Mumford says. For lunches, he invited everyone who had a birthday in a given month, 'the only way to get fork lift-drivers and accountants in the same room', without appearing to bypass layers of management authority.

Though awkward at first, the lunches became a relaxed forum where Mr Mumford got an earful on everything from parking problems to warehouses that were reaching capacity.

What Mr Mumford got in return for his changing cultural initiatives were profits double his expectations and an outpouring of staff support.

Not only did such cultural, leadership and reorganization steps smooth solving day-to-day problems quickly, they provided the groundwork for the European joint venture with competitor Mobil Oil. This alliance contributed greatly to BP's rapid improvement in profitability and revenue.

Maintaining Liaison Linkages

The continuing involvement of independent partners in an alliance, a key distinguishing characteristic of strategic alliances, dictates that careful attention be paid to liaison management. This liaison task involves managing the required continuing linkages among the partners and between the partners and the alliance. Each situation will have its own solution, which can range from having coordinating committees to having a designated liaison manager at each partner and at the alliance.

A partner alliance liaison manager needs considerable leadership skills, since this function typically does not carry much authority. In many alliance situations, success comes from persuasion not command, as well as from building personal relationships at the alliance and at the partner company which enable handling a continuing flow of problem situations. A knowledge of the industry, of the foreign country involved, and of the partner strategies, operations and personnel is also critical in performing the general management function. The difficulty of the job and the demands on the liaison manager vary by situation.

An alliance team can perform a large part of the liaison function, as seen in the British Airways' alliances. In contrast, the financial manager at the US chemical partner in Pennsylvania was able to handle the alliance liaison management functions for its Chinese alliance, since the alliance manager in China was an employee of the US partner, knew the industry well and had worked for the US partner in different positions in Asia for over 20 years. Gillette has experienced regional international managers assigned to perform the liaison management task on a continuing basis.

Another approach used by many alliances visited to create integration links is periodically to bring local alliance managers to the overseas partner operations for technical training, as well as exposure to the management culture of partner firms. Microsoft does this with its software partners; Gillette has a group of over 300 expatriate managers who have been through such a program.

While liaison management encourages integration links, it also needs to encourage autonomy and independence in the alliance. For example, several joint ventures visited wanted to install computer systems similar to those in use at the overseas partner's company. The ventures also wanted the overseas partners to pay the cost of the installation, around $5 million. In both instances, the overseas partners opted to let the joint ventures develop their own computer information systems and finance them out of their own operating budgets. This was done for two reasons: first, it enabled the joint venture to tailor the systems to their specific needs; second, it set the policy that the venture was independent and so had to learn to survive on its own. These long-term objectives were determined to outweigh short-term disadvantages.

Internal and external integration problems often arise from weaknesses in the staffing and communications areas. For example, problems arose at several ventures when a junior executive was appointed as liaison manager at one partner firm. The problems were resolved when senior managers with international experience took over the jobs. In another instance, problems arose during the interaction between the supplier shipping department at the overseas partner firm and the joint venture factory. These problem were resolved after training sessions were conducted and the personnel involved had made extended visits to each others' sites.

The difficulties were much greater in the Studds–Nolan situation, since the alliance was managed by the local partner, Studds. The overseas partner, Nolan, needed a liaison manager with superior interpersonal skills, knowledge of the industry, familiarity with the country involved and the flexibility and entrepreneurial skills to handle unusual situations. Major problems arose because Nolan did not have such a liaison manager who had time to devote to bridging the gap between the alliance and Nolan.

In order to ensure that the four criteria for effective strategic alliances (add value; enable learning; protect and enhance core competencies and competitive advantages; enable flexibility) are met, a liaison manager for the partner needs to have in place mechanisms to monitor performance, make major changes and reconcile differences. One way is have regular exchanges between alliance personnel and partner personnel. Another is to have periodic top partner management on-site visits. Several operating tools useful in liaison management described in Chapter 6 include: weekly or monthly telephone or teleconference meetings, the ones observed lasting over 2 hours each; control reports; continuing training and development programs; and the use of teams where appropriate and of state-of-the-art communication media. Another way, which was discussed earlier in the management organization section and is discussed further in the following section, is to have partner personnel with decision-making authority working in the alliance.

COLLABORATION AND COOPERATION

The concept of alliances clearly implies a balancing of power relationships through collaboration and cooperation. The reorientation required to effectively collaborate and cooperate can at times be difficult, especially in cultures where hierarchical relationships predominate.

Many of the staffing, organization structures, leadership and liaison management approaches described throughout this book are useful in nurturing collaboration and cooperation. On a day-to-day basis, however, achieving balance is difficult, since successful leadership often requires an integrated leadership style which combines participative, analytical, task-oriented, supportive and directive approaches. Failure to nurture collaboration and cooperation is one of the major reasons why one-third to one-half of all alliances are not successful (Berquist et al, 1995, p. 10).

For example, Packard Foods Inc. (USA) and Showa Foods (Japan) created a joint venture to manufacture and sell food products such as cereals and instant coffee (Yoshino, 1985). Each partner owned 50% of the venture and had equal representation on the board of directors. Showa provided all the joint venture personnel and had the right to select the president (with the approval of the board), while Packard selected the executive vice president.

A few years after the venture started, its president, who was experienced in the field and was well-known to Packard since he had handled the original negotiations, died. Showa proposed appointing someone with much less experience. The appointment apparently was based on a Japanese tradition of appointing to such a position someone near retirement whose value had diminished over the years but who could not be fired because of Japan's cultural tradition of life-time employment. In Packard's view, Showa was trying to dump a problem into the least dangerous place for it, a joint venture subsidiary – Showa had 25 other wholly-owned subsidiaries. When Packard objected to the appointment, Showa refused to budge. Showa also refused Packard's suggestion that a much younger Japanese executive currently working for the joint venture would be an ideal president. Showa pointed out that Japanese tradition did not allow for younger people, no matter how qualified, to be promoted over longer tenured executives, since length of service was extremely important in Japan.

The incident raised several other issues which had not been focused on before: the reluctance of the venture to adopt sophisticated control procedures and the fact that Packard's executive vice-president did not seem able to introduce change into the venture. These issues raised serious questions about whether the venture could continue under the present management and organization structure, since this structure did not clearly state how a balance of leadership power between partners could be maintained and how new persons could be introduced into the management system.

This situation illustrates how the cultures, as well as the personalities, of venture partners can be important. Culture greatly impacts the kind of people who will be involved in the venture, as well as how the people involved will think and act over the long run. It also illustrates why the original alliance contract should cover major human relations problems and how they can be controlled. This step is often neglected when there is good personal chemistry among the partners and their negotiators at the time a venture is formed.

Scenario writing and contingency planning may not anticipate all problems, but key ones can be anticipated and provided for, as seen in the earlier discussions of the Borg–Warner strategic alliance in France.

Nurturing a Collaborative Mindset

Several approaches to nurturing a collaborative mindset have proved useful. For example, one approach to successful alliance leadership and management has been to establish a flexible, adaptive organization that fosters and puts to work precious knowledge assets (Edvinsson and Hlavacek, 1997; Sveiby, 1997). One organization tool used to encourage the development and use of collaborative infrastructures, to promote individual effort and to help create a learning organization is the *flattened hierarchy*. This structure has many segments reporting to one person, as shown in Figure 5.3(a). Within such a structure, survival depends on increased delegation and entrepreneurial initiative – instead of on traditional bureaucratic hierarchical organization channels, such as those shown in Figure 5.3(b) – to overcome the boundaries among different working functions. In other words, success depends on developing more interactive collaborative business and human processes within the organization structure.

Many of the alliances visited have gone further in structuring their organizations to encourage more entrepreneurial interaction and initiative and so enable moving quickly to meet rapidly changing competitive market conditions. For example, a Chinese multinational computer firm revised its flattened structure into a more circular one, as shown in Figure 5.3(c). The multinational chemical joint venture discussed earlier eliminated the hierarchy entirely by making the manager only one more member of the business process. Figure 5.3(d) shows the chart used and distributed by the general manager. These structures reflect actual processes at work in the firms, processes which were instituted and embedded in the culture by the managers involved. The structure diagrams were used mainly to reinforce the working processes (business and human) and cultural changes brought about through alliance leadership (Mockler, 1996). The reason was pragmatic: it had to be done to compete internationally and any device that helped reinforce their efforts was useful.

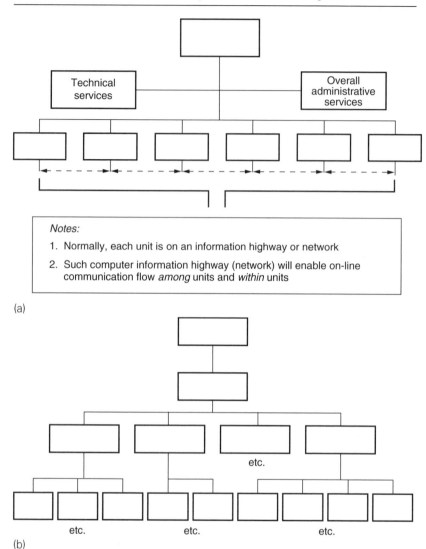

Notes:
1. Normally, each unit is on an information highway or network
2. Such computer information highway (network) will enable on-line communication flow *among* units and *within* units

(a)

(b)

Figure 5.3　(a) Flatter Network Organizations; (b) Traditional Hierarchical Organization; (c) Interactive Flat Organization (a software development company); (d) Integrative Organization Structure (a multinational chemical company)

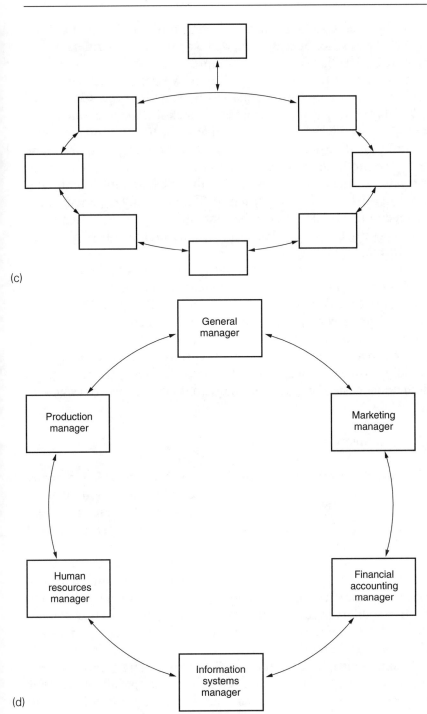

(c)

(d)

Bridging cultural differences is a continuing activity in alliances, within the alliance operation as well as among the partners. It can require both collaboration and compromise.

An organization can be viewed from two perspectives: first, as a structure of tasks, functions and reporting relationships; second, as a set of day-to-day working processes, which include integrated *business processes* as well as *human activities* such as communications, working relationships, teamwork and coordination. Tuning these business and human processes to market and business needs compensates for the many deficiencies, imbalances and inherent limitations in any organization structure. The company experiences described in this book indicate that human and business systems and processes can be as critical to success as the administrative processes and formal organization structure.

Human processes are sometimes referred to as the 'human system'. The time and effort required to realign human systems to meet competitive market needs is one reason why Philips (a Dutch electronics firm) needed 15 years to reorganize. Gillette needed 20 years to create its core of more than 350 experienced expatriate managers, which proved to be a major competitive advantage as Gillette grew rapidly through strategic alliances overseas. This is the reason it is sometimes easier for a new company to do it starting from scratch.

Using Conflict Resolution Positively

A study of 49 cross-border alliances by McKinsey & Company showed that two-thirds of the alliances ran into serious trouble during the first 2 years (Bleeke and Ernst, 1993). Resolving these conflicts can be a way to air differences and build relationships, if handled positively.

For example, it is useful during negotiations to identify areas of anticipated or existing conflict among potential alliance partners. Resolving these can be a training exercise which determines each partner's ability to resolve conflicts, as well as gives practice in doing it. This was the case with Borg–Warner whose experiences are described in Chapter 3, pp. 83–87.

Conflicts also can be useful for strengthening joint venture implementation after the venture has begun. For example, the Blackstone Group, an American investment banking firm, used conflict resolution to embed understanding of its alliances and their importance to the firm. Although the partners had alliance agreements which governed fee splitting, questions arose about how to handle fees for transactions in which one side did disproportionately more work on a deal. Blackstone's management used these occasions to reaffirm its basic philosophy that no deal was more important than the alliance itself, and so no exceptions were made to the original alliance contract (Malnight, 1991).

Effectively handling conflicts depends not only on the enabling organization, staffing and contract mechanisms in place, then, but also on the leadership exercised.

Using Teams

Initiating and maintaining human systems within organization structures to achieve balance is done in many ways besides leadership and management styles and organization innovations. Collaborative team structures are one way to achieve and maintain this balance, as was seen in the BA/AA experiences described earlier in this chapter and in the Fiat/Peugeot experiences described in Chapter 3, pp. 77–79. Team structures can range from formal ones initiated by top management to ones that form in response to daily working needs.

Special company SWAT teams are an example of a formal task team structure at the multinational parent organization level. Many multinational companies have developed SWAT teams to actively promote integrative action, respond to local needs, and rapidly transfer technology across cultural boundaries. For instance, in 1994, Texas Instruments had some 200 professionals – dubbed the 'Nomads' – who had established chip-fabricating plants in Italy, Taiwan, Japan and Singapore. U S West's CEO Callahan boasted that he could 'put a team into South Africa by Friday' to begin setting up a cellular phone system. 'We're faster than any telephone company in the world', he added. Similarly, when expanding operations in China, along with hiring experienced local Chinese professionals, Unilever dispatched a team of Chinese-speaking troubleshooters from the company's 100-country operation. They helped build detergent plants, market shampoo and other personal-care products, and even helped sell Lipton Tea to the world's largest tea-drinking population (Dwyer, 1994, pp. 84–86).

Because of situation requirements, General Electric used a different approach at its light bulb factory in Budapest, Hungary. GE used 'action workout' sessions there, sessions similar to those it uses in its US plants. These 'workouts' involve teams of workers tackling specific problems. They reflect GE's belief in a 'borderless' organization culture in which workers remove obstacles in order to work more efficiently. These and other worker/management changes, which took 3 years, were needed to change work habits left over from the communist era (Perlez, 1994).

Intel Corp. of Santa Clara, California, has teams for many projects. For example, teams formulate product sales strategies, develop new products, improve quality testing and redesign manufacturer microprocessor elements. Typically, Intel's teams work together across geographic and cultural boundaries. Team members assemble quickly, do their work and then disband and regroup with other team members for the next project.

A group of Intel intercultural managers formed a global team to determine what made high-performing teams successful. They concluded that it is important to have simple basic procedures and processes, to set clear expectations, and to have clearly defined goals, roles and responsibilities. Face-to-face meetings early in the team's development also are important. Cross-cultural training makes team members more adaptive and so helps harness the synergies possible in cross-cultural and cross-functional exchanges. These preliminary steps make later long-distance communications, through teleconferencing, videoconferencing and electronic mail, go much more smoothly. Clear agendas are needed for meetings and written minutes of the meeting must be distributed immediately to ensure that everyone understands the tasks and decisions agreed upon during the meeting. These minutes provide a means of refreshing memories and monitoring progress.

According to the study, an effective global group requires support that makes it easier for people to share information, receive feedback, and communicate. People will be discouraged by physical barriers if technology is not in place – for example, groupware for sharing documents, or e-mail and videoconferencing capabilities for rapid communication (Solomon 1995a). It is also important to include people with an appropriate mix of cultural, interpersonal, and technical expertise in global groups.

As with other leadership and management approaches, the usefulness of teams is contingent on situation circumstances. Teams are not a cure-all or universal solution and often fail, either because they are inappropriate for the situation needs and because they are mismanaged (Griffith, 1997).

Communications are important in many strategic alliance leadership and management activities. For example, the chemical joint venture was one of many joint ventures visited that had weekly or monthly telephone conferences involving the partners and the joint venture. An agenda and supporting information was circulated a week before each conference. The conferences lasted about 2 hours and covered exceptions and special operating problems, as well as progress on planned programs. Annual face-to-face meetings were held in different regional areas.

CRAFTING A WORKABLE LEADERSHIP STYLE, STAFF AND ORGANIZATION: BEST PRACTICES

This chapter has reviewed strategic alliance situations in involving leadership, staffing and organization. Several best practices guidelines can be formulated based on these experiences:

- Create an organization and exercise leadership which enables and nurtures entrepreneurial innovation and cultural change. This was what was being attempted at British Petroleum and Shell Italia.
- Anticipate operating problems, often with scenario planning. At Chongqing–Yamaha Ltd. this led to developing operating agreements to cover potential competition. Studds–Nolan failed to do this in India.
- Involve government agencies and officials affecting a venture's success where appropriate, as was done in the Chongqing–Yamaha venture, where such involvement contributed significantly to the success of the venture.
- Appoint the best people possible, people who are technical experts and perform their job well and people who are effective cross-cultural leaders and managers, as was done at Tambrands. Since these skills are often rarely found in one individual, teams are often needed. This approach was used at Matav.

- Allow adequate time to introduce the alliance and its strategic rationale, operating policies and working relationships.
- Use local talent where possible, but provide ample training, as did Tambrands and Borg–Warner.
- Work to develop synergies, as was done at Matav when it organized a top management troika to take advantage of cultural diversity and resolve conflicts.
- Nurture collaboration by the use of teams both during the negotiating phases and after the venture has started, as did British Airways, Tambrands and Fiat/Peugeot.
- Develop boundary bridgers, that is, individuals or teams who function to bridge gaps among partners (liaison managers), among the venture and its related government agencies and service/supply partners, and among the many individuals from different cultures involved with the venture. This can be done during negotiations and at a later date.
- Build on small successes to create and maintain momentum for cultural change, as did Hearnes at Shell Italia and Mumford at British Petroleum.
- Use shared management sparingly where appropriate, but only if there is a formal mechanism for handling irreconcilable differences.
- Appoint champions to key positions in order to generate and sustain enthusiasm and momentum. Tambrands and Borg–Warner did this to help overcome venture start-up uncertainties.
- Make every effort to negotiate layoffs or work force reductions prior to the signing of the venture agreement.
- Where feasible, involve those who might be managing the alliance in the preliminary planning studies of the alliance during the formulation process. British Airways structured their approach this way, as did Tambrands.
- Key management and leadership skills sought should include being comfortable with a collaborative, team-oriented environment, having the ability to deal positively with conflict and being able to delegate and govern by persuasion in a situation where s/he does not always have full authority. A sense of humor, excellent communication skills and the ability to build trust are also helpful. Human resource issues need careful attention at all phases, starting with the negotiations and continuing through partner selection and alliance staffing, development and training.

The following chapter extends this discussion to cover additional detailed operating aspects of making alliances work.

Appendix A provides a summary of key questions to be asked and answered when doing the analysis involved in making staffing and organization decisions and exercising leadership and management in multinational strategic alliance situations.

REFERENCES

Agneesseus, S. (1996). *Market Entry Decisions in South Korea*, Research Monograph. New York and Rome, Strategic Management Research Group.

Aiello, P. (1991). Building a joint venture in China: The case of Chrysler and the Beijing Jeep Corporation. *Journal of General Management*, Winter, pp. 47–63.

Beck, E. (1996). Restructured firm in Hungary offers cultural lessons. *The Wall Street Journal*, June 15, p. A10.

Beijing Business (1996). An effective tool for improving cross-cultural competencies. *Beijing Business*, May, pp. 48–49.

Berquist, W., Betwee, J. and Meuel, D. (1995). *Building Strategic Relationships*. San Francisco, CA, Jossey-Bass Publishers.

Bidault, F. and Cummings, T. (1993). *Hydro-Meca*, a case study. Lausanne, Switzerland, International Management Development Institute (IMD).

Bleeke, J. and Ernst, D. (eds) (1993). *Collaborating to Compete: Using Strategic Alliances and Acquisitions in the Global Marketplace*. New York, John Wiley, pp. 18, 34.

Chin, H.E. and Kay Mok Ku (1996). Case study of a China–Japan joint venture. In *Business Opportunities in Sichuan Province, China* (Tech Meng Tan, eds). New York, Prentice Hall, pp. 149–158.

Dwyer, P., Engardio, P., Schiller, Z. and Reed, S. (1994). The new model: Tearing up today's organization chart. *Business Week* (Special Issue: 21st Century Capitalism), November, pp. 80–90.

Edvinsson, L. and Hlavacek, J.D. (1997). *Intellectual Capital*. Chicago, IL, Irwin Professional Publishing.

Forbes III, T.M., Isabella, L.A., Spekman, R.E. and MacAvoy, T.C. (1995a). *British Air–US Air: Structuring a Global Strategic Alliance (B)*, a case study. Charlottesville, VA, University of Virginia Darden School Foundation.

Forbes III, T.M., Isabella, L.A., Spekman, R.E. and MacAvoy, T.C. (1995b). *Shell Italia (B)*, a case study. Charlottesville, VA, University of Virginia Darden School Foundation.

Graham, L.O. (1997). *Proversity: Progressive Diversity*. New York, Wiley.

Griffith, V. (1997). Teamwork's own goals: The limitations of applying teamwork methods in the workplace. *Financial Times*, July 18, p. 20.

Holusha, J. (1996). For steel-wool maker, Chinese lessons. *The New York Times*, May 28, p. D10.

Kiling, P. (1988). *Strategies for Joint Venture Success*, 2nd edn. London, Routledge.

Malnight, T.W. (1991). *The Blackstone Group*, a case study. Boston, MA, Harvard Business School Publishing Division.

Mockler, R.J. (1996). Field interviews with companies in China and Italy. May–June.

Murray, S. (1997). Back from the brink, BP finds religion. *The Wall Street Journal*, September 17, p. A19.

Perlez, J. (1994). GE finds tough going in Hungary. *The New York Times*, July 25, pp. D1, D8.

Rao, C.P., Hang I. and Smith, T.F. (1994). *Shanghai Volkswagen Corporation*. Norfolk, VA, Old Dominion University, College of Business and Public Administration.

Solomon, C.M. (1995a). Global teams: The ultimate collaboration: You think team-building in the United States is challenging? Companies such as Maxus and Intel have gone even further. They've built cross-functional teams that comprise different cultures, languages, locations and time zones. *Personnel Journal*, September, pp. 49–58.

Sveiby, K.E. (1997). *The New Organizational Wealth*. San Francisco, CA, Berrett-Koehler.

Yoshino, M. (1985). *Showa-Packard*. Boston, MA, President and Fellows of Harvard College (Harvard Business School).

6

Making Multinational Strategic Alliances Work: Management, Development and Training, Control and Termination

This chapter continues the discussion of multinational strategic alliance implementation, focusing on alliance management, training and development, communication and control.

ALLIANCE MANAGEMENT: WORKING FOR THE FUTURE

Alliance management is an internal and an external job. It involves maintaining links among all venture participants who affect the success of the venture. These participants include partners, external suppliers, customers, employees and regulatory agencies.

Managers of many multinational strategic alliances (including home country partner appointees, locals or third-country expatriates) have adopted modified versions of interactive, participative management and organization styles. Such styles are consistent with the globalization trend in multinational businesses and are especially useful when synergistically managing the kind of diversity found in multinational strategic alliances. A multidimensional integrative leadership style often is required, however, since situations at times also require directive, analytical, supportive and task-oriented leadership styles.

Many of those firms visited had managers (both foreign and local) who were observed introducing and reinforcing an integrative interactive atmosphere on a daily basis. For example, at the Chinese chemical joint venture, when a new information system was being introduced the general manager encouraged (through a kind of Socratic questioning dialogue) the systems developer and the plant manager to develop the system interfaces jointly and to come up with their own solutions – that is, to take ownership of the system and responsibility for making it work. This was the kind of management encouraged by John Mumford at British Petroleum and Samuel Hearne at Shell Italia, for example, as discussed in Chapter 5.

Such a management style was especially important at Chinese and Central European ventures because in these emerging countries workers are accustomed to hierarchical management styles and organizations, such as shown in Figure 6.1, which allow for little individual initiative. Individual entrepreneurial initiative, a process replicated in Figure 6.2, is required to prosper in a rapidly changing competitive free-market environment. This initiative is developed mainly through constant reinforcement during management/ worker interaction, mixed with a blend of directive and other leadership styles as needed. In this sense, successfully leading multinational strategic alliances requires many kinds of changes in management mindset.

CFM International (CFMI), a joint venture of General Electric (USA) and the Societé National d'Etude et de Construction Moteurs d'Aviation (France) which involved commercial jet engines, explained what made their alliance so successful:

> CFMI management paid substantial attention to making the venture work. Neumann and Ravaud (the partner venture managers/champions) had challenged their people to bring them 'solutions, not problems'. GE personnel assigned to CFMI were hand picked for the job. SNECMA assigned its best people to the program. One language, a simple decision-making structure and constant communication helped overcome the difficulties associated with the interaction of two companies and cultures.

The following section describes various problems and practices experienced in managing strategic alliances.

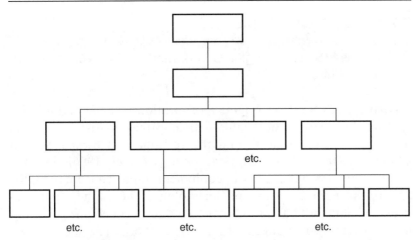

Figure 6.1 Traditional Hierarchical Organization

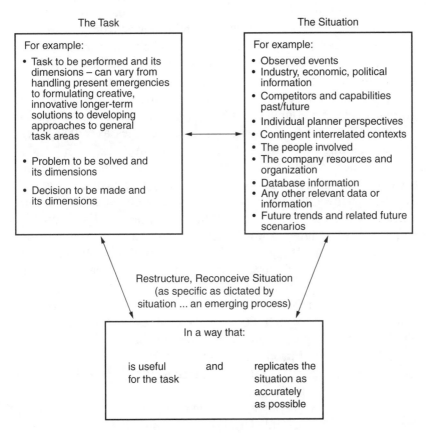

Figure 6.2 A Basic Emergent Entrepreneurial Contingency Process

SOME COMPANY EXPERIENCES

Puyi-Briggs & Stratton Engine Corporation: An Early Successful Venture in China

Puyi-Briggs & Stratton Engine Corporation is a $7 million joint venture, located in Chongqing, China. Briggs & Stratton (USA) owns 52% of the venture and the remainder is owned by two Chinese partners (Lim and Fok, 1996; Mockler, 1996). The US investment consisted mainly of equipment imported from the USA and the transfer of skills and technology. The Chinese partners provided land and buildings for the production of engine parts and for the assembly of about 20 different types of products, such as lawn mowers and outboard motors. Initially, 60% of the engine parts were manufactured in Chongqing, using raw materials from the Sichuan Province area, while 40% were imported from the USA.

Briggs chose Chongqing because it is a development zone offering tax and investment incentives (to joint ventures, but not to wholly-owned investments). In addition, the area had an ample supply of cheap labor and dozens of research universities and advanced technological support companies. Chongqing has access to the interior of China through new roadways for domestic sales, as well as access to the sea along the Yangtze River for exporting.

In preparation for the joint venture, the governor of Sichuan province and the former mayor of Chongqing visited Briggs & Stratton's Milwaukee headquarters. This visit allowed the governor and the Briggs' CEO to begin establishing a personal relationship, which helped at later times during the negotiations. The contract between Puyi and Briggs was signed shortly thereafter. The joint venture, which manufactures and sells traditionally-designed small gasoline engines (10 hp and 16 hp), took 1 year to start production.

The joint venture's production rose from 500 to 20 000 units from 1987 to 1996. It exports 80% of its engines to Southeast Asia, employs 150 people, is profitable, and during the author's visit advanced computer production support systems were being installed. While production quality was high, considerable work had been necessary to reach this point.

Initially, one problem was that the equipment brought from the USA was 30–40-years old. This is not uncommon when basic traditionally-designed products are involved; but the equipment needed to be reworked and maintained. Local unfamiliarity with the equipment and a lack of spare parts and design specifications made this difficult. In addition, importing machine parts from the USA was expensive and quality control was initially weak.

Solving these problems took several years. First, it involved finding and training local suppliers of component parts, then investing time, money and energy in supporting these suppliers. Second, the US partner provided personnel to train Chinese workers over an extended period of time, during which time quality maintenance and control programs were introduced. During this period a series of changes in the production processes were introduced at the venture. The inexperience of Briggs in joint ventures, especially in overcoming language and cultural differences, considerably delayed the operation's ability to turn a profit.

Foote, Cone and Belding (FCB) and Publicis Alliance: Managing a Complex Service Business

Because of the complicated structure of the FCB/Publicis Europe alliance, making it work initially required major efforts by all company managers (Applbaum and Yatsko, 1993; Kanter et al, 1993). A 10-member alliance transition team (five members from each partner) was formed to manage the transition over a 1–3-year period. The team prepared the announcement and explanation of the alliance and held conference calls with all the European general managers to discuss the alliance. To reinforce this effort, team members visited the European offices to discuss the alliance and its implications with all managers and staff. After eight months, all operations were formally moved to the Paris headquarters of FCB/Publicis.

Considerable time was spent determining the best way to merge FCB's and Publicis' European offices in 10 countries in a way that balanced client needs, possible client conflicts and the personal relationships with clients. The alliance partners also wanted to reduce costly duplications of services, strengthen weak offices and achieve economies of scale where feasible. The solutions varied by office and country. Some offices remained separate, some merged, some combined administrative tasks (media buying, supply purchases, and back-office systems) and in two instances existing offices were combined with those of a third-party. The transition team also had to resolve client conflicts (some were competitors) and client dissatisfaction where encountered. In several instances the team had to decide which competing client account to drop. About $6 million in billings was lost as a result.

Considerable management time and skill was also needed for the staff to adjust to working across North American and French cultures. For example, the French were used to hierarchical decision processes, the Americans to consensus decision making. Where two offices were merged, the team had to decide who would manage the new office. The situation dictated whether the FCB manager, the Publicis manager or a third-party was given the job.

Several additional years were needed to develop consistent operating procedures and processes for managing all the involved agency offices worldwide. Questions also arose concerning the division of fees when local offices provided services that led to advertising revenues at offices in different countries. Other fees involved the overhead and coordination charges to local offices to cover parent partner expenses.

Work patterns also evolved as local autonomy grew and at the same time local offices became more dependent on other units during worldwide advertising campaigns. The objective of the transition committee (eventually named the 'Alliance Operating Committee' (AOC)) was to solve small problems before they became large. Unresolved problems were referred to the chairmen of Publicis and of FCB.

In addition to cultural differences, problems sometimes arose because of the ways in which each client market functioned. For example, because it was fragmented, Europe needed a larger number of smaller offices. America was more homogeneous and so had a smaller number of larger offices. Industry billing in Norway generally was based on project fees, whereas in the rest of the world they normally were based on a commission on media bought by the client. Each of these areas required developing different organization/reporting structures and operating procedures.

All of this took management time and attention to work out initially, and continuing attention as operations became more stabile and routine. Worldwide account managers were appointed to handle international accounts and work out the degree of globalization and localization possible and needed in worldwide advertising campaigns. Continually balancing needs and working out problems became a way of life for these alliance managers, not just a management task that could be done once and for all.

In the end, the complexities proved to be too great and the alliance was dissolved in 1997 (Melcher, 1997). The reasons were many: changing strategic needs as both partners expanded into the other partner's geographic areas; pressures arising from organization structure complexities; a new FCB CEO with different growth strategies; personality clashes; the differing growth needs of two large companies in a complex business; and client complaints. In essence, the fast-changing, complex and image-sensitive industry presented problems which could not be overcome by strategic alignments and adjustments, nor by management actions.

Kentucky Fried Chicken: Personnel Management Problems

In 1988, Kentucky Fried Chicken's Tony Wang, vice-president for Southeast Asia and China, was working to resolve conflicts with KFC's two local partners at its very successful Beijing (China) restaurant (Morrison, 1989). The general manager of the restaurant in Tiananmen Square (the center of Beijing) was Sim Kay Soon. He reported to Daniel Lam, KFC's newly appointed area director for China. Lam was based in Hong Kong and reported to Wang. Sim handled the hiring of local workers who were paid 40% more than comparable factory workers and 10% more than associate professors at local universities. The hirings were based on qualifications, not on family connections (as was common in the Chinese culture), a practice to which the local partners objected.

KFC's hiring criteria included: facility in English; no former restaurant experience; high school graduates; presentable in grooming and dress; and willing to work hard. KFC hoped that selective hiring, combined with training and incentive pay, would help the company achieve its objectives. Conscientious employees could double their salary through the company's incentive program. There were 20 applicants for each of the 120 openings.

A number of cultural factors had to be overcome in managing the employees. Employees resented KFC's management practices and controls, which were designed to insure profitability and maintain levels of quality, service and cleanliness at all KFC restaurants worldwide. The Chinese had become used to accepting goods of substandard quality. In addition, since jobs were guaranteed under China's controlled economy, employees had not been expected to work hard and were somewhat apathetic towards work in general.

Before the store opening, training sessions were conducted, using adapted videotapes and hands-on training with the equipment which was in place. Four assistant managers were sent to Singapore for intensive training at KFC restaurants. The training was supervised by senior manager Anthony Leung, who later moved to Beijing as general manager. In September, the Beijing store opened for limited hours as a training exercise. Employee training was intensified when the store was closed.

Based on the trial opening, the product line was modified (no french fries) and limited (only regular chicken). After a short period, KFC quality inspectors visited the store and found quality so low that they refused to authorize the opening of the store. After problems were corrected, the store opened. Prices were set to match city restaurant prices, and so were set higher than street food. The store opened on November 12, 1987, and initial sales exceeded expectations. By March 1988 sales were well over 1000 chickens per day and customers were waiting up to 45 minutes to be served during peak hours. This led to discussions about expanding, since it appeared that the initial investment (of the Chinese partners) would be paid off in 1 year and the operation was generating a high cash flow by Chinese standards.

Before expanding, however, a number of problems needed resolution. Supervising employees was a constant problem. Employees resented being told how to do a particular job and often to be polite would agree to do a job but then fail to follow through on their commitments. For example, an employee who was asked to mop a floor said it had been mopped. When pressed the employee admitted he did not know when the floor had been mopped. He appeared to agree to mop the floor, but it later was found not to have been mopped. Constant KFC supervisor retraining was also necessary since managers were mostly from Singapore or Hong Kong and were in Beijing only on temporary assignments (18 to 30 months).

These interpersonal problems also affected relations with the partners who wanted to expand faster. Since they supplied the chickens, they discovered that they could lower quality and make more money selling chickens to customers other than the KFC outlet. They suggested that KFC buy chickens from another supplier. This raised the question of whether partners were needed, since KFC handled management and training at the outlet. In addition, KFC estimated that it had spent $250 000 preparing for the store opening and the outlet appeared to be generating only $50 000 a year in cash flow, not all of which could be converted into hard currency.

All these factors raised questions about the future. Should KFC expand at all? Would it want to expand with its present partners? Should KFC consider lowering quality and service standards to ease relations with its employees and partners since it seemed that customers neither expected or demanded such high standards? Also, the strain of managing was taking its toll on Tony Wang.

The solution appeared to be: (1) expand modestly in Beijing while maintaining quality standards; (2) expand beyond Beijing (there was considerable enthusiasm among potential franchisees in China) with new partners; and (3) engage a local general manager and assistant managers who would handle all Chinese operations, eliminating the travel demands on area managers in Singapore and Hong Kong.

Gold's Gym in Moscow: a Russian Fitness and Sports Center

Not all strategic alliances involve large companies. In 1997, two Americans (25- and 31-years-old) and a Russian (31-years-old) started a high-class athletic club in Moscow.

First, the partners studied the target market for their proposed sports/fitness center. There appeared to be a large market (estimated at 500 000) of expatriates and wealthy Russians in Moscow to support such a center, which in the USA served a middle class market. The partners estimated that they would need at least 1000 members paying annual dues of around $2000 just to break even. In early 1997 the club opened with 500 members.

The partners decided to raise capital outside Russia, since people in Russia who owe money often get murdered. They sought money from medium-sized American venture capital funds that wanted a presence in Moscow. In spite of the political and social problems, the partners raised $3 million, including $1 million from Boston's Commonwealth Property Investors.

The partners also decided to do everything in a legal way. The presence of organized crime in Moscow was notorious, especially after the 1996 assassination of American businessman Paul Tatum. The partners decided that the best way to ensure their safety was to operate in a totally legitimate way, even though operating outside the law might enable them to avoid substantial tax and regulatory problems. They also hired a local security firm, something which most businesses in Moscow do. In addition, they informally excluded from membership any suspected Russian criminals.

The Russian partner was a key enabler, since government connections were necessary to get needed equipment through customs without expensive delays. The Russian government often levies heavy storage fees for every day it refuses to release imported goods. The venture required 24 shipments, including expensive high-tech Cybex equipment and a basketball court, supplied by Nike.

The facility was designed to balance American and Russian cultures. Athletics are the pride of Russians so the gym was given a Russian flavor. The club was built in The Palace of Young Pioneers, the world's largest recreational complex – a place filled with Russian history, where Rudolf Nureyev danced and Gary Kasparov played chess. The entirely Russian staff was trained in Russian athletic instruction methods, as well as in American service standards and practices. The partners also had leading-edge high-quality equipment, a playroom for toddlers with Russian-trained nannies, personal trainers for members, tanning booths, squash courts, high priced sports accessories, two indoor tennis courts and imported coffee.

The partners opened their gym in early 1997 (Specter, 1997; Vitullo-Martin, 1997). While this experience might not be considered a strategic alliance by some, it is a cooperative venture that illustrates problems that are encountered in multinational strategic alliances in Russia and how they were resolved.

American Copier Co.: Using Local Suppliers and Maintaining Quality

As described by Mike Peng, a company he referred to as American Copier Co. (ACC) took 4 years to negotiate (1983–87) and set up a joint venture in Shanghai, China, which eventually became number one in China's growing copier market (Peng, 1997). ACC, a $10 billion dollar worldwide American document processing company, held a 51% share of the alliance, invested $15 million and licensed its technology. Bank of China held a 5% share and invested $10 million. Shanghai Photo Industry Company held the remaining 44% and contributed existing plants, equipment and personnel valued at $5 million. At full capacity, the plant could produce 40 000 units annually and employ 900 workers. Initially, ACC Shanghai employed six expatriates.

In order to better integrate the operation in China, ACC agreed to have 70% of the venture's components sourced locally and to focus production on mid-range to low-end products. To achieve this goal, ACC, through its Shanghai venture, either transferred technology or provided technical support to approximately 60 suppliers, mostly in Shanghai. In addition, ACC coached suppliers in materials management and handling, as well as in accounting. Overall, ACC spent several million dollars to train, support and monitor Chinese suppliers. Additionally, ACC Shanghai developed close working relations with the Shanghai Foreign Investment Commission, which provided funding to local companies to enable them to upgrade their plants and purchase new technology.

ACC took other steps to make the venture work. In the quality area, for example, ACC made certain that all ACC Shanghai products and their components met the quality standards ACC was known for worldwide. Further, ACC introduced its corporate quality control culture by using ACC's ongoing LUTI (learn, use, teach and inspect) system at each management level and especially with new employees.

ACC also created a Customer Satisfaction Review Board at the venture which met monthly and included representatives from all ACC Shanghai functional and management areas. The Board reviewed customer complaints and conducted customer surveys to determine where improvements might be needed and useful. ACC's success in quality control led to two awards: the Shanghai Quality Award from the Shanghai municipal government in 1989 and 1990 and an in-house quality award from the parent ACC in 1990.

Tambrands Inc.: Managing a Joint Venture in Russia

This section describes managing operations and expansion proposals at Tambrands' Russian joint venture, Femtech, after its first year of operations. Its experiences in planning, negotiating, selecting a partner and developing and structuring the alliance agreement, and then staffing, organizing, managing and implementing the venture during its first year of operation are described in Chapters 3 and 4 (De Muth, 1992; Emmons, 1990, 1993; Haslech, 1991; Knobel, 1993; Lewis, 1997; Tambrands, 1988–1995, 1996).

During the second year of operations the manufacturing manager at Femtech, Gary West, continued to train Tambrands manufacturing personnel in-house, in Kiev and in Havant, England. New production lines for tampons were set up and a stable maintenance group was developed to keep the lines running a high percentage of the time. During this period, the first fiber processing line became operational, quality was brought up to standards, additional fiber processing machines were installed and additional shifts added.

The work force appeared satisfied, judging by the low turnover (virtually zero). Gary West was supportive, took a personal interest in the 134 person workforce and was quick to praise deserving employees. Worker benefits included travel to England for training, as deemed necessary, on-site training by British and American experts, free after-work English lessons, inexpensive hot lunches and medicines for sick employees and their families. Some problems were anticipated, however, since the plant did not have worker councils, a trade union, union-owned vacation locations, childcare facilities, subsidized housing and the right to vote for managers – all of which had been provided in the past at Russian firms.

Initially all tampons were made from imported supplies. Hard currency costs were unsustainable, however, so local suppliers were developed step-by-step. First, Tambrands' engineers worked closely with the local bleached cotton supplier in nearby Cherkassy to improve quality. Other bleached cotton suppliers were consulted for assistance. Slowly, problems such as limited allocation quotas, different and conflicting government ministry regulations and limited technical skills and pricing limitations were overcome by a combination of patient assistance at the plant level and quiet diplomacy among the ministry officials. By March 1990, Femtech was able to obtain adequate supplies of high-quality bleached cotton locally. Similar problems were encountered in obtaining paper and packaging supplies. Generally there was little interest among Soviet suppliers in accommodating Femtech's special requirements, so Femtech at times was forced to work with sub-standard suppliers.

There were similar problems obtaining fuel, food, office equipment, trucks and telephones. Every basic necessity seemed in short supply and locals seemed to enjoy giving newcomers a hard time. Considerable time and entrepreneurial ingenuity, including small gifts and personal favors, were often needed to get locals to provide basic services. These problems was solved eventually by persistence, and the goal of 100% local content was expected to be achieved by the end of the second year of operations.

During the second year, pricing problems were resolved after a series of market tests and analyses. The final price was set at 3 rubles or $0.50 for a box of 10, about half the price of tampons elsewhere but still a price which yielded adequate profits. Marketing and distribution were not a problem, since there was no competition and Femtech's Soviet partner controlled all Ukranian pharmacies. Tambrands was able to sell all the tampons it could produce. Tambrands, therefore, focused its promotional efforts on preparing, distributing and presenting educational materials at conferences. Tambrands did distribute a small portion of its output in Moscow, St Petersburg and other Russian cities in anticipation of the day when sales in other locations would be needed to fulfill the joint venture's obligation to export 5% of its output.

During the second year, Femtech hired a finance manager. Since there was little knowledge of Western accounting systems in the Ukraine, Femtech had to hire competent people with potential and train them in Western accounting practices. By the end of the second year, systems to calculate profits in both Soviet and Western terms were expected to be in place. During the third year, Femtech would have to pay local taxes on venture profits (there was a tax holiday during the venture's first two years).

Femtech also attempted to export cotton fibers as a source of hard currency. Again, dozens of logistics problems involving packaging, shipping, permits and permissions were overcome by entrepreneurial 'street smarts'.

To offset cotton processing problems, Femtech started a cotton processing plant in St Petersburg (Russia) using the ruble profits from the Kiev plant. Many of the same operating problems were encountered, including shipping delays and fees, government interference and supplier inefficiencies. The situation became so bad that Tambrands closed the St Petersburg's plant in 1996.

Emerson Electric Company: Managing Employee Layoffs

Emerson Electric, which has a long history of overseas operations through exporting, wholly-owned subsidiaries, and strategic alliances, also experienced management problems in its strategic alliances. For example, a common problem with Chinese joint ventures was that the Chinese government mandated full employment. Officially, the government allowed a company to lay off employees, but from a personal cultural and informal government viewpoint wholesale reductions in the work force created problems (such reductions were considered 'impolitic').

In its Branson joint venture with Shanghai Ultrasonic Instrument Factory (SUIF), started in May 1983, Emerson for a time carried more workers than was efficient. The chemical joint venture discussed earlier encountered a similar problem in managing the work force. In both cases the problem was solved in the future by the overseas partners insisting that employee reductions be made prior to signing a new joint venture contract. This policy has eventually become widely accepted by the Chinese government with the commencement of its massive privatization program in late 1997, based on visits with their government planning group.

Similar problems were encountered by Emerson in maintaining quality at the Branson joint venture. Emerson solved these problems in subsequent joint ventures by introducing an intricate inspection procedure prior to signing joint venture agreements. Sample local partner products were tested at Emerson laboratories, identical products were purchased on the open market and then tested and Emerson conducted inspections at partner plants. Both the chemical plant and Emerson used prior-generation technology in their joint ventures to protect core technologies.

Cellular Phone Venture in Tashkent

The cellular phone venture in Tashkent in Uzbekistan, which was discussed in Chapter 3, pp. 75–76, illustrates some of the entrepreneurial steps needed to make an alliance work (Guyon, 1996).

Personnel clashes had to be resolved, differences in accounting systems had to be understood and reconciled and government contacts and family connections had to be nurtured and used. The US partners were guided through this maze of problems by their Uzbek partners, who suggested giving free phones to Uzbekistan's president, for example. This led to many government officials and agencies subsequently buying phones. Commercial customers gladly paid the $1100 needed to buy a Nokia phone, since it was impossible to do business without it given the decayed state of the local landline phone system (which was built in the 1920s).

The partners also found it necessary to adapt to dress codes, eating styles, language barriers, elevators which dropped three stories, airlines with erratic service and doubtful maintenance facilities and government steps to introduce new competitors in violation of the joint venture contract. Problems with hard currency conversion made dividend payouts difficult.

After 5 years the venture was a success. It turned its first profit in 1993 and revenues were almost $50 million in 1996 (triple 1995), at which time it had 7000 subscribers, 224 employees and an estimated value of almost $100 million. In addition, major companies such as Motorola Inc., TeleNor of Norway and Northern Telecom Ltd were wooing the joint venture for equipment contracts, communications linkups and a piece of company equity.

MANAGEMENT AND WORKER TRAINING AND DEVELOPMENT, AND COMMUNICATION PROCESSES

Management and worker training and development, and communication processes, involve balancing disparate situation factors. Cultural differences can critically affect interpersonal interaction in multinational situations. Techniques for training, development, and communication must be adapted to cultural, content, facility, people, resources, and business restraints in the situation being managed.

In 1990, Larsson – a Swedish multinational telecommunications equipment manufacturing firm – and Nagy Technika – a private Hungarian company primarily involved in computers and office systems – formed a joint venture (Larsson Technika) to manufacture telecommunications equipment for the Hungarian telephone industry. Larsson supplied the technology and Nagy Technika contributed the building, local personnel, and facilities (Cyr 1994c). Initially joint venture equity was split 50/50; subsequently Larsson had a 74% interest. By 1993, 22 of the 360 staff members at Larsson Technika were Swedish managers or technicians. The Swedish staff had been temporarily assigned to the venture to help transfer technical and managerial expertise to Hungarian managers, but were expected to eventually withdraw.

In 1991, Larsson spent $1.36 million training Hungarian engineers at its facility in Dublin. Under communism, workers had acquired a nine-to-five perspective that discouraged initiative and hard work, so training was provided to change these cultural traits. Fifty Hungarians were sent to Stockholm for training in what was called the 'Larsson way', a corporate culture based on close personal relationships and team efforts. Three people were trained to provide in-house training at Larsson Technika in four areas: technical skills, English language, 'on-the-job' training for new employees, and management skills, such as time management and marketing.

Many problems arose. Expatriate Swedish managers were paid the same as their counterparts in Hungary, which was less than they would earn in Sweden. At the same time, they were given a company car, per diem expenses and housing, which led Hungarian managers to complain that their Swedish counterparts were being paid more for the same work. Since cultural change had to be reinforced by the Swedish managers in Hungary, there were continual complaints that this reinforcement interfered with job performance, with each problem taking considerable time to explain and resolve. But these steps were necessary, if the venture was to become self-sufficient.

In many alliances, considerable time and effort is required to introduce organization and work habit changes that bridge cultural gaps effectively at the management, professional, supervisory and worker level. For example, Poland's television tubes producer, Masaryk, and Durand's Consumer Electronics division in France formed a joint venture in Poland in 1991 (Cyr, 1994b). Durand–Masaryk had 3100 employees and produced 1.1 million television tubes a year. Masaryk had been on the verge of bankruptcy and its operations were closed at the time the venture was formed.

Because of Masaryk's difficulties and the high unemployment rate in Poland, the Polish workers were receptive to change even though many inefficient work habits remained from the communist regime. These included lack of information sharing, poor work routines, lack of initiative and little teamwork. Extensive training was initiated. It was recognized that time was needed to introduce more effective and efficient work habits and routines because of human and cultural factors involved: 3000 individuals need time to adapt to new work patterns based on a different cultural perspective (Western Europe free market versus East European communist).

Middle management was key to the transition. A 12-day seminar introducing Western business practices was given to mid-level managers. At these meetings established policies were communicated: employees were encouraged to accept responsibility, provide feedback for improvement, focus on results and emphasize quality. New human resource management, marketing and financial and salary programs were also introduced. It was assumed that people were open to change and would achieve it if guided and encouraged.

Immediately after the early training sessions, many workers were confused and performed less effectively than before. Continual training was therefore undertaken through the introduction of a week-long program of 'training the trainers' for local staff members, which provided local trainers who both understood Western management methods and were familiar with Polish and Durand–Masaryk behavior. Trainers then passed on information about quality and problem-solving, for example, to the quality teams in week-long courses. Management by objectives and management by empowerment through communication and teamwork were emphasized. The development of informal communications channels by workers was encouraged.

The overseas partner's reward and performance review systems were not directly transferable to the venture because of cultural differences, and so had to be modified. For example, while workers appreciated monetary awards, bonuses had to be used more as a punishment for poor work than as a reward for exceptional work. Bonuses were reduced when goals were not met, a subtly different yet culturally significant way of presenting them. Rewards for extra effort included: special excursions, dinners, individual recognition certificates and monthly employee performance awards.

The introduction of Western free market business practices was also a difficult process at a joint venture formed by Karnovac Automobilova (the Czech Republic) and Bremen (Germany) in

1991. Bremen initially owned 31% of the venture; this share was scheduled to increase to 70% in 1995 (Cyr, 1994a). During the early years, considerable time and effort were devoted to training and managing change in a way that was appropriate for the cultural needs of the venture's 17 000 employees. The approach here was to create a learning company through integration not domination, reinforced by a shared management system. In many instances, German and Czech managers were paired so that knowledge and expertise could be transferred from the German partner to local managers through individual coaching and support.

Local managers were hungry for change, but adapting the Western Europe company's practices and methods to local conditions, customs, and culture was a gradual process, guided by these policies:

• Delegation of responsibility and employee ownership of this responsibility
• Recognition that expatriates are 'know-how partners' and share expertise with local managers
• Continued staff development
• Bilingual communication
• Intensive and continuous management training for all executives
• Continued involvement of the union
• Creation of a report- and results-oriented organization structure

Many Czech workers and middle managers were more comfortable with the previous system since it had required less initiative and acceptance of responsibility. In addition, the workers were used to electing their supervisors which gave them control of their management environment. Resistance made change slow and difficult. Sixty trainers provided 6500 employees with some form of training in 1993. There were departmental management meetings, information meetings at all management and worker levels, cross-divisional meetings which were problem-focused and shop floor meetings. These meetings and training sessions were designed to gradually introduce effective and efficient operations and to enable the transfer of control to local Czechs. The reward and performance evaluation system also evolved into a form appropriate for the local culture.

As the venture progressed, the Czech managers were given greater responsibility and decision-making power. For example, regular meetings that previously had been organized by German staff were organized by the Czechs, in the Czech language and using Czech documentation. Czech managers earned trust as workers realized that the foreign partner did not have complete knowledge of Karnovac and local conditions during the transition to a market economy. Over time, Czech management became more confident and German management became more supportive. Both sides realized that it was important to compromise to achieve common goals.

Another example of culturally-dependent management training is found in the experiences of Electronic Data Systems Ltd (EDS), a US company with offices worldwide. The company introduced a more team-, people- and vision-oriented leadership and management strategy in 1992. In trying to implement this strategy in Japan, Larry Purdy, the leadership development manager, reached two conclusions based on the first year of leadership training. First, he discovered that the Japanese and Americans shared many leadership values. These shared values, labeled the *core set of values*, included team orientation. Second, Purdy discovered that cultural differences affected the way in which values were communicated and leaders were evaluated. In Purdy's words:

As for the ways we teach our values, generally Japanese workers spend much less time than Americans doing formal classroom training. Japanese workers are educated and developed by giving them frequent new assignments; by on-the-job training; and by establishing career-long mentor-like relationships with seniors who will help them assimilate the values and culture of the company. As our training program was based primarily on a classroom, lecture-style format, our Japanese middle managers (almost all of whom have only recently joined EDS from other companies) felt they could have understood our message more clearly, and put it into practice more effectively, if we had chosen a more culturally appropriate manner of conveying that message.

The second aspect of leadership that is culturally dependent concerns how we measure, evaluate and select leaders in relation to our leadership value model. This involves judging how leaders demonstrate the behaviors associated with the identified leadership attributes or values: strong personal convictions, vision, emotional bonds, inspirational, team oriented, risk takers and drive to excel. For example, EDS expects its leaders to be team oriented. The Japanese also place great value on teamwork.

However, the motivation and the expectations of team members and manifestation of team spirit varies significantly between the two cultures. The Japanese find satisfaction in being anonymous contributors to group goals. Though Americans also value teamwork, they expect recognition for their individual contributions. American management in turn expects individuals to make recognizable, measurable contributions. Japanese managers would place much more emphasis on a team member's ability to harmonize with the group as a whole than they would on evaluating individual contribution and performance.

As a simple generalization, we might say that though both cultures value teamwork, Japanese expect individuals to conform to the group by suppressing their individuality; Americans expect the group to conform to the needs of its individuals by accommodating and measuring everyone's individuality. Thus, we need a culturally relative way in which to interpret someone's ability to be team oriented (Purdy, 1995, pp. 13–14).

Figure 6.3 shows some of the different training approaches needed when dealing with three separate cultures. This is another example of multinational contingency management. As seen in the figure, the adjustments contingent on the situation's cultural requirements can range from the timing of the sessions and training materials used, to the how the training is conducted.

The concept of such contingency management is not difficult to grasp when one studies cultural differences, such as those reviewed in Appendix B, and then manages a common business function, such as training and development, in a way appropriate for the situation. For instance, Japanese cultural bias favors group work and consensus, and protocol and status. Thus, the teaching methods that work best for the Japanese are intragroup discussions and sharing experiences with the group (but not necessarily with the instructor). The management process for training sessions is the familiar contingency process – the methods must be adapted to the audience, subject matter and objectives.

Culture differences also affect other management tasks, such as motivation and performance review. This impact can be identified and analyzed as shown in Figures 6.4(a) and 6.4(b).

Management and worker training and development, and communication, are other contingency multinational strategic management tasks. Figure 6.5 outlines a contingency perspective which is consistent with management perspectives in the other multinational management task areas covered in this book.

CONTROL AND REASSESSMENT

Internal alliance control systems, such as accounting and other computerized information systems, were also found to be tailored to individual situation needs. Most strategic alliances visited were, like their multinational counterparts, working hard to introduce the

	American	Japanese	Arab
Group Composition	Medium-sized; Mixed level OK	Smallest group; Grouped for functional harmony	Largest group; Very level-conscious
Time	8–5 with breaks	9–6 with breaks; May go until 8 or continue informally after-hours	9/10–3 maximum; No lunch break
Preparation	Individual reading; Written homework	Group orientation	Not necessary or important
Getting Started	Self-introductions; Random or by seating order	Introductions emphasizing company/belonging; Senior goes last	Introduction by status; Senior goes first
Process	Emphasize 'how to' and practical applications; Self-reliance; Specialization, reading	Emphasis on doing/discussion; Sharing experiences; Intragroup discussion; Role play; Rotation	Memorizing general skills; Coaching; Demonstration by leader; Minimal reading
Training Materials	Written; Self-explanatory	Visual with group discussion and by doing	Visual; Coaching by team leader
Tests of Knowledge	Direct questions to individual; Spontaneous, open questions	Group questions; Intragroup discussions; Directed questions	No direct, individual questions; Need preparation
Cultural Values	Self-reliance; Competition; Time conscious	Relationship; Group achievement; Group harmony	Seniority; Reputation; Individual achievement

Figure 6.3 Cultural Contrasts: Training. From *Multicultural Management 2000*, by Elashmawi and Harris. Copyright © 1998 by Gulf Publishing Company. Reproduced with permission. All rights reserved.

(a)

	American	Japanese	Arab
Management Style	Leadership; Friendliness	Persuasion; Functional group activities	Coaching; Personal attention; Parenthood
Control	Independence; Decision-making; Space; Time; Money	Group harmony	Of others/parenthood
Emotional Appeal	Opportunity	Group participation; Company success	Religion; Nationalistic; Admiration
Recognition	Individual contribution	Group identity; Belonging to group; Group contribution	Individual status; Class/society; Promotion
Material Rewards	Salary; Commission; Profit-sharing	Annual bonus; Social services; Fringe benefits	Gifts self/family; Family affair; Salary increase
Threats	Loss of job	Out of group	Demotion; Reputation
Cultural Values	Competition; Risk-taking; Material possession; Freedom	Group harmony; Achievement; Belonging	Reputation; Family security; Religion; Social status

(b)

	American	Japanese	Arab
Objective	Review based on preset goals; Identify personal strengths/weaknesses	Find out why performance is not in harmony with group	Set employee on track; Reprimand for bad performance
Structure	Formal procedure; Every 6 to 12 months in manager's office	Informal, ad-hoc with employee; Frequent reporting to administration; In office, coffee shop, bar	Informal, ad-hoc; Recorded in manager's office
Interaction	Two-way, both sides present openly own point of view; Manager as leader/advisor; Employee independent, self-motivated	Employee answers manager's concerns; Manager gives advice as parent, mentor, senior employee; Part of group/family; Continuous feedback	One-way; Manager guides subordinate; Authority figure, mentor; Random feedback; Child in family
Evaluation	Success measured by performance stated goals	Success measured by contribution to group harmony and output	Success measured by major personal contribution
Outcome	Promotion; Salary increase; Bonus; Commission; Salary freeze; Loss of title; Loss of power	Mainly affects amount of semi-annual bonus; Less important job; Job rotation; Dock bonus/salary	Bonus of 1/2-day salary; Promotion; Salary decrease
Closing	Stress agreement on expectation; Document review	Performance continually forward to personnel; Open door	Admiration or threat of punishment; One-way door
Cultural values	Openness; Equatility; Fairness	Group achievement; Relationship	Privacy; Authority; Parenthood

Figure 6.4 Cultural Contrasts. (a) Motivation; (b) Performance Reviews. From *Multicultural Management 2000*, by Elashmawi and Harris. Copyright © 1998 by Gulf Publishing Company. Reproduced with permission. All rights reserved.

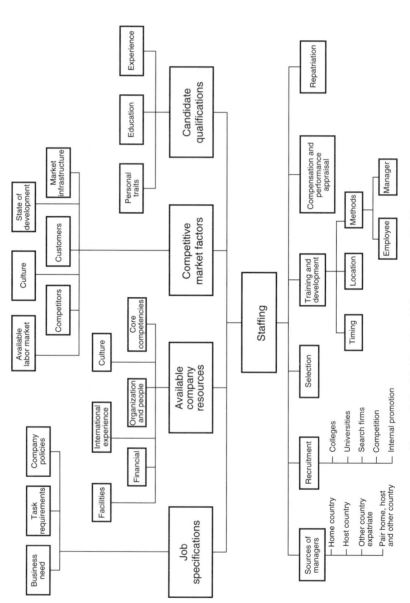

Figure 6.5 Multinational Management Staffing

latest possible information technology. This is particularly difficult in developing countries, where financial limitations, ineffective telecommunications infrastructures, lack of trained technical personnel, low levels of general familiarity with modern technical tools and non-standard local accounting, taxation and required regulatory reporting systems are found.

While these problems can be resolved with varying degrees of success locally, they often create control problems for alliance partners. For example, integrated international reporting systems may be required by partners to monitor the alliance from several local and international viewpoints. At the Chinese chemical joint venture plant this was relatively simple since the manufacturing systems were similar to those used at the partner's US plants and since the product was sold in large lots through controlled distribution channels. Integrating the alliance's reporting systems with the overseas partner's systems was therefore relatively easy to automate, making local and international operational and financial control relatively uncomplex.

This task was more difficult at the consumer products companies studied because of the large volume of different kinds of small unit sales through various sales and distribution outlets. In addition, several ventures had interlocking joint venture arrangements which had to be reported on to the government separately. In one instance, a three-man tax accounting group did nothing but work on reconciling and administering the different local government tax reporting systems. In this situation, overseas integration of the alliance with the US partner was difficult, and for the most part required manual reformulation and reporting of results.

Solutions are seldom easy and are usually secondary to solving marketing, production and other operating problems. At Femtech, for example, only in the second year of operations was a local accounting/finance manager hired and trained to resolve the problems arising from creating and integrating local and international reporting systems. This was important at Femtech because taxes were to be paid starting in the third year; this required local accounting and reporting compliance with Russian tax laws.

While the free flow of information is encouraged and a supportive enabling environment is fostered when managing an alliance locally, alliance performance must be controlled and access to knowledge that involves the disclosure of confidential information must be restricted. For example, the exchange of information has to be monitored to protect core competencies of each partner. Technology transfer can be limited by having advanced products manufactured at non-joint venture locations as was done by Gillette, by installing prior generation technology as was done in the Chinese chemical joint venture, or by specifying procedures, controls and limitations in the initial venture agreement. Proprietary knowledge diffusion can sometimes be difficult to control, however, as seen from Durawool's experiences, even where precautions are taken.

Management guidance and control systems are needed to balance diverse multinational control requirements. These systems are *formal, information-based* routines, guidelines and systems *managers* use to maintain or alter patterns in organizational activities (Mockler, 1973; Simons, 1995). These key guidance and control systems, both formal and informal systems, which impact a Business Strategy have been identified:

1. Enterprise Strategic Frameworks, which define core values and the risks to be avoided
2. Interactive Planning and Control Systems
3. Diagnostic Control and Guidance Systems

Control systems need to be balanced to manage the complex, often contradictory, rapid change encountered in today's business environments (Price Waterhouse, 1996). The paradoxical forces to be balanced include motivation and coercion, reward and punishment, guidance and proscription, stimulation and control, self-interest and the desire to contribute, and intended and emergent strategies. The guidance and control systems discussed below are used to create a dynamic tension between specific goal achievement and creative innovation.

Enterprise Strategic Framework

Enterprise strategic frameworks identify enterprise policies which senior joint venture and partner managers communicate formally and reinforce systematically to provide core values, shared purpose, and direction that senior managers want others to adopt. These core values are linked to the business strategy which is formulated as part of the strategic fit studies. They are used to inspire and focus the search for new opportunities. A formal belief system is communicated orally and through such documents as strategic objective mission and vision statements.

These systems also provide policy and other guidelines that are used to set limits for organizational participants on opportunity-seeking behavior designed to achieve the enterprise's shared vision. The policy guidelines established for the Karnovac Automoilova/ Bremen joint venture in the Czech Republic, described on p. 175, are examples of strategic boundaries.

Examples of written belief and boundary systems given in earlier chapters include Borg–Warner Chemicals Europe integration plan, described on p. 86, the preliminary general principles agreement for Femtech in Russia (Chapter 3, p. 65) and the agreements between BA/AA prior to the alliance formulation (Chapters 3 and 4, pp. 67 and 112). Enterprise strategic frameworks provide a forum for the opportunity areas that organizational participants are encouraged to exploit. In the sense that they provide direction and necessary benchmarks or standards against which performance can be measured, these two types of information frameworks function as guidance and control systems. They are generally non-quantitative and are based on the strategic alliance activities described in Chapters 2 and 3.

Diagnostic Control and Guidance Systems

Diagnostic Control Reporting Systems

Diagnostic control systems are comparative performance feedback reporting systems. They are the essence of traditional management control and are designed to ensure predictable goal achievement. Diagnostic control systems are the formal information systems that managers use to motivate employees, to monitor performance, to correct deviations from standards and to reward achievements. Several kinds of these systems used in the Fiat/Peugeot alliance were discussed in Chapter 3 pp. 77–79.

The standards, which are the key elements of control systems, may include: budgets, performance benchmarks from industry competitors, adjusted historical figures, spending limits, financial ratios, agreed-upon objectives and even financial forecasts. Cost accounting reports are an example of control reporting systems since they report on cost results and compare them to established standard costs. The simplest form of control report is a comparative sales report, such as the one shown in Table 6.1.

Table 6.1   Comparative Sales Control Report United Kingdom
Subsidiary (in £)

	Actual unit sales	Budget	Deviation
Product A	14 000	15 000	− 1000
Product B	8000	8500	+ 500

Since standards need to be appropriate for the specific situations being controlled and since variations (in labor costs, materials costs, transportation times and exchange rates) occur from country to country, international control systems are difficult to establish. For example, if the unit sales in Table 6.1 were translated into dollars for consolidation purposes, both the budget and the results deviation would have to be converted at the same rate when evaluating alliance performance to make the comparison meaningful. In addition, if an alliance's performance is compared with a similar one in another country, then local circumstances – such as a recession or labor problems, new competitors entering the market, or other circumstances or events affecting results – would have to be noted and factored into the evaluation. Because of differences among countries, comparative statements across borders have to be constructed to meet individual situation requirements.

Transfer pricing provides a typical example (Mueller, 1994). The need for determining a transfer price arises when goods or services are exchanged between international units, as in the Fiat/Peugeot joint ventures described earlier in Chapter 3, p. 77 and in the Chongqing–Yamaha venture described in Chapter 5, p. 132. When goods are transferred, the price set is not always a market price, at least in alliance agreements which allow for such flexibility and have a mechanism for making balancing adjustments. While it may be influenced by the current market price and financial impacts on each partner, the transfer price is also determined by many other situation restraints: minimizing taxes and worldwide import duties, winning host government approval, complying with other government restrictions and regulations, covering product costs, meeting competitive market conditions, enabling profit evaluations of subsidiaries and managing currency fluctuations.

Some ground rules have been developed for multinational ventures in light of these restrictions. If a country has a low tariff on imports, a high import transfer price might be recommended. If a country has a high corporate tax rate, then a high export transfer price would be preferred to minimize profits and thus taxes on profits. If expatriation of profits is restricted, a high export transfer price is one way to take profits out of a country. If devaluation is continual, a high export transfer price is one way to minimize currency losses. If a subsidiary needs to boost profits or sales by lowering its costs and selling prices, on the other hand, a low import transfer price is one way to do this. If a government has a preference for either a cost-based or market-based price or strictly controls transfer prices, any decision would take these limits into consideration.

Situations where many multiple conditions can be met are rare, since overall partner profits will be affected in alliances which export products to other partner units. For this reason, the most advantageous overall solution – that is, the most profitable overall option after considering venture and partner profits – should be chosen. Computer-analysis systems are useful in balancing these complex factors, as are clear agreements on how compensating book or other adjustments will be made.

Comparative control systems cover many areas in addition to finance and accounting: quality, productivity, sales (dollars and units), costs, unit output, inventory turnover (days or weeks), debt-to-equity ratios, customer satisfaction (monthly comparisons of customer complaints, for example), on-time performance (airlines, for example), employee turnover, compliance with government regulations (racial mix of the work force, for example), supplier performance (meeting just-in-time schedules, for example), manager performance and compliance with policies (limits on speculative currency trading, for example). These systems are useful both for internal venture control and for monitoring partner contribution to a venture.

Diagnostic Guidance and Control Processes
In addition to *reporting systems*, other kinds of diagnostic control *processes* are used in multinational alliances. Many management information systems do not contain standards or generate compari-

sons to standard measures. Instead, they provide analytic information that can be *used for* planning and control decision making. In the broadest sense, any operating report that analyzes or decomposes operating aggregates can be considered a management guidance and control system. For instance, the cost breakdowns by expense categories in profit-and-loss statements contained in a strategic alliance's periodic reports are analytical tools that can help partner management *diagnose* how healthy the venture is by comparing it to partner management's expectations. In international situations, such analyses are difficult to do if a company chooses not to translate its annual reports into the language or accounting standards familiar to the user/investor. At Gillette's joint venture in China and other ventures studied, for example, for a time special groups were needed to translate venture financial results into a form useful for partner monitoring of the venture's performance.

Interactive Planning and Control Systems

Managing and balancing stimulating creative innovation and controlling is the essence of management control. It is a balancing act which is at the heart of successful strategic alliance leadership and management.

Diagnostic control systems, such as budget comparisons, can constrain innovation and opportunity seeking while trying to ensure that outcomes are kept in line with identified strategies. Interactive planning and control systems serve another purpose. They stimulate search and learning, enabling new strategies to emerge.

Many types of control systems generally referred to as decision-support systems can be used interactively. For example, a mathematical-based analysis or forecasting software package, or a computer-based spreadsheet, that allows a manager to enter different price, production or other assumptions and then calculates the effect of each assumed change on profits is an interactive tool useful for planning and forecasting. Gillette's CEO, Al Zeien, described a computer system Gillette used to determine the best way to manufacture and supply Atra razors given the many international locations involved in this way:

> Let me give you an example of a global company as it works in the computer age. You are all probably familiar with the Atra cartridge, which is a small

razor blade shaving cartridge that we sell. About six months ago our computer optimization program was saying we really shouldn't continue to be supplying those Atra cartridges to the Australian market from our manufacturing operation in Melbourne, Australia. There was a cheaper way the computer identified in just one hour. How are we supplying Atra cartridges to the Australian market today? The steel comes from Yusugi on the west coast of Japan. It goes from there to Rio de Janeiro where it is processed into blade steel. It is then shipped out into the Atlantic ocean and up the Amazon river 1200 miles to Manaus, also in Brazil, where the plastic molding takes place and the blade steel is mounted into the cartridge, what we call a naked cartridge. Back out to sea, it goes to Singapore and there it is packaged and shipped to our Melbourne warehouse. Ladies and gentlemen at this time that is the lowest cost way to supply cartridges to Australia. Believe it (Zeien, 1995).

Interactive and diagnostic systems can be any kind of systematic use of information to stimulate thinking about new directions (planning) or correcting problems (control). The weekly phone meetings and videoconferences at many multinational companies are a good example of a systematic interactive and diagnostic exchange of information useful for planning and control purposes. Control is also exercised through the words and actions of alliance and partner leaders and managers during periodic CEO and regional manager visits to each joint venture. The manager's daily interactions at the Chinese chemical joint venture, the policy dissemination program at Foote, Cone and Belding, and the policies and their reinforcement at The Blackstone Group were other key ways observed for doing this.

Whatever the system used, continued monitoring of each partner's contribution to the alliance is needed. This requires creating standards (delivery dates, quality standards, costs and sales levels and the like), developing systems to provide control information (many formal and informal ones were discussed in this section) and monitoring performance regularly (daily, weekly, monthly, quarterly, yearly). It also requires a willingness to act quickly to correct problems, while at the same time stimulating entrepreneurial thinking and willingness to take risks – a difficult balancing act.

EXIT STRATEGIES: WHEN AND HOW TO TERMINATE

While it is prudent not to overemphasize negative aspects of an alliance, such as possible termination, the possibility should be planned for when formulating an alliance. The termination may be specified as part of the original strategy, as in the case of the Chinese government's 16-year joint electric utility venture with two French firms. Or, it may be caused by outside political circumstances, such as wars, changing partner needs, as when partner mergers or acquisitions occur, inefficient management, changing economic conditions, or by ill-conceived initial planning. For example, an aging plant needing expensive rehabilitation and greatly reduced import tariffs dictated the dissolution of the Ford Mazda auto manufacturing venture in New Zealand.

In the initial negotiations, alliance partners should establish procedures for negotiating termination of the agreement, including timing, mutual obligations and valuation. Timing may refer to a specific agreed-upon termination date or it may be linked to the occurrence of certain events (conditional termination). Mutual obligations refer to providing assistance in enabling one partner to leave the alliance while the other continues operating. Valuation procedures are probably the most difficult to establish. If the conditions are too specific and detailed, they can create distrust up front. If they are too general and easy to fulfill they will encourage alliance dissolution when the first problems arise. For these reasons it is usually best to keep termination conditions fairly general and to involve lawyers in the negotiations only during their final stages (Gates, 1993; Lynch, 1993).

Toshiba, Japan's third largest electronics giant, however, describes its alliance agreements as the corporate equivalent of a prenuptial agreement, so both sides know who gets what if the partnership does not work out (Schendler, 1997). Tsuyoshi Kawanishi, a Toshiba director and the senior executive vice president in charge of partnerships and alliances, says: 'During the honeymoon time, everything is great. But as you know, divorce is always a possibility, and that's when things can get bitter.'

Such a termination pact might have helped Procter & Gamble, when it wanted to inject more cash into its unprofitable joint venture in Vietnam in 1998. Its state-owned partner was unable to provide cash, yet was unwilling to sell its share to Procter & Gamble (Marshall, 1998). Assi/Doman, a Swedish forestry group, faced a similar problem with its alliance, Segezhabumpron, Russia's largest pulp and paper plant, and was forced to consider withdrawing from the venture (McIvor, 1998).

Royal Dutch/Shell, the Anglo-Dutch oil group, spent $2 billion to take full control of Montell, its plastics joint venture with Mont-Edison of Italy which had been created in 1995 (Taylor, 1997). The venture was mutually terminated mainly because Shell wanted to invest further in the joint venture and MontEdison was heavily in debt and so was anxious to sell. In response to global trends, Shell consolidated its other chemical business into a single global firm, Shell Chemicals, with annual sales of about $10 billion. According to the chief executive of the new global company: 'The industry is globally driven, but we have not been globally organized'.

In 1983, AT&T made a major equity investment ($260 million) to acquire 22% of Olivetti's common stock. Through the alliance, Olivetti sought access to new technology, greater financial resources and access to the end-user market in office equipment (personal computers, electric typewriters and the like). AT&T, in contrast, sought to enter new markets outside the USA and to develop new office equipment products. It was essentially an unrelated diversification for each firm.

Historically, AT&T, through its focus on telecommunications, had developed an operations-driven, long-cycle regulated business style. In contrast, Olivetti had focused on specific, discrete products such as typewriters sold in short-cycle, competitive businesses, and so had developed a marketing-driven business style. This led to problems, as AT&T's style and operations were not suited to the requirements of office equipment products (end-user, market-driven) and so clashed with the dynamic, entrepreneurial style of Olivetti's marketing and design-driven management. As a result of conflicts between operating and marketing executives and managers, AT&T eventually sold its share in Olivetti for a large financial gain (Taucher, 1993; Taylor, 1989).

Strategic alliance terminations are not always dramatic or complex. Airline alliances often consist of integrated computer systems, airline sales offices and phone reservation services, and at times some combined airport facilities. The termination of such airline alliances often are relatively painless, except for situations such as the one involving USAir and British Airways, where USAir sued to collect damages.

The difficulties of and approaches to strategic alliance termination are contingent on a variety of situation factors, including: how well preplanned exit strategies can be or have been defined

(Toshiba); the specification of predetermined termination dates (GM–Toyota); the difficulty of meshing of cultures (AT&T/Olivetti); the mutuality of strategic goals and availability of financial resources (Shell/MontEdison); and the difficulty or ease involved in separating the two parties (BA/USAir).

MAKING AN ALLIANCE WORK OVER THE YEARS: BEST PRACTICES GUIDELINES

The following best practices guidelines have been developed from the company experiences described in this chapter. They are generally applicable, but like rules they may be broken when the situation warrants a different approach.

- Work ethics differ from culture to culture and this will affect training practices and management styles, since considerably more supervision time and attention may be needed in running overseas operations. As was seen at Kentucky Fried Chicken in Beijing, it is common for Chinese workers to avoid confrontations with management.
- Where cultural differences have to be taken into account when managing a venture, a synergistic balance should be the goal when possible. The troika management team of a Hungarian, American and German manager at the Hungarian telecommunications company was an example of a synergistic approach.
- Because of the many cultural gaps in a strategic alliance that need to be bridged, constant communication and management attention is needed on a continuing basis, as at Durand–Masaryk in Poland.
- Where possible, problems should be dealt with immediately. This was done by Jack Welch, CEO of General Electric, in the Toshiba/GE alliance. Building an early communication and personal chemistry base was the key to enabling such direct handling of problems as they arose.
- Cultural differences dictate that considerable time may be needed when trying to transfer Western business practices, as will a variety of organization, leadership, staffing, management and information systems approaches.

- Because training is a continuing job, as much as possible it is necessary to have in place a permanent 'train the trainers' program, which makes ample use of local personnel. This was done at Puyi–Briggs, Tambrands and Durand–Masaryk.
- Considerable time and money are needed to develop quality and service standards in many overseas operations, especially in developing countries, as was seen in the American Copier situation.
- In developing countries, such as China and Russia, be prepared for substantial problems in marketing, since both countries had controlled economies where marketing infrastructures were almost non-existent. In addition, be prepared for major government delays (and often payoffs) in getting approvals and the tendency of local suppliers to miss performance schedules.
- Considerable time and attention should be spent in developing supplier and distribution relationships. This often requires providing equipment and training. This was the case at Tambrands and American Copier.
- Language differences need to be taken into account. For example, remember that 'yes' often means only 'I heard you', not that they understand or agree. 'No problem' may mean none for them, but a great one for you. Asians have a preference for avoiding giving a direct 'no'.
- Allow for different accounting and control systems to be used but always provide for a reconciliation system that permits all partners, as well as strategic alliance management, to control and measure performance. This was done at Gillette.
- Periodic reviews are critical to success.
- Allow adequate time to introduce the alliance and its strategic rationale, operating policies and working relationships, as was done at Durand–Masaryk in Poland.
- Technology transfer and development must be well defined and controlled, as Durawool found out in China and as Motorola encountered in Japan.
- Champions involved in the initiation of an alliance can help sustain commitment, enthusiasm and momentum if they are given key roles in the continuing management of the venture, as was seen at Tambrands and Borg–Warner.
- When problems arise, work together to solve them, partner to partner or partner to alliance managers. Any means that

involves interpersonal interaction among key participants is good, since ultimately the success of an alliance depends on the people involved. The attention of key people interacting with each other is the single most important key to multinational strategic alliance success.

Appendix A at the end of this book provides a summary of key questions to be asked and answered when doing the analysis involved in making decisions and managing such multinational strategic alliance activities such as development and training at all levels, control, and terminating alliances.

REFERENCES

Applbaum, K.D. and Yatsko, P.A. (1993). *FCB and Publicis (A)*: *Forming an Alliance*, a case study. Boston, MA, Harvard Business School.
Cyr, D.J. and Schneider, S.C. (1994a). *Creating A Learning Organization Through HRM: A German-Czech Joint Venture (A,B)*. Fontainebleau, France, INSEAD.
Cyr, D.J. and Schneider, S.C. (1994b). *Creating Change Through Human Resources: The Case of French-Polish Joint Venture (A,B)*. Fontainebleau, France, INSEAD.
Cyr, D.J. and Schneider, S.C. (1994c). *Creating Cultural Change in a Swedish-Hungarian Joint Venture (A,B)*. Fontainebleau, France, INSEAD.
De Muth, J. (1992). The east is (in the) red. *World Trade*, November, pp. 44–46.
Emmons, W. (1990). *Tambrands Inc.: The Femtech Soviet Venture (A)(B)*, a case study. Boston, MA, Harvard Business School Publishing Division.
Emmons, W. (1993). *Tambrands Inc.: The Femtech Soviet Venture (A) (B)*, a case study. Boston, MA, Harvard Business School Publishing Division.
Gates, S. (1993). *Strategic Alliances: Guidelines for Successful Management*. New York, The Conference Board.
Guyon, J. (1996). Some good old boys make lots of money phoning up Tashkent. *The Wall Street Journal*, June 21, pp. A1, A6.
Haslech, R. (1991). Whither free enterprise? The difficulties for Western investors in the Soviet Union. *Europe*, April, pp. 15–18.
Kanter, R.M., Applbaum, K.D. and Yatsko, P.A. (1993). *FCB and Publicis (B): Managing Client and Country Diversity*, Boston, MA, Harvard Business School.
Knobel, B. (1993). On the waterfront Russian-style. *International Business*, December, pp. 43–45.
Lewis, D.E. (1997). Returning to market as undisputed leader, Tambrands buy would give P&G 50% of tampon market. *Boston Globe*, April 11, pp. D1, D6.
Lim, Y.T.P. and Fok, M.K. (1996). Puyi-Briggs & Stratton Engine Company: A case study of a China–US Joint Venture. In *Business Opportunities in Sichuan Province, China* (Tech Meng Tan, ed.). New York, Prentice Hall, pp. 137–147.
Lynch, R.P. (1993). *Business Alliances Guide*. New York, John Wiley.

Marshall, S. (1998). P&G squabbles with Vietnamese partner. *The Wall Street Journal*, February 27, p. A14.

McIvor, G. (1998). Assi poised to pull out of Russian plant. *Financial Times*, February 12, p. 9.

Melcher, R.A. (1997). A marriage made in hell. *Business Week*, December 22, pp. 40–42.

Mockler, R.J. (1973). *The Management Control Process*. Englewood Cliffs, NJ, Prentice Hall.

Morrison, A.J. (1997). Kentucky Fried Chicken in China – expansion and consequent problems. In *Business Strategy: An Asia-Pacific Focus*. Singapore, Prentice-Hall, pp. 407–415.

Mueller, G.G., Gernon, H. and Meek, G.K. (1994). *Accounting: An International Perspective*, 3rd edn. Burr Ridge, IL, Irwin.

Peng, M.W. (1997). The China strategy: A tale of two firms. In *Business Strategy: An Asia-Pacific Focus*. Singapore, Prentice-Hall, pp. 441–446.

Price Waterhouse Change Integration Team (1996). *The Paradox Principles: How High-Performance Companies Manage Chaos, Complexity, and Contradiction to Achieve Superior Results*. Chicago, IL, Irwin.

Purdy, L. (1995). Leadership: Is it culturally dependent? Presentation, Mexico City, Mexico: Strategic Management Society Annual National Conference, October 15–18.

Simons, R. (1995). *Levels of Control*. Boston, MA, Harvard Business School Press.

Specter, M. (1997). Moscow Journal: Mrs Lenin's palace survives to serve the fittest. *The New York Times*, February 4, p. A4.

Tambrands (1996). Letter to Shareholders, White Plains, NY.

Taucher, G. (1993). AT&T and Olivetti joint venture. In *Strategic Alliances: Guidelines for Successful Management*, (Gates, S. ed.). New York, The Conference Board, p. 12.

Taylor, J. (1989). The American Telephone & Telegraph Co., Ing. C. Olivetti & Co. Spa, and Note on the office automation industry. In *Managing the Global Corporation*, (William H. Davidson and Jose de la Torre, eds.), New York, McGraw-Hill, pp. 266–274, 275–284 and 285–295.

Taylor, R. (1997). Deal long in the making. *Financial Times*, July 3, p. 20.

Zeien, A. (1995). Gillette's global marketing experiences. *Talk at St John's University's Annual Colman Mockler Leadership Award Ceremony*, New York, February 27.

7
Conclusion: Guidelines for Developing and Managing Multinational Strategic Alliances

This book has provided a systematic, disciplined approach to multinational strategic alliance development and management. Many company experiences have been described to introduce readers to a wide range of alliance situations and their different requirements, an approach used by most successful alliance companies studied (Harbison, 1997c).

This chapter and the concluding sections of Chapters 2–6 give best practices guidelines for developing and managing alliances. In addition, Appendix A gives checklists covering important questions to asked when analyzing a specific potential alliance situation. Chapter 7, the concluding sections of Chapters 2–6 and Appendix A provide a quick reference summary of the highlights of this book as they relate to helping managers do the job more effectively. They also provide a basis for helping to develop a rigorous, disciplined approach to building an corporate alliance capability, a step most successful alliance companies take (Kelly, 1997; Pekar and Harbison, 1998).

Like 'rules', these guidelines and checklists are 'made to be broken' where situation requirements dictate different approaches. In addition, each one by itself does not guarantee success. Foote, Cone and Belding (USA), for example, did many things right when developing its advertising agency alliance with Publicis (France). Ultimately it failed, however.

This chapter explores some of the key reasons for alliance failure and reviews some key ways to avoid failure by building a best practices alliance capability within the firm.

CAUSES OF FAILURE

Surveys confirm the causes of failure described in the company experiences covered in this book. For example, a Conference Board survey of 138 firms indicated the following causes of alliance failure (Troy 1994, p. 19):

Reason for failure	Per cent of Respondents
Drastic changes in environment	56
Cultures too different	44
Poor leadership	43
Ambiguous leadership	43
Overestimated market	35
Poor integration process	34

Bain and Company reported that in 48% of the alliances they studied the cause of failure was inadequate strategy development (Rigby, 1994). Studies by Booz-Allen & Hamilton over a 6-year period involving 500 CEOs gave these reasons for alliance failures: selected wrong partner, overly optimistic expectations, lukewarm commitment, poor communication, undefined roles, unclear value creation, loose agreement, little relationship building, weak business plan, lack of alliance experience and not bridging partners' styles (Pekar and Harbison, 1998).

Many aspects of these causes have been discussed in preceding chapters of this book. Specific company studies were explored to illustrate how these failures came about in practice.

In spite of these failures, the point made by Jim Kelly, CEO of United Parcel Service (UPS), is that alliances are a necessary part of doing business successfully today. A company can learn from both successful and unsuccessful alliance experiences. Eventually a company can and should develop a core competency in alliance capability, which can give it a competitive edge (Kelly, 1997). The concluding sections of Chapters 2–6 have provided some best practices guidelines to help develop and strengthen such a core competency.

The checklists in Appendix A include useful lists of questions which might be asked during each analytical and action phase of the alliance development and management process. The answers can provide a situational basis for the decisions and actions involved in multinational strategic alliance development and implementation – appropriate decisions and actions which most often are dictated by specific situation requirements.

These guidelines and checklists are based on the discussions of company experiences in this book, the author's personal experiences, and studies and surveys of companies involved in alliances by industry groups, consulting firms and individual consultants (for example, Garone, 1996; Gates 1993; Harbison, 1997a,b; Hart, 1994; Lynch, 1993; Pekar and Harbison, 1998; Troy, 1994). These studies show:

1. A high percentage of both domestic and international companies – more than 50% – are engaged in some form of strategic alliance activity. This participation was increasing in the mid-1990s.
2. A high percentage of these alliances are not successful, but the percentage of successes is increasing.
3. It is possible to dramatically improve the chances of success through both one's experiences and studying the experiences of others.
4. Companies using alliances have higher overall return on investments (ROI) for the alliances than for their companies as a whole.
5. Return on Investment grows as alliance experience increases.

Because of the differing situation requirements, the best practices guidelines and analytical questions given in this book are not prescriptions for success in every situation. Ultimately success depends to a large measure on a company's ability to adapt these guidelines to fit its own specific requirements and to manage changing events on a continuing basis.

REDUCING RISK

Paradoxically, strategic alliances can both reduce risks and increase them, depending on how they are developed and managed. After each partner's strategic needs are identified, it is possible to move by steps incrementally into and through the alliance, which was the approach used by the European Paint Manufacturers discussed in Chapter 4, p. 124 who began their alliance with a co-purchasing joint venture. Tambrands used another incremental approach, as over two years it carefully explored the territory, gradually increased production, developed the knowledge and contacts needed to make the alliances work and later financed expansion out of venture earnings. Even then the Femtech alliance in Kiev worked, but the Tambrands' alliance in St Petersburg did not.

Such incremental approaches can reduce risks in many situations by allowing time for partners to become acquainted as they work out unforeseen details, and by reducing the commitment during the early stages of a relationship when major uncertainties exist. An incremental approach is not always possible, however. Another way to reduce risk is to limit the equity investment, as, for example, in the Femtech and Rawley Dawson alliances.

The best practices guidelines discussed in each chapter are effective ways to anticipate and reduce strategic alliance risks (Harbison, 1997a). Where these basic best practices guidelines are not followed, as in the Studds–Nolan situation, alliances can be very risky. The following sections summarize this book's discussions of the lessons learned from analyzing key activities involved in successful multinational strategic alliance development and management.

Strategic Fit

When planning for strategic fit, the approach is to find complementary supporting and synergistic strategic needs and activities among the partners. Alliances where this match seems to have been well-identified, structured and managed involved: General Motors/Toyota; Femtech; Chongqing–Yamaha; Borg–Warner; and Puyi-Briggs & Stratton. Situations in which strategic misalignments existed were the AT&T/Olivetti, Durawool and Shell Italia alliances.

Because of the variety of relationships among alliance partners, the best strategic fit is not always readily apparent. This is one reason why time is needed to explore the operational fits, as well as the relative present and future competitive positions, of the partners. Detailed explorations often reveal the exact nature of the fit and the best way to structure and incrementally time the different alliance development stages to effectively mesh partners' strategic goals – the strategic reasons driving the alliance need – and to avoid counter-productive partner competition.

In essence, the objective is to create a significant win–win situation for all partners. When the driving strategic needs diminish or diverge, an alliance moves towards failure, as when MontEdison encountered capital availability problems in the Shell Italia venture. Overoptimism and undefined roles have also been shown to be key reasons for alliance failure (Harbison, 1997a).

Negotiations

Effective negotiating skills are needed during all phases of multinational alliance planning, creation, management, and implementation. This requires specific knowledge of cultural differences and ways to handle them at all alliance management levels and during all phases of the alliance process. The initial negotiations are a good testing ground for forming judgments about the personalities involved, especially during conflict resolution phases. For this reason, negotiations should be face-to-face when possible until the partners have gotten to know each other well. Because of the multiple purposes they serve, negotiations almost always take longer than planned and require more personal involvement and face-to-face meetings than might be expected.

At times, competitive pressures may require rushing negotiations. This was the case when the Otis Elevator Company was entering Russia and competing firms were vying to ally with the same Russian firm. This can increase risks, however. In Otis' case this haste led to severe financial and operational problems in the alliance (Fey and Killing, 1995; Prescia, 1997).

The key is not the amount of time spent in alliance negotiations, however, but how the time is used. Tambrands used the time to ask specific questions related to strategic fit and operational fit, and used the process to get to know the partners involved. In an entirely different situation, British Airways needed the time to negotiate with different government bodies, further delaying the British Airways/American Airlines proposed alliance in early 1998.

Surveys indicate that lack of relationship building and failing to bridge partners' styles and cultures are key reasons for alliance failure (Pekar and Harbison, 1998).

Selecting Partners

In one survey, poor partner selection was listed as the principal cause of alliance failure by 85% of the 500 CEOs questioned. The process of getting to know partners continues both during and after selection. The most obvious criteria when selecting a partner is the compatibility of strategic goals: what each partner intends to get from the alliance (focusing on realistic, achievable expectations) and the degree of commitment that can be expected. Compatibility also refers to complementary relationships – how each partner's goals strengthen and reinforce the other's and so provide for each to gain value from the alliance. Adequate time should be spent raising and answering these questions, since rushing the negotiations can be dangerous. Unclear value creation and lukewarm commitment were cited in surveys as major reasons for alliance failure (Pekar and Harbison, 1998).

The compatibility of values, cultures and personalities is also a good predictor of future responsiveness to problem solving and conflict resolution. This 'personal chemistry' is an important basis on which to build trust, a key ingredient in an alliance's success. Partners should, therefore, take time to understand each other's values, as well as to gain knowledge of their own values, something that was not carefully enough considered in the AT&T/Olivetti joint venture.

A third criteria for partner selection involves competency, both in relation to the strategic match of partner competencies with strategic needs and in relation to the effective operating of the alliance. Partners sought should have high levels of needed skills and experience, high standards of excellence and a high degree of entrepreneurial ingenuity in solving unusual problems. All partners should have exhibited the ability to outperform aggressive competitors both on their own and when working with partners.

Protecting Core Competencies

Protecting core competencies is an important consideration when structuring an alliance and writing the contract – for example, when giving only prior-generation technology to a joint venture, as did Gillette and the US Chemical firm when entering China. Personnel must thoroughly understand and adhere to the limits placed on information and technology transfer when interacting with partners over a continuing time period.

General Alliance Type

While it is useful to understand the distinct types of alliances shown in Figure 1.4, p. 18, all alliances require situational tailoring to meet specific situation needs. The alliance form selected must be shaped into a structure which fits the needs of all the partners.

For example the terms used to describe alliance type are not generally understood in the same way by all people. In addition, some of the terms have specific legal connotations. For instance, the term 'partnership' can imply legal obligations which might not have been intended. General terms such as 'alliance' should be used in written documents and legal advice should be followed on how the alliance type is worded in communications with partners and potential partners. Early feasibility/discussion documents exchanged with potential partners should not be called 'letters or statements of intent', since this may make them legally binding in some nations and cultures.

Some experts feel that alliances without equity investment are 'transactional' alliances rather than 'strategic' alliances. Field studies show, however, that contractual alliances, such as those in the international airline industry, are so extensive that they are, in fact, strategic. In addition, they often lead to more comprehensive alliances and in that sense are building blocks in the strategic alliance continuum.

Operational Fit

Operational fit is a critical, but at times seemingly unending, activity in designing successful alliances. This activity involves developing and constructing scenarios of the different operations involved in the alliance and the different possible outcomes over time. In the Tambrands situation, the operational fit study led to the development of feasibility guidelines that were used as a basis for negotiating the structure and final contract for the joint venture. This step might also help to pinpoint unforeseen strategic fit problems, as in the Studds–Nolan and FCB/Publicis situations.

Assessing operational fit can be an exhausting and time-consuming task for managers, but it is an important one for finding what has been called 'the devils in the detail'. In addition, the process provides good training for those who will be working at or with the alliance in the future, either as partner liaison managers or alliance managers. The process also helps to get buy-ins, since people tend to support what they help create, provided credit is shared.

Environmental problems are one of the surprises which often are encountered as alliances operate. When anticipated, they can be planned for, as was done in the Chinese chemical joint venture, where the managing director assigned was an expert in environmental issues.

Structure

Entrepreneurial ingenuity may be involved in developing appropriate alliance structures, since the structure must fit business needs and partner strategic and control needs, as well as enable handling unforeseen future changes.

Alliance managers need a degree of autonomy because of the many entrepreneurial problems and challenges which can arise. This autonomy must be balanced with control. Control can be created through such structural mechanisms as equity division (one partner may have more than 50% of the equity), composition of the board of directors, decision-making guidelines (for example, having alliance co-managers who need to agree on actions, which are referred to partner managers when there are irresolvable disagreements), designating which partner appoints or approves appointment of new alliance managers or CEO and the like.

There seems to be an infinite variety of permutations and combinations in the way alliances can be structured. The business needs and partner relationships most often require situation-specific solutions. For example, Foote, Cone and Belding/Publicis was structured around a network of services and differing partner needs, Airbus around the needs of firms located in four different country and industry requirements, and the Tashkent cellular phone venture around the local, industry, investor and partner requirements.

The guideline, then, is to tailor the structure to the requirements identified up to this point in the strategic alliance development process. In addition, legal documents should contain terms and conditions specific to the needs of the partners in the particular alliance under study. Loose alliance agreements were found in surveys to be a major cause of alliance failure (Pekar and Harbison, 1998).

Flexibility

Each partner should retain flexibility and not be overly reliant on any one partner. As seen from Motorola's experiences, the strategic environment – the internal company needs and the external competitive market – can change over time. In addition, changing industry and political situations can affect the alliance. A company has to be prepared to try different types of alliances (as well as alternatives to alliances, such as mergers and acquisitions, as did Royal Dutch Petroleum), to explore new partners (as did British Airways), to revise existing alliances (Airbus), and where necessary to terminate alliances (General Motors/Toyota and Shell Italia).

The Liaison Role

In addition to strong partner commitment, each partner firm needs a liaison manager and champion to actively and continuously work at making the alliance work as it is implemented. This person, where possible, should be involved from the start in initiating interest in the alliance, and continue to participate in the detailed development of the alliance.

At British Airways, the liaison role was performed initially by the coordinating team which created the alliance and subsequently by that same team in combination with steering committees and working groups. Tambrands used a feasibility study group and international vice-president to develop its Femtech alliance. Both the international manager and personnel drawn from the feasibility study group were later used for liaison purposes and to fill key alliance management roles. The same was true for its Russian partner.

A liaison manager or management group is essential for the continuing health of an alliance. Preferably he or she or the group members should be champions for the alliance, possess the requisite integrative and communication skills and have the personal chemistry needed to further alliance objectives synergistically and reconcile conflicts positively.

Above all, liaison managers and other alliance leaders and managers should understand that trust is built in small steps over years. They should have the ability to continually achieve small successes, as did Samuel Hearne at Shell Italia and John Mumford at British Petroleum. They should strive at all times to avoid actions that undermine trust and confidence. Poor communications were found in surveys to be a major cause of alliance failure; such problems can often be overcome by effective liaison management (Pekar and Harbison, 1998).

Human resource issues need careful attention at all phases, starting with the negotiations and continuing through partner selection and alliance staffing, development and training.

Conflict Resolution

When organizing alliances, a mechanism for resolving conflicts which arise should be in place. One way is to have partner liaison managers who know each other, as in the Femtech situation. CEOs (Toshiba/General Electric) or teams (British Airways) can perform that function. Many alliance contracts contain arbitration procedures and designate outside arbitration agencies to handle irresolvable disputes.

In general, conflicts provide opportunities for partners to get to know one another better and build a base for synergistic creativity by using diversity to build new directions, communicate and reinforce policies and create new opportunities, as was the case at Femtech and The Blackstone Group.

Alliance CEO

Alliance agreements should specify which partner (or combination of partners) has the authority to select the CEO. The partners also need to agree on the amount of expertise CEO candidates should have in the field and the amount of time the CEO should be expected to commit to the alliance. The agreement should specify how subsequent managers at the alliance will be selected. This helps avoid the problems encountered when key alliance personnel die, retire or must be replaced.

A CEO with skills related to the alliance type and mission should be selected. For example, when an alliance's objective is to create a new market, the alliance manager should be a confident change-manager, who is able to judge risks and make things happen under difficult circumstances. A manager who is a control-oriented and measurement-driven evaluator is likely to fail in such situations.

Key Managers and Operating Personnel

Appointments made throughout the alliance should be based on skill contributions, not on family ties, political payoffs or other non-business reasons. Appointments also should be balanced with partner interests. Ideally, people who participate in the alliance negotiating and plan development processes, and so are familiar with the different parties and operations involved, should be appointed to key alliance positions. Femtech and Borg–Warner encountered many problems, many of which were anticipated by people who worked on developing the alliance and who eventually worked in the alliance to manage those problems. In general, top-notch people should be assigned to the alliance, as was done in the CFM International alliance.

Collaborative/Team-Oriented Management Style

Key alliance management and leadership skills needed include: being comfortable with a collaborative, team-oriented environment, having the ability to deal positively with conflict and being able to delegate and govern by persuasion in a situation where one does not always have full authority. A sense of humor, excellent communication skills and the ability to build trust are also helpful. This was the approach used by John Mumford at British Petroleum and Samuel

Hearne at Shell Italia. Alliance situations frequently require a mix of leadership styles, even though the concept of alliance places focus on collaborative styles. Chapter 5 described the use of teams at US West, British Airways, Volkswagen Shanghai, Gillette, Briggs & Stratton, and Intel.

Control Balanced with Autonomy

Balancing control and autonomy is a difficult activity in alliance structuring and management. At the partner level, controls can be built into the alliance structure, as they were at Tambrands (which did not have majority equity control), at Shell Italia (where the equity was divided 50/50) and at Foote, Cone and Belding (where there were several different levels of equity investment). Control is balanced with entrepreneurial autonomy at the operating level in part through the way management is exercised and in part through reporting systems and formal controls.

Control reporting systems include those used by the alliance to control its operations and those required by each partner to control the alliance in terms of its needs. Gillette initially had such a dual system: the reporting system for Gillette control purposes in Boston at its headquarters was developed manually by a special group, based on the reports used by the alliance management to control its operations. The alliance management control system at Gillette also had a third dimension, common in many developing countries, which was created to meet the different reporting needs of local government regulatory bodies.

Financial forecasts are often illusory and unreliable in foreign ventures because circumstances can change rapidly. This happened at Otis Elevator in Russia where sales of elevators were dramatically below forecasts. Steps were taken to acquire service businesses which were needed to provide the main source of income for the alliance in Russia (Fey, 1995; Prescia, 1997).

Most often, controls are not the key to success. Entrepreneurship, creativity, persistence, the ability to sell and manage, cooperation, trust, and many related skills are what make for success. The control systems should be designed to nurture these skills as much as possible.

Cultural Issues

Managing cultural differences is important not only during early negotiations and partner selection, but also during the phases involved in making an alliance work.

Meshing cultural diversity is a common problem which can be handled in many different ways. One study suggested that the most effective way at the functional level was by setting up unifying processes and structure, such as John Mumford did. At the policy group and top management levels setting up cross-cultural groupings can be effective, as was done at the companies which used teams (Parkhe, 1991).

The AT&T/Olivetti alliance provided an example of the situation circumstances under which inherent differences undermined the specific strategic needs of both partners and so turned out to be insurmountable.

The nature of cultural differences and their impact on multinational strategic alliance development and management are discussed in Appendix B.

Termination

While it can be unwise to overemphasize termination conditions, the alliance agreement should, at a minimum, outline the principles and general terms guiding any termination.

A Continuing Job: Collaboration, Cooperation and Continuing Commitment

Alliance success ultimately depends on effectively managing the alliance on a continuing basis. Unforeseen events and the need to work in partnership alone can create enormous risks. That is why commitment, flexibility and superior entrepreneurial and interpersonal skills are important to an alliance's success.

INSTITUTIONALIZING STRATEGIC ALLIANCE CAPABILITIES

The effectiveness of a company's alliances generally improves as its experiences with alliances grow, especially where it systematically takes steps to institutionalize or embed and preserve alliance capabilities within the firm (Kelly, 1997; Harbison, 1997c). Successful companies also are more disciplined in following a defined alliance development and management process, according to these same surveys (Pekar, 1998).

Companies without experience often in the past approached alliances in an *ad hoc* way, through trial and error. This does not have to be the approach, since books such as this one are now available that describe disciplined approaches and best practices. In addition, many experienced consulting firms provide alliance development and management services.

Recognizing the importance of alliances, many companies have taken steps to improve their chances of success during the 1990s. As a company's experiences grow, leaders in alliance management emerge. These leaders, who are essentially alliance gurus with experience and knowledge, are the firm's initial imbedded alliance capability. This initial experience base is extended in successful alliance firms in several ways, in an effort to institutionalize, capture and use that experience. First, formal processes and procedures and a staff capable of managing the alliance process are developed. This provides a knowledge repository for future use and dissemination. The steps taken to collect and disseminate knowledge and to organize and train people in order to institutionalize alliance capabilities vary at different firms.

Hewlett-Packard (H-P), for example, found that general seminars for managers on alliances were not enough. Managers needed H-P specific information on the best practices guidelines formed from H-P's alliance experiences. Training programs were developed to provide case histories, tools kits, checklists and best practices to follow. The material was reinforced with studies of the best practices of other companies. Learning from a company's own experience, combined with learning from the experiences of others, appears to be the formula for alliance success. H-P has conducted 50 two-day seminars on alliances for its top 1000 executives.

In order to provide executives with company-specific information, a database repository which goes beyond gathering historical information on past alliance structures and performances is needed. The database should include what the company has learned from its own experiences and the best practices emerging from these lessons. This requires continual self-assessment by the company, alliance management and alliance partners. Partner surveys can be especially useful in obtaining information on ways to improve alliance success – through communicating, appointing the right people, being forthright and the like. This is especially important for US companies, which are frequently good at planning alliances, but seem to be behind Asian and European partners in alliance integration and implementation (Harbison, 1997a,b,c).

On the simplest procedural level, a best practices database might include a specific company's experiences with each of its alliances in each of the applicable best practices guideline areas discussed at the end of Chapters 2–6. Companies such as Ford, IBM and Dun & Bradstreet are in various stages of creating such company-specific repositories. Such repositories or alliance information clearing houses would also include information on alliance partners, market reactions to alliance moves and press releases related to company alliances. Several companies, such as Oracle and Xerox, have gone so far as to create Web sites to disseminate alliance knowledge bases.

Training programs are increasing at alliance-oriented companies. BellSouth, for example, offered a two-day alliance workshop for 150 senior managers. This workshop showed that company specific information was needed, that managers learned much from each other and that specific disciplined processes do work. Networking developed through these seminars providing important supplementary information exchanges and learning.

The best practices guidelines at the end of Chapters 2–6, and the checklists in Appendix A, supplemented by the experiences described throughout this book, are one kind of data base. Other examples of transferable best practices tools given in this book include Borg–Warner's evaluation of human resources on p. 83, and the analysis of strategic fit in Figure 3.1, p. 72. The Tambrands and British Airways preliminary objectives and principles statements prepared early in the alliance development process are another example of best practices observed at successful alliance companies that are in some form transferable to other companies.

Organization steps are also important in imbedding alliance capabilities. These steps vary by firm. According to Booz-Allen &

Hamilton, the most successful companies have alliance functional groups only at the corporate level (Xerox) (Harbison, 1997c). Alliance liaison relationship management is also most likely to be performed at the corporate level in successful alliance companies. Business development groups (H-P) and strategic business units (Unisys) are used at other companies to house the alliance coordinating and management functions.

These experiences are indicative of a movement towards Centers of Alliance Excellence within companies in order to embed and institutionalize strategic alliance capabilities. Such a step was what United Parcel Service CEO Jim Kelly indicated was needed in order for a company to establish a core competency in this very important multinational business area (Kelly, 1997).

STRATEGIC ALLIANCES: A KEY MULTINATIONAL STRATEGIC MANAGEMENT ENABLER

As shown in Figure 7.1, strategic alliances are a key enabler in multinational strategic management. They can be used in almost every multinational task area outlined in Figure 7.2, from method of entry (often equity joint ventures) through marketing (such as co-distribution agreements) and technology development (for example, multifirm research consortia). As also shown in the two figures, the development and management process depends significantly on the situation context analyses, an essential step covered in the checklists in Appendix A.

Alliances strategies often are not identified initially in precise, feasible terms. Rather, they often emerge over time. The same is true in the overall multinational strategic management process, as shown in Figure 7.3.

The initial focus in strategic alliance development is on basic values, as in the outline of the strategic framework of multinational strategic management in Figure 7.4. In the overall process, planned steps are identified and developed and the alliance is implemented. During this process, diverse factors must be balanced. The implementation requires doing whatever is necessary to get the job done within well-defined general moral, legal, ethical and policy guidelines.

Like multinational strategic management, developing and managing strategic alliances is a circular iterative process, as shown

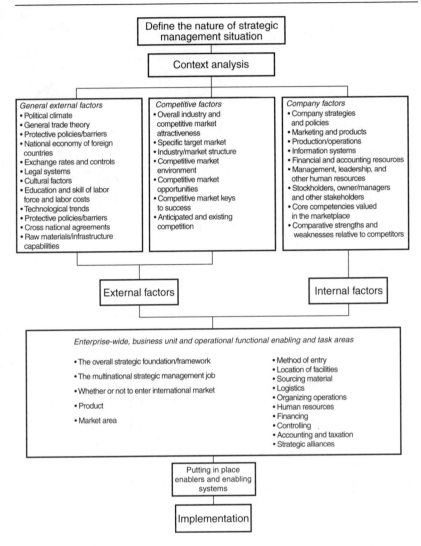

Figure 7.1 The Multinational Strategic Management Process: A Linear Situational Overview

in Figure 7.5. Alliances are developed in stages, as negotiations proceed, partner relationships are explored and developed, strategic and operational fits are studied, structures are developed and alliances are implemented.

Because of the fluidity, uncertainty and continually changing international context of multinational strategic alliances, a high level of entrepreneurial skills is needed, as outlined in Figure 7.6.

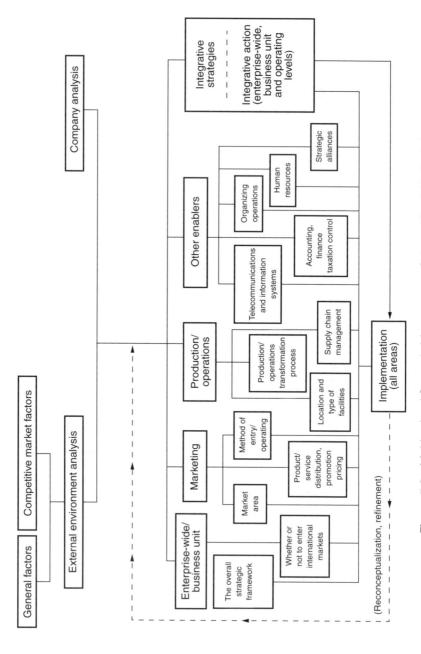

Figure 7.2 Multinational Strategic Management: Selected Decision/Task Areas

The Focus: An Emergent Entrepreneurial Leadership Process
The Process
1. *Strategic vision/mission:*
   'I knew exactly what kind of company I envisioned; I Just didn't know precisely what it would look like.' Precise definitions, in other words, often emerge over time, through the experiences involved in doing it.
2. *Strategic guidelines:*
   This is the map, the path, the planned steps. The secret here is KISS – 'Keep It Short and Simple.' That means one page written, five minutes oral, maximum length.
3. *Implementation:*
   'Doing whatever was necessary to get the job done, within well-defined general moral, legal, ethical and policy guidelines.' This often involves reconciling and balancing diverse, conflicting and often paradoxical forces, on a continuing basis, in a complex and rapidly changing competitive market environment.

The Activities
- Creating an overall vision (values, mission, strategic focus on core competencies, opportunities in future) and strategic framework (the guidelines or map). Specific strategies and strategic plans (enterprise-wide and in business units and functional areas) often emerge over time, through the enabling systems and processes.
- Activating, energizing, putting into place and monitoring enabling systems and processes, such as: functional area operations; telecommunications/information systems; accounting and finance systems; organization and business structures, processes and cultures; and strategic alliances.
- Nurturing enabling human resources and processes through: organization development; understanding cultural diversity, staffing, training, and communicating; and effective flexible leadership and integrative management at all levels.
- Ensuring that a core management staff (with appropriate interpersonal, communication, entrepreneurial and management skills and potential) is in place and functioning.
- Communicating and implementing the strategic framework, as well as the cultural benchmarks that are needed to enable the core management staff to translate the desired vision into action. The actual process involves superior visionary and pragmatic leadership appropriate for both the managers and people/groups involved in the situation.
- Leaving managers relatively free to manage, and pushing decision making as close to the customer as possible, but intervening where appropriate to make certain integrative activities are operating efficiently and effectively to achieve the company's strategic short- and long-term objectives.

Figure 7.3 Strategic Management: Multinational and Domestic

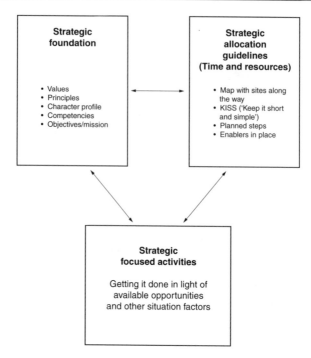

Figure 7.4   Strategically Focused Management: The Strategic Framework

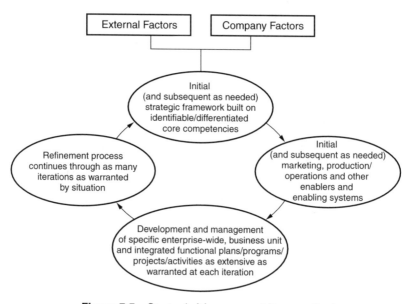

Figure 7.5   Strategic Management Process Cycle

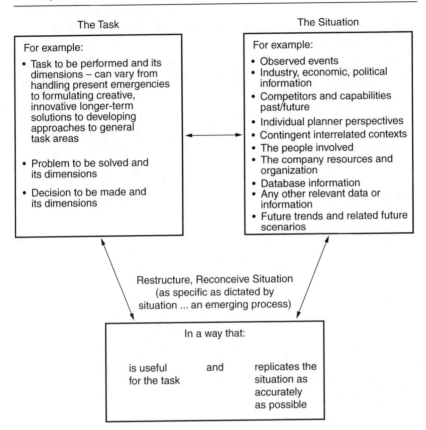

Figure 7.6 A Basic Emergent Entrepreneurial Contingency Process

This entrepreneurial process has been referred to and used through-out this book.

These overall multinational strategic leadership and management perspectives provide an overall focus for the multinational strategic alliance discussions in this book. Alliances are best understood, developed and managed within the context of this perspective in each business firm. A comprehensive discussion of multinational strategic leadership and management, the overall context for this book, is given in the author's latest book on the subject (Mockler, 2000).

This perspective also is important on a practical level in multi-national strategic alliances because many of the techniques useful for effective multinational strategic leadership and management help alliances succeed, in all phases from determining strategic fit through managing and making them work.

The following appendices explore two areas important to multinational strategic alliance success. Appendix A provides checklists for analyzing situation factors during all phases of multinational strategic alliance development and implementation. Appendix B discusses cultural differences and their impact on all phases of multinational strategic alliance development.

REFERENCES

Fey, C. and Killing, J.P. (1995). *Otis Elevator Company: Russian Joint Venture.* Western Ontario, Canada, Richard Ivey School of Business.

Garone, S.J. (1996). *Strategic Alliances: Gaining a Competitive Advantage,* Report Number 1168–96–CH. New York, The Conference Board.

Gates, S. (1993). *Strategic Alliances: Guidelines for Successful Management,* Report Number 1028. New York, The Conference Board.

Harbison, J.R. and Pekar, P. (1997a). *A Practical Guide to Alliances: Leapfrogging The Learning Curve.* New York: Booz-Allen & Hamilton.

Harbison, J.R. and Pekar, P. (1997b). *Cross-Border Alliances in the Age of Collaboration.* New York, Booz-Allen & Hamilton.

Harbison, J.R. and Pekar, P. (1997c). *Institutionalizing Alliance Skills: Secrets of Repeatable Success.* New York, Booz-Allen & Hamilton.

Hart, M. and Garone, S.J. (1994). *Making Strategic Alliances Work,* Report Number 1086–94–CH. New York, The conference Board.

Kelly, J. (1997). All together now. *Chief Executive,* November, pp. 61–63.

Lynch, R.P. (1993). *Business Alliances Guide.* New York, John Wiley.

Mockler, R.J. (2000). *Strategic Leadership and Management: A Context Specific Process.* Taiyuan, Shanxi (People's Republic of China), Shanxi People's Publishing House. (This is a Chinese translation of the book originally published in New York by the Strategic Management Research Group in 1999.)

Parkhe, A. (1991). Interfirm diversity, organizational learning, and longevity in global strategic alliances. *Strategic Management Journal,* fourth quarter, pp. 579–601.

Pekar, P. and Harbison, J.R. (1998). (Of Booz-Allen & Hamilton). Implementing alliances and acquisitions. *The 1998 Strategic Alliances Conference.* New York, The Conference Board, April 30–May 1.

Prescia, D. and Mockler, R.J. (1997). *Otis Elevator Method of Entry Into China and Russia.* New York, Strategic Management Research Group.

Rigby, D.K. and Buchanan, R.W.T. (1994). Putting more strategy in strategic alliances. *Directors and Boards,* Winter, p. 16.

Troy, K. (1994). *Change Management: Strategic Alliances,* Report Number 1090–94–RR. New York, The Conference Board.

Appendix A
Asking and Answering Relevant Questions

This Appendix provides checklists to help stimulate and guide situation analyses useful for understanding and doing each phase of multinational strategic alliance development and implementation. They supplement the best practices guidelines given at the end of Chapters 2–6 and summarized in Chapter 7. Given the wide range of possible multinational strategic alliances, not all questions apply in all situations.

The checklists are divided into five sections, one each for Chapters 2–6. This Appendix is intended to provide a quick reference resource – a handy summary perspective of the book and of the multinational strategic management process.

CHECKLISTS FOR CHAPTER 2: DETERMINING STRATEGIC MANAGEMENT FIT

The following checklists assist in analyzing the initiating partner's profile and marketing position, the existing and anticipated industry and competitive market conditions, and the profiles of the other partners. These analyses provide a comparative basis for matching strategic and operational requirements and determining the strategic fit, and for suggesting ways in which a strategic fit might be developed. They also provide a basis for partner matching and selection and for negotiating as the multinational strategic alliance process continues.

Initiating Alliance Partner: Profile

- What is your firm's strategic objective and what are your firm's key strategic needs, especially in the international area?
- What are your major core competencies?
- What are your weaknesses in relation to your strategic objectives?
- What does your firm have to offer prospective alliance partners?
- What is your management and decision-making style? Is corporate culture hierarchical, cooperative, or a combination of the two?
- What are your firm's and its top managers' basic values and philosophy?

Initiating Alliance Partner: Market Position

- Is your company under competitive pressure in your domestic market?
- Is that market maturing?
- How important is overseas expansion to your firm?
- Do overseas markets under consideration have restricted entry/ operating requirements and what are these restrictions?
- What moves are multinational competitors likely to make?
- Identify potential alliance partners within and outside the overseas markets under study.
- Does your firm have the financial resources and know-how to penetrate strategically important overseas markets on its own?
- In which specific strategic and operating resource areas does your firm need alliance support?
- What experiences does your firm have in the overseas markets under consideration?
- What experience does your firm have with strategic alliances?

The Industry and Competitive Market

- Is the industry growing, maturing, or in its early growth stages, in general and in the overseas market under study?
- Is the technology changing rapidly?
- Is the market changing rapidly and if so in what way, in general

and in the overseas market under study?

- Does the overseas market under study have distinctly different requirements from those in other countries?
- How intense is the competition, who are the competitors, and in what ways are they a threat, overall and in the overseas market under study?
- Describe the ways in which your move into a specific overseas market can strengthen your position in relation to any of your competitors.

Potential Alliance Partners

- Answer the initiating partner profile questions listed above as they relate to potential partners identified.
- What is the competitive position of potential partners within and outside the overseas market under study?
- Comparatively match potential partners strengths and weaknesses with your firm's in all areas including: corporate culture, market presence, management, technology, materials, manufacturing, customer service, product/service lines, promotion, distribution, and capital.
- Based on this preliminary comparative analysis, how good is the strategic fit or potential for strategic integration? Which are the greatest fit areas and the weakest ones? In what ways can you compensate for, or neutralize, the weaknesses?
- What is your relationship, if any, with potential partner(s) in the following areas: existing or potential competitor; supplier, distributor or contract manufacturer; technology source? In what ways, if any, would an alliance relationship with each partner affect your comparative competitive positions?
- Can additional steps be taken to improve the alliances chances of success? If so, name them.

CHECKLISTS FOR CHAPTER 3: NEGOTIATION AND PARTNER SELECTION

The following are detailed analyses useful during the negotiations and partner selection phase of multinational strategic alliance development and implementation.

Compatible Partner Selection: More Detailed Business Profile

- In the manufacturing area, what are each partner's production capabilities, condition of its facilities, dedication to quality, technical expertise, R&D capabilities, supplier relationships and state-of-the-art equipment and processes?
- What is each partner's financial situation, including cash flow, available investment capital, profit and loss experiences and credit rating? Have there been adequate financial disclosures and access to financial records?
- In the marketing area, what are each partner's brand and product/service strengths, consumer or business marketing experience and market penetration, distribution systems and advertising competencies, new product/service history and potential, depth of marketing personnel, sophistication in Western market mix planning and management, trade relations and relation to competitive products and services?
- Does the partner have good relations with vendors, suppliers and customers, and have you independently verified this?
- Is the firm involved in any lawsuits or other industry disputes?
- What is the status of the work force and will major layoffs be necessary in order to operate the alliance successfully?
- What are the partner's skills in strategic thinking, its organization culture and structure, the character and competencies of its work force and its ability to respond effectively and quickly to competitive pressures?
- Is the partner currently or has it formerly been involved in other alliances, and what has been its experience?

Partner Selection: More Detailed People Profile

- Who are the people championing the alliance and what are their positions in the potential partner firm.
- How long has the present management been in place and how likely is the management to work with the new alliance in the future? Have you taken the time to get to know the background of the managers?
- What are their personal and business values which could affect the success of the alliance and your ability to work with them and develop trust?

- How committed is top management to the alliance?
- In general, what are the company's and its management's reputation in the industry for honest dealings and for quality service and products?
- Are others currently negotiating an alliance with this partner?
- Is the personal chemistry strong among people in your firm and the potential partner company? Do you feel there are ways to strengthen that chemistry?
- Are there people involved in the negotiations who might be effective working in the new alliance and would they be willing to do so?
- Is it likely that government officials involved in alliance approval are accessible?
- Based on initial analyses, what problems are anticipated and what steps should be taken to avoid and solve these problems early in the negotiations?
- In what ways do you plan to use negotiations to get to know the potential partner's personnel better, assess the depth of your compatibility with them, and test and nurture personal chemistry and trust?
- Is its management style collaborative or hierarchical driven?
- How is management control exercised?
- In general, what is the morale of the work force?
- Are you aware of the cultural differences among the people involved in the situation and are you prepared to take steps to adapt to and synergize these differences to the degree needed to make the alliance work?
- Do you feel that an alliance relationship with this partner will add mutual strategic value, enable learning, protect and enhance core competencies and enable flexibility?

Negotiations

- Do the potential partner's business and personnel profiles sufficiently match your firm's profiles? Are you satisfied that good operational and strategic fits exist or can be developed to a degree that will justify entering into lengthy negotiations with them?
- Are you prepared to devote the time needed during negotiations to develop a long-term relationship with both the company and the people involved?

- Have you collected enough information about the people involved and the business of the potential partner to be certain you are seriously interested in the alliance and the potential partner you are dealing with?
- Have you determined who has the power to negotiate, who will make the final decisions, and what the role of each negotiator is at the potential partner firm?
- To what degree will other parties (government agencies and other industry participants) be involved in the negotiations, what approvals will be needed from them, and what direct access is available and necessary with them?
- Are you prepared to formally record all negotiations, even if unable to use tape recorders or videos?
- Who has been assigned to negotiate for your firm and have you left them free enough from other duties to be able to do this effectively? Are some of these people likely to be involved in key ways in the alliance's operations? Do they have any special relationships with the country or potential partner involved?
- Have you adequately verified the ability of the potential partner to fulfill commitments it makes during negotiations?
- Are you prepared to deal with problems as negotiations progress and not defer them until later?
- Have you identified and found a use for outside parties to further and influence negotiations?
- Have you calculated the bargaining power of the potential partner in such areas as the relative importance of the alliance to it and to you, its alternatives to partnering with you, your options and its knowledge of your options, the degree to which its survival depends on your partnering with it, the importance of the technology you offer to it, and its and your urgency in needing to strike a deal.

CHECKLISTS FOR CHAPTER 4: DETERMINING TYPE AND
STRUCTURE OF STRATEGIC ALLIANCES –
THE OPERATIONAL FIT

The following checklists analyze situation factors relevant to the development of alliance type and structure. This checklist helps insure that detailed operational fit studies are done to anticipate and plan for potential problems, as well as for nurturing synergistic opportunities.

Alliance Type

- In light of your studies of available partners, have you restudied your initial choice to pursue a strategic alliance as opposed to other methods (exporting, wholly-owned subsidiary) of entering and operating in your chosen overseas location?
- Have you reviewed the different types of alliances, explored the impact of using each in your situation and determined which is best for yours and your potential partner's situation requirements?
- Have you discussed your analysis and conclusions with each potential partner?

Operational Fit (or Integration): Crafting a Specific Workable Alliance Structure

- In reviewing the profiles developed of each potential partner and comparing those profiles with your firm's, have you specifically identified the areas of mismatch and potential problems, as well as the areas in which strong complementary synergies exist? Areas of possible differences might include organizational culture, personalities of CEOs, available resources, planning time frame (long- or short-term), management styles, technology, skills of key personnel, the character of the industry each partner is involved in, the understanding of what is involved in making an alliance work, the willingness and commitment to make the alliance work, each partner's perception of the future of the industry and market involved, and the cultures of the countries involved.
- Do the mismatches and problems mean that the alliance will not work? Or, is it possible to take steps to neutralize them or solve potential problems?
- Have you developed plans for resolving potential problems or improving the chances of success by creating a better match?

- Further, have you developed scenarios of possible problems that might arise due to unforeseen external problems, such as competitor moves or supply and distribution developments, and adjusted the alliance structure to enable handling these?
- Have you discussed these problems and plans with each potential alliance partner and worked with them to refine the plans and adjust the structure to enable handling such problems in the future?
- Have you explored ways in which you might further exploit and build on identified potential synergies?
- Have you used a devil's advocate to question the validity of your initial decisions and avoid being so focused on potential synergies that you may have overlooked potential problems?
- Have you used areas of disagreement to build a closer relationship with each potential partner?
- If the problems involve excess personnel, have you made a major effort to have any layoffs required take place before the alliance agreement is signed?
- As much as possible during the later phases of alliance structuring have you worked on developing alliance operating plans as a means of finding the 'devil in the detail' and facing up to problems which will be encountered?

The Alliance Structure: Calculating and Reducing Risk

- What will be the composition of the board of directors and the rules governing its decision making?
- What are the rules governing the appointment of top management by the alliance partners?
- Does the alliance agreement specify steps to be taken if disagreements occur in the future?
- In equity alliances, what will be the equity division and will there be any provisions for increasing or decreasing each partner's share?
- Have you studied ways in which the alliance might be structured incrementally, in order to reduce initial capital outlays and to allow time for a relationship to develop?
- Has your initial structure taken into account the different geographic settings in which the alliance might operate?

- Have all financial sources been explored to minimize capital investment or spread it as much as possible over the life of the alliance in a way that lets the alliance operation finance itself out of earnings?
- Have adequate steps been taken to identify all the legal and legislative factors that affect the alliance and has time been scheduled to prepare required documents?
- Have written records been made of informal agreements reached during the negotiations and have these been incorporated into the alliance agreement?
- Have detailed financial analyses and projections been made to determine the investment required, initial start-up costs in all operating areas, continuing costs, profits, the possible financial impact of different scenarios arising from possible events in the future and all tax and fee requirements?
- Have you studied the risks involved in competitive market moves, new technology developments, the history of such ventures for all parties, environmental concerns, political risks and the depth of each partner's financial and personnel resources?
- Has a statement of the principles underlying the overall agreement been drawn up, covering such areas as: the alliance's strategic objective and policies; its strategic plan; the scope of products, services, markets and customer groups; financial and timing philosophy and targets; each partner's contributions; decision-making mechanisms; division of authority, responsibilities and obligations; rules governing change management and for handling future problems; and benefits expected from the alliance.
- What steps will be needed to communicate and explain the alliance plan to the staff of all concerned partners?

Additional Details

- Does the final agreement include details about: the nature of each partner's contribution; the timing of investments and what happens if more money is needed; how confidential information will be handled; allocation of profits and losses; patent and technology rights; branding of products/services and distinctive features of products/services; products/services excluded from the alliance; rights to distribute products/services in different ways and locations; obligations of partner liaison managers; funds and profits transfer and other financial transaction guidelines; the specific structure of the alliance; and the transfer price of products/services among the alliance and its partners.

- What rules govern alliance dissolution?

CHECKLISTS FOR CHAPTER 5: MAKING MULTINATIONAL STRATEGIC ALLIANCES WORK – MANAGEMENT STAFFING, ORGANIZING AND LEADING

The following checklists analyze situation factors which have an impact on staffing, organizing, leadership and operational planning and management.

Staffing

- Has a genuine effort been made by all partners to appoint the best possible people to lead and manage the alliance?
- Have the original champions of the alliance been given key roles in the alliance?
- In staffing the alliance, has maximum use been made of people who were involved in planning and implementing the alliance?
- Have specific staff been assigned to handle government relationships and regulation administration?

Leadership

- Does the alliance leader have skills to synergize cross-cultural differences and match his/her style to the requirements of the cultures of the various parties involved in the alliance?
- Has change management been planned for, since often the reason for an overseas partner to join an alliance is to introduce new technology, skills and work ethics and practices?
- Is the leadership to be chosen intended to nurture entrepreneurial thinking, where appropriate?
- Has alliance leadership and management assumed the responsi-

bility of introducing the alliance and its strategic rationale, operating policies and working ground rules to all involved?

- Is this process also intended to resolve ambiguities and build trust?
- Is conflict perceived and used as a means of furthering the cooperative culture and the feeling of trust in the alliance?
- Have high-level liaison teams and/or managers been appointed to handle the transition and continuing operations?
- Do the alliance leaders appointed have the necessary leadership skills – visionary initiators, risk takers, new idea and direction generators – and have these skills been distinguished from leadership and management skills that make the alliance work day to day?
- Is there positive personal chemistry among alliance and partner top management and are steps planned to nurture that positive personal chemistry?
- As much as possible, has the alliance been placed in a position of self-sufficiency rather than being overly dependent on alliance partners for support?

Organizing

- Is the organization structured to meet the needs of the alliance rather than just being a copy of the structure at either partner organization?
- Is shared management a viable alternative and, if used, have provisions been made to enable reconciling differences?
- Has the organization been designed to enable cooperation if that is considered important to success?
- Have teams and working groups, in addition to committees, been used to further enable effective cooperation?
- Have communication process and tools that make interaction among the alliance and its partners easy and productive in a time efficient manner been put into place?

Planning for Successful Operations

- In general, have tasks and responsibilities been assigned in areas such as: financial forecasting, developing operating plans, budgeting for operations, competitor analysis, sales projections, promotion, pricing and costing, purchasing, manufacture, product/service quality, product engineering, service support, screening and hiring, and administration, including procedures development?

* Have plans been made to extend the scope of the alliance among partners, to extend the geographic areas of its operations, or to expand its product line or services offered?

CHECKLISTS FOR CHAPTER 6: MAKING MULTINATIONAL STRATEGIC ALLIANCES WORK – MANAGEMENT, DEVELOPMENT AND TRAINING, CONTROL, AND TERMINATION

The following checklists guide the analysis of the situation factors relevant to the four key aspects of the multinational strategic alliance process covered in Chapter 6, management, development and training, control, and termination.

Management

* When required, do alliance managers have the skills, training, and capabilities to be effective interactive/participative managers, capable of managing cross-cultural diversity synergistically?
* Where needed, do alliance managers have experience and skills in managing workers in developing countries, where hierarchical managing styles have been used for years?
* Have adequate liaison management linkages and communication channels among alliance and partner management been established to ensure that needed information flows among all parties are maintained?
* As much as possible have alliance managers and supervisors been drawn from the pool of people who worked on different aspects of the alliance during its development phases?
* Have managers been appointed based on their technical, interpersonal and intercultural skills, rather than on family ties or political connections?

- Have adequate incentives and clear career paths been established for expatriates from alliance partners who serve in the alliance for a limited time?

Development and Training

- Have provisions been made for continuous training at all levels?
- Have the training approaches and tools been adapted to, or developed specifically for, the cultures involved?
- Where appropriate has this training included both expatriate experts on the job at the alliance and training conducted for key personnel at overseas partner facilities?
- Where teams or work groups are used, are facilitators available to help in training and making work groups effective?

Control

- Are there adequate financial and accounting and control systems for internal alliance management, control by partners, and compliance with local government regulations, even if this may mean that three different financial reporting systems have to be reconciled?
- Are operating control systems available to make control by alliance managers and partners feasible in such areas as sales and sales forecasts, costs and prices, quality, interpartner transfers, production, customer service, research and development, and worker performance?
- Are there regularly scheduled interpersonal contacts and communications among alliance and partner managers and among managers within the alliance which enable effective control and coordination at the strategic and operational levels?
- Are control and reporting systems used both for compliance monitoring and for stimulating entrepreneurial creativity and innovation?
- Have adequate controls been developed to protect partner proprietary information and core competencies?
- When identified, are problems corrected quickly?

Exit Strategies: Termination

- Do guidelines specify how the alliance will be terminated should circumstances change so that it no longer meets the strategic or operational needs of either partner, without overemphasizing the negative implications of such considerations?

Appendix B
Bridging Cultural Gaps

Culture refers to shared values, beliefs, attitudes, expectations and norms found within countries, regions, social groups, industries, corporations and even departments and work groups within a business firm.

Cultural differences impact on many aspects of multinational strategic alliance activities. In many Asian countries, for example, initial negotiations may be lengthy since getting to know each other, building personal relationships, and developing trust is extremely important before getting on to the details of the deal. This was not done in the Studds–Nolan study, but was a major success factor in the GM, Borg–Warner and Tambrands situations. Contracts are also less likely to be detailed and cover all contingencies in Asia, India and the Arab states – a barrier which at times has to be surmounted when dealing with multinational strategic alliances.

In bridging cultural gaps (in negotiations, in selecting partners, or in managing strategic alliances), it is useful to examine six aspects of potential cultural differences. These six perspectives are described briefly below. Their impact on alliance effectiveness is discussed in detail in Chapters 5 and 6 as it relates to managing and leading alliances.

THE ROLE OF PERSONAL RELATIONSHIPS: BUSINESS OR PEOPLE FIRST?

The social context and human aspects of a situation are emphasized differently in various cultures. They are, for example, very important to Asians, who prefer to *develop personal relationships* with the parties involved before negotiating the specific alliance terms. GM encountered this during their negotiations in China. This explains in part why family relationships often are important when doing business in China.

At the other end of the continuum shown in Figure A.1 (Section A), Americans are likely to get to the point more quickly and to rely on superficial friendly remarks as a quick way to get things started. This cultural bias is reflected in such phrases as: 'I don't have to like someone I do business with'. Like most cultural biases, this statement is generally true and the bias can be useful in cultures similar to that in the USA. It can, however, create problems in other cultures (Engholm, 1991).

Along a second continuum shown in Figure A.1 (Section B), at one cultural extreme there can be a tendency to keep relations harmonious by not talking directly about problems, as in Asian and some Latin American cultures. In cultures where human relationships are highly valued, confrontations are avoided. This can create problems when trying to develop working relationships during the planning and negotiating phases of strategic alliance development.

FOCUS ON THE INDIVIDUAL OR ON THE GROUP?

Succeeding in managing cultural differences does not depend on becoming or acting like the nationality being dealt with. Success generally requires being aware of differences and adapting to some degree, something that was done in the Tashkent, Chongqing–Yamaha, and GM situations described in the text.

Relative to other cultures, Americans are very extreme in the value they place on individualism. US history and its educational system support an individualistic culture. This trait can cause problems during negotiations. For example, Americans often expect the Japanese to make decisions at the negotiating table. In turn, the Japanese are continually surprised to find individuals on the American side advancing their own ideas and opinions, and at times contradicting one another. This creates a cultural gap which has to bridged by one side or the other, through initiating a dialogue about the gap and reaching an understanding on how to bridge it. Again,

A. Importance of personal relationships

B. Dealing with difficult problems

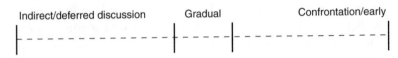

C. Working in teams

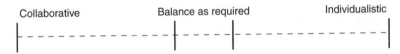

D. Importance of status and position

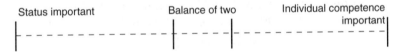

Figure A.1   Sample Continuums Representing Range of Cultural Differences

this usually requires more time than Americans originally were prepared to spend on negotiations.

Cultures with a high social conscience, such as in China, tend to believe 'God helps those who help each other' and prefer to *work in teams and for group consensus*. As shown in Figure A.1 (Section C), at the other extreme there are cultures, such as in North America, that place a high premium on *individualism* and individualistic reactions, and so tend to believe that 'God helps those who help themselves'. Such people are more likely to be *individualistic* rather than inherently natural team players.

In collectivist, group-centered cultures, harmony is an important goal – harmony with groups and society, and harmony with traditions that may have developed over hundreds of years. This dictates careful judgment and restraint as to the timing of outspoken criticism and objections during business negotiations. Where appropriate, business people should resist the urge to get down to business and into the task of establishing bargaining positions prematurely.

STATUS: IS EVERYONE CREATED EQUAL?

As shown in Figure A.1 (Section D), some cultures, such as those in Asia, Northern Europe and South America, place great value on social status. This may be reflected in seating arrangements and other protocols based on position. British Petroleum's John Mumford had to overcome this barrier in Malaysia. At the other extreme, Americans tend to give more importance to competence (Engholm, 1991). The USA has an egalitarian culture which holds the belief that all men are created equal. Next to Australia, it is probably the world's most informal culture.

In many cultures, formal protocols are important, however. Early in business relationships, people are referred to by their formal titles – Mr or Mrs, for example – not by first names as in the USA. Gift-giving practices also vary by culture, as do the timing and length of business meals. Dinners are much later, close to 11 pm, in Spain; expect three-hour lunches in Buenos Aires. It is important to learn these protocols as quickly as possible.

Embracing egalitarianism leads to a willingness to speak frankly to anyone as an equal, a very direct approach. US business people tend to speak frankly no matter what the rank of the listener. Protocols based on status or custom dictate a somewhat different approach. In cultures where rank and position are considered important – such as Mexico, Italy and even France – such directness can appear vulgar, harsh and impersonal. Many other cultural values dictate ambiguity and indirectness in order to maintain harmony, respect status, elaborate points within larger contexts and save face. Status values may dictate that it is prudent to praise contributions in order to increase a listener's status before offering any criticism – a good idea in any culture.

LANGUAGE/INFORMATION FLOW FACTORS

The most immediate and obvious cultural difference is language. Naturally, in multinational management the more languages one speaks the better. In practice, most people are fluent in only one language. Since English is the generally accepted language of business, most international managers will have English as a second language, but not necessarily as their primary one. This can cause problems. People may be uncertain, self-conscious and hesitant when using a second language. They may have difficulty finding the right word to convey their intended meaning.

The way information is conveyed also varies by culture. For example, a typical Western trait, especially in Germany and the USA, is 'getting straight to the point'. In other cultures, both the speed and path of information flow can vary. Getting to the 'point' may first involve 'getting to know each other', a more time-consuming task. Also, more than one point (including family affairs) may be discussed along the information flow path as a means of getting to know each other.

Body language interpretations can also vary among cultures. For example, people from the more socially-oriented cultures tend to stand very close while talking, while others, including Americans, prefer to keep a little more space between speakers during a conversation. Eye contact also has different meaning in different cultures; not looking indirectly at someone might be interpreted in India as a sign of respect, whereas intensely looking someone in the eye is thought a way to show personal interest in someone in other cultures, such as that in the USA.

A QUESTION OF PRIORITIES: WHAT IS THE VALUE OF TIME

Northern Europeans (strongly) and Americans (moderately) tend to favor treating events one at a time, in an 'orderly' fashion. This is a monochromic time perspective. Monochromic time is linear, with things done separately and sequentially. Time is compartmentalized, organized and controlled. Time is a commodity that has value because of its scarcity and its usefulness in defining the context in which activity occurs.

Polychromic time, on the other hand, is more circular. It is endless; there is plenty of it and it has no beginning or end. Most important, many things can happen at once. This cultural perspective is prevalent in Arab countries, Central and Southern Asia and Latin American countries. At conferences in these countries it is common to find many topics, involving family and business, being discussed at the same time – because it is part of the 'getting to know each other' ritual and there is less pressure to stick to an agenda.

SOME GENERAL GUIDELINES

When putting to use one's sensings about cultural differences and communicating across cultural boundaries, it is useful to remember several general guidelines:

- While it is useful to explore generalities and their implications, individuals do not always conform to general cultural stereotypes. Not all Japanese, for example, are 'typical' Japanese, and 'typical' Japanese may vary by age, sex and other demographic categories. For instance, young women in all countries now share many common values, as was demonstrated in the August 1995 United Nations Conference on Women in Beijing, which has led to significant differences in Japan between the values of younger and older groups of women (Kristof, 1996; Tyler, 1995).
- Differences are not always culturally based. Some arise from individual personality differences and some from personal, institutional or business factors. This is true in any country. In addition, any given action may be stimulated by various cultural biases that reinforce each other, not just one bias.
- Do not assume that because something works in one culture, it will work in another. Sometimes there is communality across cultural boundaries, as in the common frameworks described earlier in this book (for example, see Figure 1.1, p. 9) and the increasing trends towards more global products, services and communications. This is especially true among younger generations in all countries. However, differences will always exist, even among teenagers in different countries who share many common values (Warner, 1996).
- Understand yourself and your own culture first so that you may be more aware of your own biases or mental set and have a benchmark against which to study others.
- Study cultural diversity within your own country, since such a study yields clues to cultural differences and how to handle diversity. The USA, for example, is known as the melting pot of

the world since it has such a wide range of cultures within its borders.

- The discussion above focuses on continuums, that is, on sets of two extremes between which there can be many varied gradations. Try to avoid thinking in terms of extreme black-and-white stereotypes.
- Ultimately, it is best to learn as much as you can about cultural and personal sensitivities specific to the situation you are dealing with, in much the same way you would in any situation involving other human beings.
- The same words often have different connotations in different cultures: for example, the French sense of 'individualistic' is very different from a North American's sense of 'individualism' and both are different from a Latin American's understanding of the words.

Understanding these cultural differences provides some clues as to how the different partners and individuals involved in the alliance might be expected to act. This understanding, added to an understanding of other personality factors (such as values and working styles), as well as personal chemistry, helps in anticipating some of the problems which may be encountered and provides a means of managing more effectively collaboration and cooperation during the life of the alliance.

REFERENCES

Engholm, C. (1991). *When Business East Meets Business West.* New York, John Wiley.

Kristof, N.D. (1996). Japan is a woman's world once the front door is shut. *The New York Times,* June 19, pp. A1, A8.

Tyler, P. (1995). Forum on women agrees on goals. *The New York Times,* September 15, pp. A1, A3.

Warner, F. (1996). So much for an MTV world: Teens are far apart on hopes and values. *The Asian Wall Street Journal,* June 20, pp. 1, 8.

Company/Alliance Index

Subject Index

Index compiled by Indexing Specialists